JESUS VERSUS CHRISTIANITY

JESUS VERSUS CHRISTIANITY

RAYMOND GARDELLA

LIBERTY HILL PUBLISHING

Liberty Hill Press
2301 Lucien Way #415
Maitland, FL 32751
407.339.4217
www.libertyhillpublishing.com

Paperback ISBN-13: 978-1-6628-0839-5

Hard Cover ISBN-13: 978-1-6628-0840-1
Ebook ISBN-13: 978-1-6628-0841-8

To my Wife, Ardis, and my children, Carey and Sean, and their spouses, Scott and Ann, and my grandchildren, Kyle, Lily, Owen, Abigail, Cayla, Elle, Emmet, and Lauren.
A Family is a Fortress.

JESUS
IS
NOT
CHRISTIANITY
AND
CHRISTIANITY
IS
NOT
JESUS

"The next day John was there again with two of his disciples, and as he watched Jesus walk by, he said, 'Behold, the Lamb of God.' The two disciples heard what he said and followed Jesus. Jesus turned and saw them following him and said to them, 'What are you looking for?' They said to him, 'Rabbi…, 'where are you staying?' He said to them, 'Come, and you will see.'" (J.:35-39)

Jesus began to speak to the crowd about John:

"What did you go out into the wilderness to see? A reed swayed by the wind? If not, what did you go out to see? A man dressed in fine clothes? No, those who wear fine clothes are in kings' palaces. Then what did you go out to see? A Prophet? Yes, I tell you, and more than a prophet. This is the one about whom it is written:

'I will send my messenger ahead of you,
Who will prepare the way before you.'

Truly I tell you, among those born of women there has not risen anyone greater than John the Baptist; yet whoever is least in the kingdom of heaven is greater than he. From the days of John the Baptist until now, the Kingdom of heaven has been subjected to violence, and violent people have been raiding it." (Mt.11:7-12)

CONTENTS

Introduction. xv
Prelude: Consciousness is King xxv

Chapter 1: Context is Everything 1
Chapter 2: Soft Jesus 13
Chapter 3: John the Baptist ("No Greater Man") 21
Chapter 4: Jesus Out of Peacemaking 31
Chapter 5: Systemic Evil. 43
Chapter 6: Equality. 53
Chapter 7: Condemnation For Sure 61
Chapter 8: Lying is a Profession 73
Chapter 9: The Very Narrow Gate 85
Chapter 10: Which Jesus? 97
Chapter 11: Born From Above 107
Chapter 12: God's Vision 117
Chapter 13: Out of Eden 127
Chapter 14: Sola What? 139
Chapter 15: The Real Sola .151
Chapter 16: The Imperatives. 161
Chapter 17: Accommodation (Selling Out God's Laws) . .171
Chapter 18: A Relationship, Not A Membership 181
Chapter 19: Conscience Aborted 199
Chapter 20: Jesus, the Unifier? Really! 217
Chapter 21: Piety vs. Morality. 225
Chapter 22: One Final Word. 235

About the Author. 249

Acknowledgement

MUST ACKNOWLEDGE A FRIEND OF MANY YEARS for his inquisitive mind and demanding questions about topics engaged in this book. Michael (Duke) DeLong led me and pushed me to enter my thoughts into a book and I took the challenge, for which I am most grateful. Thanks Duke.

INTRODUCTION

OUR GENERAL SCOPE AND ENDEAVOR COVER A
large number of topics that demonstrate the inefficacy of
Christianity in the United States. It dramatizes the ineptitude and fickleness of Christian teaching and church principles brought forward by the leading members of the churches.
Above all it exposes the inability of church leaders to take up
arms against the falsehoods and lies of a nation that has followed the culture and its political establishments to by-pass
the most essential laws of God. Whereas Jesus exposed evil and
condemned it, the churches of this nation succumb to the rav-
ished morality of these times without a word of rejection. The
pulpits of today are all suspect if the principles of Jesus Christ
are what they internally and clandestinely profess to, but externally and publicly avoid. Jesus did not come all the way from
his Father's house to preach placebos. If there is a separation
of church and state, then the church portion should speak ada-
mantly and openly about its professed message, not accommodate the self-serving ambitions of public opinion.

Our analysis takes to task the vital issues Jesus himself raised
while on earth. It brings out of the wilderness such topics as
self-discipline, the amassment of wealth (Did Jesus "really"
mean selling everything and following him?), the utter evil of
lying and the despicable use of slander against political opponents, the maniacal corruption of power, the dissolution of

truth in an atmosphere of Media directed hate. One major recurring theme is the sheer defection of conscience in a proclaimed Judeo-Christian society, especially as it is related to the Killing of the Unborn.

Of necessity we also cover such topics as Baptism and the Eucharist that Jesus himself covered rather extensively and conclusively (using John's memory in the gospel as authentic guide), that may not be ignored by a partial application of the gospels. Another chapter of the book covers the reliance of faith on consciousness as a fundamental source of knowledge and conviction; with consciousness there is nothing blind about faith. Associated with the faith topic is the matter of Sola in fides: what is the real Sola?

We state emphatically that what the Christian Church is obliged to do is proclaim the gospel of Jesus Christ, not deliver some melted down version of love and peace and piety that has been sifted through the approving heads of government and the culture and MEDIA. Jesus came on this earth loaded with bear, and he delivered it with bear claws.

Also manifested is the fact that while the culture and government and all things political are "amassing" to become more radical, the churches are walking in silence keeping their tax exemptions under guarded protection. In an age of chaos and evil the churches pretend "there is no evil," that all can be overcome with a little more love and a lot less division. While John Lennon once said that the Beatles had bested Jesus and was rightly condemned for it, you have a political party and its propaganda machine today that overtly subvert the law and truth and kill babies, but there is no public condemnation by the churches. Instead the churches stay indoors to light candles of peace.

Above all we affirm superlatively the preeminence of Jesus Christ. There is no other who has descended from heaven and has manifested his divinity to mankind and who alone can and will raise others to his Father's house at the end of time. Jesus is not only Number One, he is the Only One. There is no other. Jesus did not come for political approval by any party or media apparatus, or king, or church. His approval came from his Father, not from the sullied hands of dictators and the squeamish minds of his followership.

Without the authentic Jesus of the gospel "according to Jesus," the Christianity we know is second rate at best, and false otherwise. My book introduces Jesus without any references to former theological authorities and without the heterodoxy of the leading churches. Jesus, the name and the person, originate with the Father in heaven, not from the historical "Summas" of past centuries. Too many condescending assumptions have allowed Christianity to walk away from Jesus and ameliorate his message and his urgency.

Finally, we celebrate Jesus but not Christianity. The voices who most claim responsibility for the message of Christ are themselves often short on the facts and weak on conviction. As a consequence, Christianity demonstrates impotence. It speaks peace as impotence. It emphasizes love as impotence. It confers forgiveness out of impotence rather than out of absolute necessity. It hides from confrontation. Jesus was none of that. Jesus and impotence are an oxymoron. Jesus' life and his messages challenged humankind to reawaken to his Father's life and laws—indeed, to become perfect like the Heavenly Father. If we are not becoming perfect, we are becoming nothing. We are advocates for the Devil.

If Christianity condones Lying, Slander, Greed, Killing the Unborn, Accommodation for the Culture, Acceptance without Condemnation for any Political View, then it has crossed over to the Devil's side. It used to be that governments, cultures, and societies' life styles and ambitions threatened and persecuted

Christianity without Christianity wavering and losing its foundation principles. But now governments and cultures have driven inroads into Christianity and all attempts at withstanding their enclosure has become futile. If there is but a narrow gate into heaven, there is a broad gate into Christianity. That was never the case 50 and 60 years ago when Christianity stood firm in its basic principles and never joined the rabble trying to tear down its gates. It is the task of Christianity to convert the reprobates in society, rather than the reprobates converting (transforming at minimum) Christianity to its ways. Society today equates good and evil, clouds the difference between good and evil, threatens those who uphold the good over evil, and defies and will destroy anyone who gets in its way.

If ever there was a lame duck situation applied to something today, it is to Christianity. It has walked away from the battle and left the battlefield. "Try not to offend anyone," is the excuse. P.C. has neutered Christianity. There is corruption everywhere and Christianity refuses to say anything. There is self-indulgence everywhere and nothing is done. This country interprets freedom as license to demand everything and refrain from nothing, and we insist Christianity has no say in it. We are gluttons, eating our way to sickness and disease, and we say nothing. Obesity is a "disease," says the culture, and gluttony is a sin, says earlier Christianity, but of course they are not related anymore according to "progressive" Christianity.

In Baptism the newly washed one has been committed to Christ. The "former" person is gone, and a new person is born—born into Christ. The person is newly constituted in the life of Christ. Moreover, through Baptism the newly washed "swears" that he or she "believes in Jesus Christ." Thus, to say that "I believe in Jesus Christ" constitutes an oath that must out of necessity validate the Baptism. If the oath is absent or refused, there is no Baptism. Hence to be baptized is to swear an oath of allegiance to Jesus Christ. It is an oath "super omnia" of other oaths and superseding all other oaths and all other obligations. Jesus must be first in belief and performance. He is first, his words are first, his commands are first, and his ultimate designs are first. Believing in Jesus is a consummation devoutly to be wished and walked and witnessed.

The problem with Christianity today centers around the ambiguity of witnessing. To believe in something and profess it but allow it to be overshadowed by the loudness and lewdness of the crowd beggar's deplorability. To believe in something godly and let it be equalized with moral madness and depravity is sheer incredulity. To believe in something of conspicuous intrinsic value and let it be suffocated by politically corrupt correctness borders on a lost baptismal oath. Jesus does not suffer such stupidity and disbelief with deference. "Whoever disowns me before others, I will disown before my Father in heaven." (Mt.10:33)

The oath made at baptism is taken for life and encompasses all of life without exception. There are no loopholes or exemptions, no family excuses, no societal exclusions, no political waivers, no adjustments for privilege or power or wealth. Oaths make you accountable. "If anyone is ashamed of me and my words in this adulterous and sinful generation, the Son of Man will be ashamed of them when he comes in his Father's glory with the holy angels."(Mk.8:38) Jesus came not only to bring salvation but to make men believe and "express" that belief. To believe and then really believe in that belief requires saying it vociferously and with his principles as guide.

What is happening today is that Christianity has a lock on its mouth—locked up by episcopal heads, or church elders, or church assemblies, or church policies, or big church contributors. The gospel of Jesus Christ is preached through human filters, not according to the original mind of Jesus. There is one gospel, but it has voluminous handlers who carry the water buckets for society and its sycophants, not for Christ. Jesus is so often sidelined by the big-league religious quarterbacks who adopt and conform to the multitudes. Thus, Christianity becomes a measured religious influence in the bigger game of politics, commerce, entertainment, sports, education, and every other temporal endeavor.

America is a melting pot, so we are told. "We are a nation of many becoming one" is fine if you are trying to teach a respectable compatible norm for a society of many different immigrants. We melt away the differences in order to form a uniform culture. We adopt a facade of oneness. But it is all very fragile. In that vein we adopt a God who becomes more generic every day— "Generic" so he can fit into the nondescript, inoffensive melting pot of America. The word God refers to a generic person, perhaps real, perhaps myth. People everywhere use the word and people everywhere mean different things. We prefer it "generic" so that no offense is committed in its usage and so that we all just peacefully "coexist.

However, "E Pluribus Unum" gets you in trouble if you are talking about Christianity. Jesus was not interested in a soft, fragile and elusive melting pot that produces a democracy that in turn elects a disparate body of minds that in turn creates a government of vast disparities with unending proclivities to more disparity. He was interested in an adamant, determined and exclusive commitment to himself and his Father. There is nothing generic about his divinity and his authority. Jesus is the One, not One of the Ones. Exclusivity is written all over his gospels.

When John the Baptist came and preached his message of repentance, he set the tone and created the atmosphere in which Jesus would surround himself. What is most antithetical to repentance is a lying tongue. No one needs or seeks repentance if lying is a habit of action, and the inevitable companion to lying is the quest for power. The devil can never seek repentance because he can never forgo lying because power is his only appetite. Two things that prohibit any form of repentance are lying and the quest for power. Both drive repentance into oblivion.

Repentance is about more than sin, or forgiveness of sin. Repentance encompasses the very essence and life of Christianity. It includes humility above all, plus a deep acceptance of powerlessness, an urgency of forgiveness of others, a willingness to surrender all judgment to God, and living temporarily with no attachment to temporality. Never, however, does it surrender principle and belief to anyone. Repentance stands firm and solid for Jesus, for justice, for righteousness, for the life to come. Neither acceptance or silence over injustice and falsehood fit into the scheme of repentance. Repenting does not employ silence or surrender to a violent lying society. John the Baptist surrendered nothing to Herod, or malefactors.

The quest for Jesus does not necessarily mean a subscription to Christianity. There is Christianity everywhere—churches, theologies, religious practices, ministers and members—but there is not always the Jesus who walked the earth and talked unceasingly about his Father's kingdom, the Jesus who did not create a religion with dogmas and rituals and piety, but who awakened us to the vast realities of his Father's world. "Come and see," he told Andrew. It was an invitation to something outside the pale of this existence. Jesus was about something else beyond today and tomorrow and here and now. He never led us into structures and institutions, or fixed narratives about reality and spirituality. Jesus was an itinerant preacher with a defining message from his Father.

His call to us was to believe in him directly and to fasten ourselves to his person, his name, his values and realities, not to seek adherence to a myriad of intermediaries with human trappings: "Unless you believe in the One who has been sent, you will not enter the kingdom of heaven," was his constant refrain.

"I do not belong to Christianity, I belong to Christ," is the affidavit of a follower of Christ. Baptism is between one person and the triune God with specific focus on Jesus. Jesus is not Christianity and Christianity is not Jesus, and anyone who thinks they are synonymous has been fooled. Jesus and Christianity are in so many ways and thoughts and expressions an oxymoron. Christianity is a human development with human attachments; Jesus has only two other attachments—his Father and the Spirit. Nothing else intervenes.

Early on after the Ascension there may have only been one form of Christianity as expressed by the apostles, but that singularity soon past. Almost from the very beginning there have been multiple strains of Christianity—Eastern, Western, Arianism, Nestorianism, the schools of Tertullian and Origin, then later Lutheranism, Anglicanism, Calvinism, Presbyterianism, the Quakers and Methodists and Baptists, then Mormons and a vast host of others. There is no lack of Christian groups.

However, group thought, group identity, group solidarity, group reservations and regulations and restraints and conformities were not Jesus' frontline requirements. Group conformity leads to containment and often a forgery of Jesus' spirit and the dynamic revelation of his Father's commands. Jesus did not ask for containment. At the final moment of his ascent into heaven he said, "Go into all the world and preach the gospel to all creation." (Mt.16:15) Jesus is bigger than anything imaginable. Jesus' coming was just a beginning and its evolution had no lockbox attached to it. However, the early disciples had acquired a mode of comfort and confinement that Jesus had not envisioned. As a result within a few short years after his departure Jesus enlisted the energy and passion and imagination of Paul to extend his message to the entire world of foreigners for the simple reason that the disciples in Jerusalem had formed a consensus, perhaps an inertia, of thought and action that constrained his message. Peter was one of a few who reached out to the non-Jews and received an awakening one night when a sheet full of religiously prohibited animals descended on him in a dream and he awakened to a realization that broke the Jewish code for exclusion, which became a metaphor for non-Jews becoming Christian. It was Paul who eventually brought Jesus out of Jerusalem to dissolve the restraints placed on Gentiles.

After Paul arrived Christianity became more clearly defined as a personal experience rather than a group encampment. If your head is fixed on Jesus, then Christ rules; if you are fixed on Christianity, then the group rules. If there is any current clarity coming out of today's Christian institutions, it is the awareness that group power focuses on its own existence and its own permanence. It demands submission to its own order and perpetuity. There is an underwritten acknowledgment of its preeminence. However, through baptism there is only one allegiance, and that is to Jesus. Any action or thought that limits and retards allegiance to Christ is fallacious. He tied no one to a monolithic institution. He tied everyone to himself and a life of unconditional goodness. Institutions, or groups, even families, do not confer salvation on anyone. Jesus is the Savior.

Probably what the churches are called to do essentially is to announce Jesus' message(s), then stand aside to permit the Holy Spirit to activate and develop what they are called to proclaim. In other words, do not stand in the way, but stand on the sidelines with motivating and guiding voices both clarifying and accelerating Jesus' "way and truth and life." Jesus' call is to himself, not to the myriad institutions holding up his cross.

The key focus is Jesus. He came in person; he spoke in person; he healed in person; he is his Father's witness in person; he left himself in the Eucharist, and that is IN PERSON. In the case of Jesus, the divine mystery is not a mystery, it is a reality. And if so, why would anyone want to siphon off that mystery with surrogates? Christianity therefore becomes an Aide de Camp for the real one who gathers and lifts up everyone to the Father.

Jesus is not an outsider. His name is household. His words resound with stampeding logic. His message for most of the world is one of selfless service. His principles, if examined with care, are easily and readily understood. He did not come to rival the authority of others, but he did with emphatic clarity demand adherence to his authority and his Father's. In a very real sense Jesus authorized the way to the next life. He also "exclusivized" his authority over that life. "Sine qua non" comes in the middle of his name: Jesus "Sine qua Non" Christ. He was given authority by his Father and he used it abundantly. There is no other authority on earth that can superimpose its authority over his. His death was not a defeat. It was a defining moment in the life of a man who first died but, then, rose from the dead. He overcame the impossible and thus becomes unquestionably the "the way and the truth and the life." Unsurpassable event! Unsurpassable Man. Unsurpassable God!

Prelude

CONSCIOUSNESS IS KING

IN THE VERY FOREFRONT OF HUMAN LIFE EXISTS a faculty known as consciousness. It stands in the center and at the core of human existence. It is superior to everything we have and everything we are. Without it we are matter and brain without a window to self-awareness and self-fulfillment: "I exist but I don't know who I am or where I'm going." Consciousness is space without matter, capable of feats unleashed from territorial boundaries where gravity rules, and as a consequence it can advance into unbounded spheres. This is more than intellect and brain. There are innumerable animal creatures surrounding us that mimic our own physical constitutions so we are not unique in comparison. What gives us exceptional uniqueness is the consciousness we possess.

A philosopher of renown once said, "I think, therefore I am"; another philosopher also said in the reverse, "I am, therefore I think." Neither one is right or wrong, but what is more correct is to say, "I am conscious, therefore I am and I think." Without consciousness there is no identifiable human existence. We come close to the divine image primarily through the enormous beneficence of consciousness. Consciousness is tantamount to spirit. It is not Spirit but it invades spirit space. This explains precisely why consciousness has the deep affinity

to the infinite and limitlessness and God. It defines our inclination to things spirit and to God. To be conscious in the human
condition is to be spirit formed and God bound. Consciousness
makes us God friendly. We are in his zone. We sense his existence and even his presence. We are quasi inhabitants of his
world. We are under his tutorial influence.

When Thomas Jefferson argued in the "Declaration of
Independence" that all men are created equal and to them
accrue certain unalienable rights, he made exclusive reference to
the fact these truths are "self-evident" by the fact that they are
"endowed by the Creator." This declaration did not come from
the King of England, or from the Bible, or from his Anglican
heritage, it came out of a conscious revelation that God's spirit
placed on him. Consciousness delivered this self-evident fact.
Our deeper awarenesses emanate from sources beyond the tangible and merely visible. Truths we espouse and truths that we
inscribe in our laws are the products of the self-evidence of God
and his spirit working through our consciousness.

The physical instincts we are all aware of preserve and safeguard our earthly existence; they rule and direct daily life; they
are built-in and mechanical. Consciousness, however, reaches
sources outside and far beyond anything temporal. It literally
outsources information. Before the electronic internet there
existed an internet of spirit far more extensive and pervasive
than anything manmade. It comes with consciousness. It was
God invented. The physical instincts help us operate in the
world in the flesh, consciousness draws us out of ourselves and
into a world not only of intellectual concepts but into a world
far beyond the circumference of this planet. Instincts operate
in the world of the seen, consciousness deals with the world
outside and far beyond, and so far never seen.

Consciousness is the gateway to the unseen. Consciousness
enables us to enter into a world of spirit and God and infinite

futures. Without consciousness we would be incapable and unknowing of God and the infinite life beyond. This is our admission slip into the unfathomable eternal world. We are physically deeply limited but with consciousness we are exceedingly unlimited.

However, we can only think eternity, we cannot reach eternity. We can think immensity, but we cannot overcome gravitation. We are capable of such lofty infinite forevers but temporality pins our feet to time and death. Moreover, in spite of the limitlessness of consciousness we are kept in the dark: God and spirit remain a mystery; we have no final assurances about the future; we hope without confirmed evidence; we imagine without uncovering tomorrow's footprints. No one has ever returned to assure us that an infinite beyond is a reality. The Bible indicates it, the prophets proclaim it, saints are celebrated as having arrived there—somewhere..., out there..., way beyond here—yet no one has seen or knows where the "there" is. Consciousness and its affinity for the infinite drives this consensus. But consciousness alone cannot give evidence for its affirmation. It remains locked in a premise—that God and the infinite exist, but they remain speculation.

The rescue to this dilemma occurs when a well known aid arrives by the name of faith. It is not an unknown phenomenon. We are born with it. We live daily with it. We survive with it. Even death is peaceful because of it. Faith is our survival kit. We are literally wrapped in faith. We eventually come to know things but in the meantime we are sustained by faith. We live by faith, not by sight. The future thrives inside the mind only because of the forces of faith. Hope itself is faith driven; it is an extension of faith. To believe is to aspire forward. Today's faith is tomorrow's hope.

In essence we really do not know anything. Knowing is a gathering exercise. Unless you are the inventor-creator, your knowledge is second hand. More precisely, unless you create from "nothing," you really do not know something. Your knowledge is second hand and incomplete. Knowledge "derived" involves dissecting and exploring the evidence, it never absolutely arrives at the essence. Knowledge is forever inconclusive. Only the creator knows, everyone else observes. You are a witness. Knowledge gives credence to what the creator has provided. You see but you do not see. You know but you do not know. Only the creator knows with certainty and complexity.

Human knowing consists principally in "believing what is revealed." If we really authentically knew something, we could then dispose of faith. But that cannot and will not happen. Knowledge is not our biggest suit. We busy ourselves with exploring, but in the midst of all this activity and at the final conclusion we remain believers. In every moment of life we are consigned to faith. Faith is the rudder of life. It is never a case where you "know something," it is always a fact that you "believe something." Indeed, we believe something with greater intensity than we know something. Moreover, we believe in more things than things we know.

Furthermore, the believing we engage in surpasses all boundaries. To say "I believe in my wife and my children" has finite justification and verification, but to say "I believe in God" reaches into the boundless where there is no verification. We could not accomplish this feat without consciousness. Knowing does nothing to advance me toward God; consciousness does that effortlessly. We are believers before we are knowers because consciousness comes first and paves the way for knowing. Any activity into the boundless unknown is the gift of consciousness. With consciousness believing in God is the centerpiece of its function and activity. With consciousness all roads lead to the infinite and to God.

Consciousness introduces us to spirit and God. The church presence and its functions are accessories to that introduction. We are not religious because of the church, we are religious because of our consciousness and its subsequent awareness of and believing in God. God is an innate phenomenon in consciousness. He is reality and dogma simultaneously. To say that God comes accidentally and externally (by way of others and by institutional forms) falsifies the reality of the experience. God comes more directly and intimately. Consciousness experiences the immediate present such as sights and sounds, but it likewise transports things distant and unseen that cannot be verified with the physical senses. There is a presence of God in consciousness. He is neither an outsider or an intruder. He is part of the very landscape we call human consciousness. To be destined for immortality and not know the source and the party responsible for that outcome would constitute a colossal contradiction. The inclination to immortality is accompanied by the very source of that immortality—God himself. Jesus' whole coming to earth simply confirms that outcome (immortality) and that source (God, the Father).

In a very real sense Ralph Waldo Emerson was correct in saying, "To your own self be true." It is in self-reliance, that you will find the truth. It is God given, not introduced from outside. Our essential God-source is in our own consciousness. Reading thousands of books on theology or listening to similar amounts of sermons and lectures on God will not replace the conviction one has about the veracity and profundity of God in one's life. God is real not because of someone else's word but because of God's word in one's head. It is specifically God's imprint in one's consciousness. Faith comes by God, not by some other voice. Jesus confirms this process: "No one can come to me unless the Father who sent me draws them..." (J.6:44)

The gospel of Jesus Christ has one singular ring to it, and that is that the Father in heaven draws the individual to himself, and Jesus is the only intermediary. There are others who may suggest the truth, but they are outside the direct message coming from the divine authority and divine power. God does not require translators. If human life is God's creation, and human consciousness bears evidence of God's spirit, then God himself is at the forefront of that activity. Anyone who wants to hear will hear. All others will pass over to some other non-authoritative power that speaks insufficiently of the truth and its reality. God does not have to reinvent himself in a world he has already invented. And what he invented, he sustains. And what he sustains, he directs. A conscious mind housed in a truly conscious spirit will hear and abide by the authority of God and no one else.

Leaders who claim top affiliation with Jesus because of their clerical rank in society must always endeavor to preach a message of self-reliance to all audiences. "God is near," "God is in heart and mind," "God comes to those who are open and listen," is not a mystic's phantasy. If we are God made, we are God driven, and furthermore God led. A man without a bible, without a church, without a family, without a friend, alone on an island, is in the solitary presence of God and his spirit, whether he knows it or not. His omnipresence defies denial. Human consciousness corroborates that denial.

In the end the statement, "I am," confirms a state of consciousness. That realization produces an unlimited ability to reach not only seeable realities but also, and importantly, the unseeable realities. In that state of consciousness we maneuver between knowledge and belief, with belief taking precedence in almost every stage of knowing. We are believers in every pursuit and believers in every outcome. It is in that makeup we can and must say that, "I am, therefore I believe." Most of what "I know" is attributable to what " I believe." God is the exclusive holder of knowledge—without exception.

The human "I am" and the divine "I am" are not on the same planet, nor in the same galaxy. My "I am" gives me a glimpse of my existence and an awareness of my individuality as separate from everything else. God's "I am" is an indescribable statement into the very essence of his existence that has no origin except itself. My "I am" is the result of my existence at the hand of someone else. His "I am" is self-produced without any other intervention. For this reason God does not really know anything because he is everything. Essence is his nature and knowledge can only follow the path of essence. If you are essence, you are simultaneously knowledge. In God's case knowledge becomes superfluous, because essence surpasses knowledge. In the case of human beings knowledge is acquired and only verified and retained through belief. We are essentially only believers and knowers superficially.

For human beings consciousness is king. Without it we would be totally immersed in matter and confined to instincts, and therefore without any awareness of space and infinity, and, therefore, God. For God consciousness and existence and essence are all indistinguishable. His "is" is synonymous with consciousness. In fact it is pure consciousness. His consciousness does not require matter and form. His "is" is a consciousness that manifests itself without action or movement. In a real sense the opening sentence of John's gospel sums up God's eternal essence: "In the beginning was the Word, and the Word was with God, and the Word was God." God as Word—as consciousness— is the magnanimous reality in the divinity. God is most often referred to as Spirit; however, God as pure consciousness better delineates God in his most unique role as creator and provider. In the very first lines of the book of Genesis God is referred to as Spirit "hovering over the waters" and speaking life into existence. But God is not some form, albeit Spirit. He is formless. He is Vastness. He is pure Consciousness. God surpasses Spirit, because Spirit conjures up a form, in spite of its invisibility, but God is formless. Nothing anthropomorphic attaches itself to God. Consciousness best approaches the formless vastness that describes God. God creates without any form, without any necessity of shape or structure. We, on the other hand, cannot operate without body and form; consciousness gives us capacities far beyond matter, but our operational environment is limited to the world of matter. God's consciousness surpasses all matter, form, and structure. It suffices in itself. It is simply plenipotentiary.

We humans are the recipients of a quality that in God is his very essence, and, above all, his power. If we could reach a semblance of that essence and its power we could "move mountains." When Jesus claims that faith the size of a mustard seed can transfer a mountain from one place to another, he is talking about empowering consciousness through faith to execute that action. God has shared a power that fully describes himself and with that power we not only experience ourselves and the world around us, but the vastness that is beyond and also the divinity itself. Consciousness is our connection with God. It is not a void, but a vessel filled with his virtues and his presence.

Hence, if consciousness is king, then each human being has the innate ability to experience and benefit from God's creative existence in one's life. We are not foreigners in a wasteland of matter and instincts, but genuine participants in a vast unimaginable odyssey called life and as a consequence invited into the very mind of God Himself. God transcends everything and we, fortunately, are able to enjoy some of his transcendence.

Chapter 1

CONTEXT IS EVERYTHING

WE WHO HAVE FOR CENTURIES ESPOUSED Christianity as a lifeline to God have believed that we had entered a zone of pristine truth and unquestionable morality. Christianity stood for the most and for the best. If Jesus is the way and the truth and the life, and we had adopted that same Jesus, then we had adopted nothing but the best of God for humanity.

We came to believe in Jesus no matter the odds. What he said was not only in the gospel but was gospel. Jesus did not beat around the bush. Jesus was never a sell-out. Truth in all things must do the selling; it does not abandon its roots. We came to believe in someone above us but for us. We came to believe in something irrevocable, something uncreated, something beyond creation. Jesus was not a mystic, a soothsayer, a prophet; not a marvel, a genius, a prodigy. He left no writings or artifacts, but left an image that even the ugliest of humanity knows has inviolable credentials. At the very mention of his name humanity beckons to take a knee. Jesus, the name and the image, calls humanity out of its selfish, narcissistic shell to a place of honesty and integrity.

Jesus, in spite of his commonplace name, did not come to provide coverup for human immorality. He did not come to

1

walk around the commandments Moses brought down from the mountain. His mission carried him into a battleground with evil, both individual and collective, and he was steadfast in facing that evil every day and at every moment. He forgave but he did not excuse. He talked patiently, but did not submit to hypocrisy and slander. He upheld love for neighbor, but he did not let love become an excuse for inaction and Political Correctness. Jesus did not have time for mob rule and conservative complacency.

He had to take evil on and refused to let it pervade the human condition. Prophets of old did this, but their authority and influence never lasted. Jesus' authority came unmatched and continued un-ended. It possessed an eternal chronology. If Jesus is eternal, then his truth is eternal. His directives reach forward into the future and beyond. What he said then in person way back then commands us today. He stood on top of the mountain preaching the beatitudes, but never let the beatitudes become mere platitudes.

The primary dilemma today, and for many years past, is that Jesus is portrayed as a platitude. Nice guy, nice words, nice performances, even nicer miracles and death raisings, but his portrayal today matches that of a stage performer who wants to make everyone feel good, feel comfortable, feel wanted, and feel all together. Christianity has become a club for nice people who have to say nice things and give even nicer performances. That means getting along with evil. That means checking your principles at the door. That means "staying away from offending anyone." This is not the Jesus message. Love is, but love without principle is not. Kindness is, but kindness without steadfast truth is not. Justice is, but justice without God's laws is not.

Jesus today has a limited vocabulary. His original vocabulary has been trimmed and modified to meet the demands of later generations who were not able or willing to receive his message. Over the centuries numerous adjustments have been made and as a consequence the message becomes whatever the listener can bear. For centuries Christians mocked Christ with the brutal system of slavery. The South was full of church going Christians who abused and brutalized men and women as slaves. Can anyone explain how they marched into a "Christian church setting" on Sundays and professed a belief in Jesus but before and afterwards chained, beat, sold, raped, separated the families of, and even murdered those men and women they kept as slaves? Can anyone of a Christian faith explain how Jesus' name could be raised amongst those slave holding members who brutalized the bodies and spirits of those kept in bondage and brutality? The answer is Jesus was not there. Jesus could not be there. Jesus would refuse to be there. Jesus would have condemned them for their depravity. If he had used a whip against the money changers in the temple, he would have used a bigger whip against the owners of slave quarters. A whip? No! Fire and Gehenna!

But somehow Christianity was compromised for slave owners. It accepted the practice of slavery and all of its brutality and inhumanity. It gave unchallenged reign to those who would buy and sell humanity, then encumber it for a lifetime. This may have been the Christianity of the 17th and 18th centuries and beyond, but it never was the gospel of Jesus Christ. Those who professed a belief in Jesus and proclaimed his gospel in the churches during those times shamed and desecrated his gospel by not condemning those who practiced that awful testament to inhumanity. Christianity lost its virginity to a weak and misconceived preaching class. It further demonstrated that Christianity is a commodity "for sale." The "goodies" of love, peace, patience, goodness, joy, happiness, and long suffering are the commodities for sale and that beckon customers to congregate around them. They are mere generalities that satisfy the masses and produce a general feeling of goodwill but turn silent and easily submit to the evil that the masses engage in and sanction.

Throughout so many periods of human history from the beginning of Christianity, the gospel of Jesus has been turned into a cultural stamp of approval. Society adopts something and the church concedes. The force of his message is re-decoded to match the prevailing external pressures in society and in the culture. So much so now that the message of old has been edited and re-edited to mimic the mind of the beholder, not the mind of bestower. Jesus did not ask for interpretation and re-interpretation of his message. He spoke clearly and acted clearly and did not ask for modified versions of his messages. "Do as I tell you and as I have directed you, not as you misconstrue me and my message," would be the paraphrase of his message. Parables were used to keep things simple and colloquial, out of the range of philosophical dichotomies and legalistic parsings and theological ruminations. Jesus was literal and mater-of-fact, not inclined to obfuscation. If you read the gospels with a clear and open mind, you will glimpse at the steadfastness and determination in his words. Once you modify his message, you have completely destroyed the message. A believer has only one path to follow, and that is to accept the seriousness and severity of his words. He once told a crowd of listeners, "Be perfect as your Heavenly Father is perfect." Anything less is not of Jesus. Anything less is a distortion and a destruction of Jesus' words. Even though he said to love your enemy, he never indicated that we endorse the enemy, or let the enemy take over his words, or reconfigure his words, or reinterpret his words, or take the necessity out of his words, or slander another human being, or pillage another's property, or brutalize and kill another human being. The Heavenly Father

4

does not collaborate with evil. Promoting love, peace, patience, goodness, joy, happiness, does not mean surrendering for the sake of these to evil. Evil is to be cast out, not adorned and equalized with the good, as if the good to prove that it is good must walk into the den of evil and lay down and be cursed. Evil will be met by a vengeance, perhaps not by us but certainly by the hand of divine justice.

One very obvious observation in the gospels is that Jesus did not work to satisfy the masses. He met with the masses and talked to the masses and performed miracles before the masses, but never caved to the masses. His message was sent to the world and for the world, but the world had no input in that message. Currently, there are Liberal forces in this country that dedicate themselves to rewrite the constitution of the United States and use the very courts that are obligated to uphold that constitution to mutilate its contents. And there are judges and justices in the courts who apply with bias their ideology on the constitution. They insert the liquidity of the culture of the masses on a document that has frozen meaning in time and without that frozen meaning the country no longer exists. Similarly, the meaning of Jesus' words are frozen for all time and any rewriting of those words turns Jesus' message into an absurdity. One word wrongly unfrozen from his entire messaging can mutilate the entire meaning of his message. One word tossed into the cauldron of the culture can obliterate Jesus' purpose and focus. One word without its context dissolves into mass mush, where anyone can distill a new meaning anytime of the day. There is no meaning of Jesus' words without its context. The word "love," for instance, has no significance without its incorporation in the gospels, otherwise it is not the word-meaning Jesus applies but what someone personally unfreezes to push his or her word bias.

Any word a human being uses springs from an emotion and a preconceived bias, and these, in turn, spring from a myriad of contexts—families, cultures, peers, environments, vistas, experiences, opportunities, even tastes and smells. No word we use hangs in a vacuum or is as pure as the wind driven snow. It is processed through multiple filters that shade the very makeup of the word. And all of our contexts issue from the personal and societal masses we find ourselves in. Everything we have and are is delivered to us. We are not islands separated from other islands. We are a speck of sand surrounded and crowded by trillions of other specks of sand, and we are simultaneously crowded by their influences and words. Our contexts shift us from one place to another. We are pushed and led by them. Nothing is frozen. We move with the tides. But Jesus does not. And his words do not. His context is not ours or anything like ours. His context is the Father, nothing else and no one else. His context is frozen in time because it is out of time. If you want to see and know his word, you have to see and know his context. Both are frozen, but neither is static.

Jesus came to introduce a new context, the context of Father, Son, and Spirit. They are out of time and place. Out of words with nuance and disfiguration. Out of earthly ties and attachments. Out of shifting contexts of emotion and expectation. Out of now into forever. Out of mortality into immortality. Hence his resurrection becomes the centerpiece of his work bringing earthly into eternal. He came from another context, not this one. "My kingdom is not of this world," he said. And at another time he said, "Who are my mother and sister and brother." His context was elsewhere, and he was informing us of it and attempting to lead us there.

Jesus' words have no meaning if they are not seen in the context that he placed them. Out of their context they will irrevocably be misused and misunderstood and totally abused. Living temporarily for an eternal destiny was Jesus' primary center of attention. There is no kingdom on this earth. None. Tomorrow is the Kingdom, tomorrow is the context. If Jesus' words are not found in his context, they are completely lost. Indeed, they become anathema to what he really said and expected. Anyone supporting and creating a kingdom on earth has lost Jesus' context and Jesus himself. More than once Jesus told his followers "to leave everything and come follow me." The follower, the believer, must take Jesus on as his or her new and total context.

As long as one's vision of life does not change, then we will not see and experience Jesus in his own declared context. This is precisely why the Jesus of Christianity is not for the masses. Without his context Christianity is something else. Something re-worded. Something out of order. Something modified. Something dressed up. Something merely embellished like art. A word taken out of context has no validity. Jesus taken out of context has less validity. Without his context Jesus loses his credentials. He may look like Jesus, talk like Jesus, even proclaim himself Jesus, but he is not Jesus. When you take Jesus out of the whole context, you have sacrificed the real Jesus. He is more than one word, more than a phrase, more than a few miracles, more than a litany of beatitudes. Jesus is a new world, a new order, a new life.

Over the centuries we, the human race, have installed Jesus into "our" context and "our" milieu. We have built cavernous churches, elaborate shrines, vast institutions for religious learning; we have written uncountable theological treatises on his dual natures, have over-examined his gospels, have superimposed our thoughts on his words and ruminated about the scriptures picking and choosing our favorite launching quotes for the sake of more commentary. All the time we have fitted Jesus into our context. We have managed and arranged his "way and truth and life" into our sinful, selfish, temporal and earthly style of living. Jesus has become convenient fodder for the masses not the Eucharist for eternity.

Jesus' words have segued into commodities. Our religious organizations sell his words and proclaim a doctrine that excludes his seriousness and severity. If the masses want "Nice," then that is what we give them. If the masses want "peace and comfort," then that is what we give them. If the masses want "succor and compassion," they get it. If the masses shout slander and lies, we step aside. If the masses teach same sex marriage, we step aside. If the masses declare Leftist speech means no speech for the religious right, we shut up. If the masses declare a death sentence on unborn babies, we stay silent and condemn no one even when catholic politicians promote and vote for their deaths. The masses rule.

There is no "Jesus Context" in Christianity any more. We have a name, an institution, lots of dogma, lots more ritual, and heavy on devotion and administration, and we are entirely committed to the masses. This commitment includes not offending the masses. The masses have to be respected and given a wide path. It's an untouchable area. Their context overrules any other context in spite of the fact that their context has no substance, no rules, no discipline and no permanence. But they have power, and power means might, and might is always right.

Once you engage the masses for admission, you have surrendered your independence and righteousness. In order to enter inside their denizen you must allow them to filter your message and intentions, and your fundamental activities. They drive the engine and you are in the baggage compartment. The masses drive society and create the majority opinion, in spite of overwhelming evidence of its malfeasance and corruption. The Christian Churches stand aside and allow the masses unfettered dominance over public thought and morality. The masses issue a "cease and desist" order to the conservative flank of society and all activity stops, including the Christian elements in society that purport to adhere to the mandates of the gospel. The churches do not talk back. Their silence supposedly signifies "objectivity" and furthermore exemplifies the presumed "non-combative" spirit of Christ. This gives the masses self-righteous justification for their reckless behavior and dominance. No opposition means reticent consent, or at minimum a superiority over all others especially those least informed and least morally inclined.

The masses can debase politicians and call it free speech. The masses can debunk police and call it police brutality. The masses can demolish statues and call it historic cleansing. The masses can defame the flag because it belies universal freedom. They can remove the American eagle because it represents a white-headed Supremacist vulture. They can burn buildings and call it retribution. They can scream racism every minute of the day when there is nothing else to disclaim. The masses can destroy the Unborn and call it women's rights. And there is no kick back. We simply gather up our tools and clean up the mess they leave behind.

Christianity is a great thing if you can keep it. Jesus did not say let his words be brought to the whole world so that the whole world can remake them. He brought his message in a very specific context to the world in order to remake the world. However, the world has been remaking Christ from the very beginning. Peter tried it. Judas betrayed Jesus because he couldn't accept Jesus as he was and for what he was. Martha tried her influences and pretty much failed. The townsfolk of Nazareth thought they could buy some miracles and they were shut out. The Pharisees tried their cunning over and over again and failed miserably. The masses who received abundant feeding at the miracle of the loaves and fishes tried for more of the same and were rejected. Herod hoped for gems from Jesus and came away with utter silence. Jesus was not someone else's man, he was his own man, the Son of Man, with a commission from and a responsibility to his Father.

Jesus stood down all powers and influences and mobs and masses. No majority and no minority silenced Jesus, nor drove him in a direction outside of his Father's commission. If Christianity has a commission from Jesus, it is to proclaim the truth as it came from him in "his" context and with "his" determination and decisiveness. Less than that is to fall short in huge proportions from his commands, as the rich young man fell short when Jesus asked him "to sell everything and give it to the poor and then come follow him" and subsequently left Jesus with a saddened countenance. Selling Jesus "without reserve" in the selfish and power-manipulative atmosphere of the culture and its media abandons the whole Jesus of the gospels. Once Jesus gave the young man the full context of his message, the young man sulked and left. This is what Christianity has done for interminable ages. It preaches his "nice" words but leaves out the full context of his message. And that message is part word and part context, and that context is part today and very much tomorrow.

In Jesus' parlance tomorrow is always part of today because tomorrow will be today. And today is merely the handmaid of tomorrow. Yesterday has already become today and today will surely become tomorrow. The only today we have is the tomorrow it is becoming. The only today that counts is the tomorrow it is becoming. Indeed, there are no todays until they are defined by tomorrow. The very essence of Christianity is that it wraps itself into and around tomorrow. If resurrection is the key point of Christianity, then tomorrow is what it is all about. Resurrection is a tomorrow event. If you are a Christian, you are becoming tomorrow by the way you live today.

There is a distinct difference between Christ and Christianity, and there is necessarily no comparison between the two. When we are baptized, we are baptized into Christ, not Christianity. Christianity is more than Christ but also less than Christ. There is only one Christ but there are many Christians, which means the one Christ can easily become more and different than he really was. Jesus in the gospels is one person and Jesus in the pulpits of thousands and thousands of churches is someone else. These pulpits preach his words but leave out his context. They know his storyline and his dogmatic demands, but fall short in giving evidence of the context of his life and sayings. This is borne out by Paul (1 Corinthians 1:12-13),when he complains about the many versions of Christ in the early church: "One of you says, 'I follow Paul'; another, 'I follow Apollos'; another, 'I follow Cephas'; another, 'I follow Christ.' Is Christ divided? Was Paul crucified for you? Were you baptized in the name of Paul?" Even in the very beginning of Christianity Paul struggled to keep Christ, not someone or something else.

Christianity is full of people. Christianity is full of ideas. Christianity is full of people trying to get the ideas right. Christianity is full of people making heterodoxy a primary focus. However, Christianity's singular task exists to deliver Christ in his words and in his context, and in his seriousness and boldness, all of which validate his authority and authenticity. If there is any heterodoxy to be found, it will be found in finding the whole Jesus—words and context.

Chapter 2

SOFT JESUS

FOR SO MANY, TOO MANY, CHRISTIANS, JESUS is a name on a book cover. The book starts with Bethlehem and ends in Jerusalem. The book is never opened. And all the time those preaching what's supposedly in the book is Soft Stuff, Good Stuff, non-threatening Stuff—peace, joy, forgiveness, do unto others, don't let your anger go to bed with you, the godly get rich, love conquers all, hope is all you need, every good deed will get rewarded, Jesus loves, Jesus saves, Jesus does anything you want.

All the while no one peeks inside the book to discover who the real Jesus was and is. Jesus is defined by the churches, by the culture, by the behavior of leading Christians, by the many schools engaged in teaching theology, by politicians who claim allegiance to Christianity but legislate something else, by business moguls who live exclusively by profits not by the words of any prophet, and lastly Jesus is defined by the many faces and mouths in the Media and entertainment world. Jesus even rallies around Abortion believers.

The book with Jesus' name on the cover is almost anything to everyone. There is comfort and compassion. There is justice and forbearance. There's faith, hope, and charity. There's unmeasured forgiveness. There's congeniality and universal acceptance. There is something for everyone. Everyone can reap benefits and applause from it for the simple reason that they never open the pages and digest the contents.

According to a lot of clever minds Jesus invented an omnibus of nuanced placebos. He came quietly, then spent 30 years working on wood, finally made an effort to gather a group to follow him for the betterment of humankind before he was killed for being honest. His efforts were primarily gentle and Jesus was not a radical pushing an outrageous message to overwhelm the world. He was a lamb not a lion. Apparently he came all the way from the divine world to carefully and thoughtfully nudge the earth's inhabitants into a kinder, gentler world always respecting their freedom and righteous objections.

Harshness and an aggressive behavior cannot be attributed to Jesus' past, at least not from what modern day historians describe. The country is full of Christian Churches, sects, communities, societies, groups, families who espouse a Jesus who lives outside the pages of the New Testament. There is genuine chaos related to what Jesus said and taught, not to mention how he lived. There is even greater chaos and consternation about what Jesus demanded from everyone. But because Jesus taught peace and love, whatever consternation exists among followers has to be turned into appeasement among the groups. Condemnation stands outside the boundaries of Christian love. The ruling formula of response is "Love your enemy." Disagreement does not lead to condemnation, even if the issue of disagreement is as irreconcilable as Abortion. Love tolerates no exceptions.

In the end Christianity has morphed into a collection of meaningless pleasantries. No one condemns and no one gets condemned. Christians have adopted the golden rule: "do not judge others and you will not be judged." The pretext is that Jesus doesn't condemn, so we can't either. You may be allowed to object but you can't condemn. So if your brother, or sister, is caught in moral jeopardy, your only response is objection not condemnation.

The end result in this Christianity of restraint is that the real Jesus never gets preached. He is subdued by the power of his own words. Those who preach the gospel of Jesus Christ preach only the Jesus of kindness, of congeniality, of long suffering, of self immolation, of turning the other cheek, of forgiving malefactors. A placid love overrules all justice and righteousness and morality. And if a placid love doesn't deter condemnation, then a demand for privacy will. Privacy is the newest exemption for condemnation. It's the latest "New Testament" coverup exclusion from accountability and condemnation.

What we have is placid love and placid Jesus. The churches have commandeered Jesus and the New Testament and as a consequence morality now conforms to culture, not culture conform to morality. The preachers and ministers almost across the board preach what the attendees and the church administrators want to hear not what they should hear. Jesus' message has to pass through PC and liberal filters. Moral orthodoxy emanates from cautious conservative minds on the right while it is shouted down by the blatant progressive views of the leaders of the Left. A prophet must restrain his mouth and parrot the Media of the masses.

However, Jesus' message did not run parallel with the masses. His commission came from his Father who sent his son to convey his (the Father's) message to the masses. We can logically conjecture from the life Jesus led that the substance of the message was not one of slight consequences. If the Father sent his son for a trivial visit of peace to the inhabitants of the earth, then Jesus' horrendous death on the cross does not bear this out. There is nothing trivial or lighthearted about Jesus sojourn on earth. From beginning to end the message was straightforward and it wasn't about peace on earth.

Hence the Christmas moment does not foretell the actual purpose of the event. The full meaning hides somewhere in the swaddling clothes of the infant and the revelation will not be unveiled until the infant is a man. All we can do now is surmise that God came to earth for more than a peace agenda. There is a lot hidden in the swaddling clothes and it's not the message of Peace on Earth.

For God to have reached the decision he did to enter his Son on earth must have come with staggering purpose. To say the least it was a monumental event, which means his coming had to have had catastrophic origins. God sending God to Earth exceeded even extraordinary events. The actual events leading up to the Son of God becoming man forecast in the annals of divine history an underlying frustration with humanity. God was perturbed. In the past He had expressed disgust with creation and entered such disgust through the prophets. These were invariably emissaries, second hand messengers, who transported the divine disgust to men. Never had God come in Person to confront the malfeasance of mankind. He stayed at a distance intervening through selected agents. Most of these initially refused, some ran, but in the end performed their task. But always God stayed away. He could not come. He did not have the requisite body and voice. The divine message, however, was desperately urgent. It had to be delivered. All previous emissaries had insufficiently completed their tasks. Yet the divine message had to be delivered and this time in Person. No more surrogates, no more secondary conscripts. God had to come in Person.

The question was, "How could this be accomplished?" God is unseeable, untouchable. His invisibility is his greatness, it is his nature. How do you take that nature and expose it to mankind without losing its essence. If God becomes other than God, He loses his "godness." A secondary existence diminishes God; a stand-in personality detracts from the divine Person. God is God as God. Crossing natures is against the primary nature of any species. When we make a dog speak with a human voice, it is staged not real. A bird that screeches with human words does not have human nature sequestered in the background. Human and animal natures resist crossing over; in fact, cannot be done and has never occurred. For God to cross over to human nature crashes into an identical insurmountable incongruity. There exists a chasm beyond infinite proportions between the divine and the human. God crossing over to man appears in the slightest as out of bounds and inconceivable. It is too much, too far a reach. God cannot, must not, become man. But it happened. God defied the totally impossible. He took his Divinity and entered a nature inundated with imperfections and consumed with selfishness.

The more puzzling factor beyond the fact that he came as human is the way he came. Not just as man but as a meager man. Born to a poor woman, to a poor carpenter, in a poor town, to a hostage country, to a religion suffocated by ritual rites and bloated with insufferable leadership arrogance. Amazing that he came but equally amazing is how it happened—that he came in swaddling clothes and lived incognito at the bottom of the economic scale. For thirty years he was invisible and unknown. The divine arrives on earth and is hidden away in Nazareth. The invisible remains invisible, without Divine recognition, without Divine-Royal trappings, without any acknowledgement from mankind. After the shepherds and angels and kings at his birth, he is a nobody with no assets. In his earliest childhood years he is in a foreign land away from all family and relatives. Had he died before the age of 30 he would have left a void in the history of the world.

Peace covers up and disguises the underlying meaning of Jesus in Bethlehem. Peace on Earth was not the message of Jesus at his birth. The real meaning was hardship and insignificance. Mary and Joseph traveling to Bethlehem for a census report on foot and on a donkey conjures up an arduous journey especially for a young woman who is pregnant. There is hardship written all over this story, from the dangers of traveling on foot, the risks of encounters with unsavory individuals, the requirements of finding food and water, exposure to climate uncertainties, the exigencies of nature, finally arriving in a village without reservations. Mary and Joseph were at the mercy of time, climate and circumstances. They found a resting place in a small barn already occupied by animals. Straw became the bedroom furniture of that night. And that night Jesus was born with Joseph and incidental domestic animals in attendance. This all bespeaks of hardship and, as an observer looking on centuries later, much insignificance.

God, the Father, chose hardship and insignificance for his Son's entry into human history. An insignificant mother, an insignificant adoptive father, an insignificant birth place, an insignificant time, surrounded the advent of the Son of God on earth. In reality, the Son of God has no surroundings. But he wants nothing. He has his Father, nothing else matters. His birth and his birth place display a detachment from his surroundings. His mother is adopted, his father even more so, his crib is someone else's and the dwelling is donated for the night.

Was this an accident? Hardly. It is at the heart of Jesus' coming. His birth is divested of everything—of culture, self-assurances, possessions, physical preconditions and preconceptions, and every element of the known world—after which we are left with Jesus alone and nothing else. The baby is the focus. He becomes the singular focus in an empty room.

One amazing fact is that no aristocracy surrounds Jesus at his birth. No plumage, no epaulets, no golden slippers, no jewels and crowns, no knights and military guards, no castle and bedecked audience chamber encompasses Jesus. He is very much alone. He is Jesus in a cloth wrap in the midst of a few domestic animals with one mother and one father. He is Jewish because he is born to a Jewish woman with a Jewish adoptive father which gives him no distinction except exclusion as a member of a race and religion that is surrounded by hostile enemies.

Jesus' birth has been transformed over the centuries. Pomp and circumstance was not present in its original form; there was Mary and there was Joseph, and that was it. It was beyond simple. It was austere. It was invisible and un-trumpeted. But through the centuries Jesus' birth grew in ceremony and fanfare, in ostentation and pageantry. The austerity of Bethlehem vanishes out of sight. The stable is still there, indeed, but the Son of God gets smaller every year.

What is surprising in all this is that the Son of God does not come to govern but to hide. In Bethlehem he is virtually alone and shortly afterwards he is whisked away to Egypt. There is the visit of the Magi and his presentation in the temple; however, these events produce no widespread attention outside of a few mysterious kings from unknown lands and a couple of seniors in the temple who privately and clandestinely await the savior of the Jewish Nation. No crowds attend either events and no aftershock about the event is recorded.

What is fundamentally evident in all this is that Jesus does not come to rule. He is Son of God, but his actions reveal him as Son of Man. Nothing of privilege surrounds him and nothing of power draws attention to him. If he is God, or of God, no one knows it.

His lineage is a secret and everything about him is secret. His birth comes with insignificance. It comes with meagerness. It comes in poverty. With austerity and simplicity. He is unknown and unattended. Without assets and possessions. No inheritance, or wealth.

Jesus' birth reverses everything. He comes as a model for mankind. Wealth and distinction are ruled out. Lineage is of no consequence. Insignificance is Significance. Poverty suffers no shame. Free of possessions is freedom indeed. "Foxes have holes and birds have nests but the Son of Man has no place to rest his head." Unencumbered and unpretentious are jewels of character. Attachment to God becomes the ultimate source of life. Jesus' only attachment was his Father. He spoke of him always and with deep and abiding connection and obedience.

Jesus' birth and the nature of his birth is the first of his messages. Everything Jesus does and how he does it becomes a teaching. Picking Jesus' birth but isolating it from the actual circumstances violates Jesus himself and his coming. It's like saying "I believe in you but I don't believe in what and how you are doing it." We pick Jesus but not the nuances of his movements and circumstances. Jesus himself is the message and everything surrounding him is the message. Absent these movements and circumstances Jesus becomes a fabricated man-made phenomenon. It is a makeover of adulterous proportions. At his birth Jesus is not a king adorned in splendor, but a very tiny barn born baby surrounded by a smaller group of even less significant attendees who give evidence of no power and no wealth. There is no king here.

Chapter 3

JOHN THE BAPTIST
("NO GREATER MAN")

CONTEMPORANEOUS WITH JESUS WAS HIS cousin John the Baptist. Their conceptions were 6 months apart, giving John just six months seniority over Jesus so that when Mary came pregnant with Jesus, John would be anointed in his mother's womb in Jesus' presence. Only one man in all of Israel prepared the nation for the coming of the Savior. John held a singular and privileged position among all the Jews. No scholar, no religious elite, no prominent business figure, John lived away from the fray of Jewish life and affairs. He prepared himself in the wilderness and upon entering into the lives of his fellow countrymen he preached a salvation of awareness and repentance. He possessed an unassailable reputation not only among the average citizen but from everyone on top including the notorious Herod, who secretly came to listen to John's talks and admired his words.

John's entire life was devoted to "preparing the way" for Jesus. God hand-picked John to perform the introductions for Jesus and he did so from a distance keeping himself out of the mischief of daily life. There were no failings in John's life and no mishaps. He was the real thing, the one man sent to proclaim, "the lamb of God," "the light of the world," "God among us."

John met Jesus in the womb but never saw Jesus until Jesus' appearance at the Jordan where he was baptizing. John's life was bitterly austere living frugally and with the barest of necessities until his death. God called him to prepare the way of his son and that is exclusively what he did. No deterrents, no deviations took John from his designated task. He was always on message. God relied on one man to proclaim Jesus' coming. One was enough.

John, the prophet, was not for profit and completely disconnected from the Jewish Elite. John belonged solely to God, performing for God, and advancing God's Son to the world. Perhaps without any risk of exaggeration John is the most guileless human being in all of Scripture. Jesus himself referred to him as the greatest of all human beings. John could not be bought, could not be compromised, could not succumb to threats or imprisonment. He was untouchable. He was the perfect forerunner for Jesus whose life exemplifies austerity and who had only one continuous and consistent source of influence, who was his Father.

John spoke only One Language, the Language of God. That language was serious and severe. It was not the language of a peacemaker. When he called out the Jewish leaders for their deceit and referred to them as "Vipers," he unleashed all restraint to denounce them. Prophets have short messages and short lives, and John was the most perfect example of both. He spoke clearly and pointedly delivering a lethal analysis of what truth demanded and that truth did not reside in the mouths of the Sadducees and Pharisees. Not one of either party ever defected to John, in spite of overwhelming evidence of his mass appeal, his God delivered messages, and his persistent exposure of their hypocrisy.

In John there was no ambiguity. He spoke firmly and unequivocally. No one doubted his words; they just stayed away from them. John may have been in the "wilderness" but he spoke with God's voice calling all Israel to a baptism of repentance. All Israel knew of him. Prophets were heard in those days in spite of no telegraph and no wireless. Word of mouth carried far and swiftly by eager ears that awaited news from abroad and from above.

God called John to the wilderness for two reasons. The first was to keep John in close touch with the Spirit away from the cities and the distortions of everyday life. The city corrupts mind and spirit dragging human consciousness into the quagmire of deceit and falsehood. From John's conception the spirit had dwelt inside of him and as a consequence there was no further need of "other" influences. He had been dedicated to God and had been destined for one unique task and nothing was to deter his preparation and coming. Anything outside the sphere of the spirit would have and could have delayed and misled his coming as the one and only messenger for Jesus.

The angel appearing to Zechariah announcing John's coming states clearly the scope and nature of John's life: "He will drink neither wine nor strong drink. He will be filled with Holy Spirit even from his mother's womb, and he will turn many of the children of Israel to the lord their God. He will go before him in the spirit and power of Elijah to turn the hearts of fathers toward children and the disobedient to the understanding of the righteous, to prepare a people fit for the lord." (Lk.1:15-17)

The Spirit of God encompassed the entirety of John's life. God wanted only one man, one life, and one mouth proclaiming the "the way of the Lord." Unconditional dedication and separation from the world would be crucial in this one man's life and words. Very early in his life John left for the wilderness and there received his commission from God. With the Essenes or near the Essenes he studied and absorbed his task. There he remained secluded and protected from any influences of culture and theocracy.

In addition to his dedication to God's spirit John lived a life of diligent self-discipline. Spirit without discipline is futile. The necessary path to spirit is discipline. A life undisciplined removes the influence of the spirit. The two are most compatible and required companions. John's life exemplified that union of spirit and discipline. "Neither wine nor strong drink" is the prelude to a disciplined life. Every activity of human existence must conspire to live in disciple and with discipline. Spirit without discipline is an oxymoron, and discipline without spirit borders on mere odious repression.

Living in "the wilderness" further describes John's modified environment. However, hibernation from society is not the essence of self-discipline nor does it fully describe John's personal life, but a degree of hibernation must accompany anyone attached to the spirit and not the world. It is hard to imagine someone in the midst of public noise and chaos staying focused on the Spirit of God. There are many activities in life that can tolerate a dalliance between a dedicated vocation and flirting with frivolity, but a true dedication to the life of spirit does not. Before bringing his son into the world society God wanted a messenger of pristine credentials and unquestioned ability to handle the lies and onslaughts of unredeemed fools like Herod and the blemished self-idolatrous Pharisees and Sadducees. The testing of John was done "in the wilderness" many years before he came forward to "prepare the way of the Lord," which required unbroken persistence and eye on the goal.

John the Baptist is the essential and only lead-in to Jesus. Before Jesus would one day soon tell his followers "to leave everything and come follow me" John had already reached that point. Self-denial and self-discipline were trademarks of John's life and necessarily qualities to be adopted by those to become followers of Jesus. John leads to Jesus and his life in the spirit and his life of self-discipline must continue after Jesus with those who follow him. Jesus never questions John's qualifications or his behavior; his praise is unconditional and exceptional. John is an exemplar among men. That includes his dedication to God and his self-discipline, both coming together to execute a perfect task.

The self-discipline of John ranks second to none of qualifications for someone aspiring to follow God. It is a sine qua non for those preparing for Jesus, as was John, and similarly for those following Jesus. If God is a discipline one is attempting to reach in life, then self-discipline is the necessary companion. Nothing attains its goal without the handmaid of self-discipline. Even in the secular world of any career self-discipline is the essential background for achievement and success. It becomes an absolute pathway to achievement. An aspiring violinist starts his or her career at the age of three. A mental memory genius starts reading at the age of two. Genius starts very early and never abandons its quest without a dedication to self-discipline. Any quest for success requires a life of focus without the distractions and limitations of debilitating excesses.

John becomes the first role model for Christians. If he is the first to usher in Christ, he subsequently has the task of ushering in his followers. If he was good enough for Christ, he is certainly good enough for those who follow behind Christ. John's devotion to self-discipline cannot be classified as excessive, only exemplary. When Jesus is accused of behaving like a glutton and drunkard because of some of the company he kept, he is contrasted with John whose reputation for austerity and abstinence had spread far and wide.

John's personal life had assured everyone of his integrity and authenticity. He possessed an irreproachable character, unbendable, unyielding, and adamantine in every circumstance including issues with the Jewish religious elite and any political heads of state. He readily condemned the Pharisees who came for a baptism of repentance at the Jordan insisting their repentance was false. He likewise condemned Herod for his adulterous marriage to Herodias, the wife of his brother, which became the very cause of his imprisonment and death. Without his dedication to self-discipline in every instance of his life, he could not have ventured into battle with the moral evil in his environment. His strength of character started with himself—his physical habits, his intake of food and drink, the complete jurisdiction of his mind, and lastly the conformity of his spirit to God. He endured the world outside because he was able to subdue the world inside.

In every way, John is the lead saint for all of Christianity. He was everything a prophet should be and could be. He was flawless to an extreme. He was the forerunner to Jesus, the "Lamb of God" he announced at the Jordan. His mother conceived him as a direct promise from God.

He was touched by the spirit before he was born and anointed by Jesus in his mother's womb. His years of sacrifice and self-discipline in the desert eventually led him to the shores of the Jordan where he spread his twofold message of repentance and the arrival of a savior. No one doubted the truth of his message, they simply kept their distance.

Like every other prophet he preached repentance and like every other prophet he condemned evil. Hypocrisy was number one on his list of evils and he never hesitated to condemn it, so when the Pharisees came to him for baptism he exclaimed, "You brood of vipers! Who warned you to flee from the coming wrath?" (Mt.3:7)

John's life of discipline endowed him with the fortitude and strength of conviction to not only come to the truth but to exact it from those who chose to ignore and violate the truth. He had no tolerance for violators. He executed his role as primary prophet of the age with exceptional distinction and with much notoriety, only because he was constantly in someone's face. His single advantage for the truth was his direct connection with the spirit. In other words, he had God's ear, or, rather, God had his ear. John was not a Jewish religious leader; he was a prophet of God. His truth and courage emanated from the spirit. He was outside culture and religion. His informant was God himself. Unlike other prophets who wavered and faltered, John pursued a course of industrious, unflagging demand for the truth and integrity. No one was above his prosecuting voice and unrelenting condemnation.

Prophets come seldom in history and they match a common profile of someone who comes reluctantly later in life, requests for exemption from the calling, performs with modest success, then either dies a martyr or is banished from society. John came with his calling from the womb, prepared for his vocation in the wilderness, gave evidence of his calling all along the Jordan, preached and baptized unceasingly and passionately for repentance, connected the dots between repentance and the coming of the Messiah, then witnessed his coming and baptism and anointing, and finally was martyred for his defense of the truth.

John was privy to the truth and privy to the coming of Jesus. He was declaratory about both. His gift was to define the truth and then defend it. He backed off to no one. He called a spade a spade and left no one unscathed. After John is imprisoned Jesus defends and describes the magnitude and forcefulness of John: "What did you go out to the desert to see? A reed swayed by the wind?" (Mt.11:7-10) The question is rhetorical. Nothing sways John. John is the superlative force for truth and the good. He cannot be bought nor compromised. And Jesus continues; "Then what did you go out to see? Someone dressed in fine clothing?" No, that's for palace life. Then Jesus tells them what they really came to see: "Then why did you go out? To see a

Prophet? Yes, I tell you, and more than a prophet." John exceeds the role of the prophet not because he dies for his beliefs but because he stands steadfast for the truth and confronts anyone who attempts to thwart the evidence for the truth.

John was a man for all seasons, for all men and for all times. The austerity of his life and the boldness of his convictions converged to create a man, a prophet, a champion, for the truth never seen before and not seen again. He is that one man, "a voice in the wilderness," declaring and crying for all mankind to repent of its evil and selfishness and come to the Savior, Jesus Christ. He doesn't ask, he demands. And for those who refuse, the consequences are lethal.

According to John's testimony God's principles and truths are not optional. They are not for sale and they are not for compromise. And there is no hiding behind a secular culture or secular laws or religious laxity and ineptitude claiming an exemption. You never heard of exemptions issuing from John's mouth. On the contrary, John issued condemnation for those who deviated from righteous behavior and unaccommodating disapproval for anyone committing offenses against another human being. No one escaped his eye of justice. For those who came to the Jordan seeking true repentance he proclaimed a litany of righteous behaviors.

John enters Christianity as the centerpiece for the life of a follower of Christ. Dedicated, decisive, devoted, determined to do God's bidding to stand firm for truth, justice and the arrival of the Savior. He is not swayed by any wind or threat of personal danger. He lives in God's bubble. He chose to live outside the environment of weak and evil men in an environment that allowed God's spirit to nourish and strengthen him. The Jordan was not an escape, but an advancement to things closer to God's mind and his power.

The message John's life gives us is one of certainty in the truth and an ability to stand firmly in its presence and defend it. John's message is this: Where evil exists, it is to be condemned not accommodated or compromised. Evil is a fact of human existence. Where there are human beings, there is evil, some of it personal and some of it collective. So much of it is the result of a collective "conscience" that allows individuals to adapt to evil without personal guilt. The collective "conscience" escapes and removes personal judgment and condemnation, so if your behavior allies with evil you can feel safe and secure knowing that the "big conscience" guarantees you free passage. Not for John: "Who told you to escape from the wrath to come?"

We live in a society and culture and world that celebrates slander, lies, deceit, sexual perversion, the redefinition of God's laws and language and creation, and above all abortion. More and more each day these are protected by a "collective conscience" that is broadcast 24/7 into our ears by a Media (social and public) of ritual accommodation. Truth is not truth, it is ideology. Truth is not tradition, it is evolution. Truth is not fact, it is party propaganda. Truth is not discipline, it is self-indulgence. Truth reveals no crime, it covers for personal privacy and rights. Men and Media fabricate the truth. God is a mere bystander with no voice.

John's adherence to truth came from his adherence to God. If you get your truth from your environment and the cacophony of messaging in the environment, then you become subject to the evils professed by that environment, but if your spirit is attached to the Spirit given to you in your mother's womb then that Spirit will lead you to the truth. John's ear was for God not man. His life came from God, his calling came from God, his messaging came from God, and subsequently he was able to proclaim the Son of God to the world and the truths and principles his son wanted proclaimed to the world.

Finally, John was a truthsayer, and a very tough one at that. His mentor was God. He was the pathway to Christ. He was handpicked. He not only announces the arrival of Christ, he sets the moral stage from which Jesus will act and concur. John is not a mere harbinger for the Savior, or some sort of announcer, a heralder, or introducer. His words spoke volumes about the evil that existed at the time and the corrective measures needed to overcome and repent for that evil. John ushered in a moral dynamic that had not been preached before. Whereas the Pharisees called for adherence to a set of external ritual demands, John spoke to the morality of personal and interpersonal relationships: "And the crowds asked him, 'What should we do?' He said to them in reply, 'Whoever has two cloaks should share with the person who has none. And whoever has food should do the likewise.' Even tax collectors came to be baptized and they said to him, 'Teacher, what should we do?' He answered them, 'Stop collecting more than what is prescribed.' Soldiers also asked him, 'What is it that we should do?' He told them, 'Do not practice extortion, do not falsely accuse anyone, and be satisfied with your wages." (Lk.3:10-14)

The torch of morality was passed from John to Jesus, and with the same consequences: "John answered them all, 'I baptize you with water. But one who is more powerful than I will come, the strap of whose sandals I am not worthy to untie. He will baptize you with the Holy Spirit and fire. His winnowing fork is in his hand to clear his threshing floor and to gather the wheat into the barn, but he will burn up the chaff with unquenchable fire." (Mt.3:11-12)

John was not a mere stage-hand waiting to open the curtain for Jesus' appearance. John was a critical part of the act, a vital part of the performance, a performance that brought God to the limelight, and along with him all the unabridged demands for moral uprightness and steadfastness.

Chapter 4

JESUS OUT OF PEACEMAKING

ONE GIGANTIC PIECE OF FAKE NEWS THAT SUR-
rounds Jesus is that he came to deliver peace in the world.
Over and over again we are submitted to the notion that God
sent his Son to earth to make a heavenly paradise out of an
earthly chaos. Jesus was to become the Peacemaker of all time.
His arrival as an innocent babe is more or less proof of that,
implying that Jesus the defenseless one in the manger would
herald a time of no resistance, of no retaliation, of no vengeance, of non-violence. The star of Bethlehem after all universally symbolizes peace. So Jesus, by no design of his own or
his Father's, becomes the peace baby.

The only problem with that theory is that the baby Jesus'
arrival caused the massacre of hundreds of other babies at the
hand of Herod. Apparently, Jesus' reign of peace didn't last
very long. And for the next 30 years while Jesus remained in
seclusion the world around him and beyond him continued its
irrational pace of iniquity. No visible signs of peace appeared.
Herod continued his slaughters and Caesar never reformed,
and Jewish leaders maintained their religious grip over the
Jews. God came to earth, but nothing happened. Peace did
not quite make it.

It is the misconception of gross proportions to believe that peace was the objective of God the Father in sending his son to earth. Once Jesus' sabbatical of 30 years was over and he joined John the Baptist at the Jordan the first thing that takes place after his baptism is that John in acknowledging Jesus as the Messiah passes the torch of repentance and righteousness on to Jesus. There is no transfer of an Olympic Peace Torch. If anything, the torch resembles a warning sign not a peace proposal. Hours before Jesus showed up on the shores of the Jordan John told his inquiring audience, "I am the voice calling in the wilderness, 'Make straight the way for the Lord.'" John was not on the shores of the Jordan river passing out olive branches, he was there to demand repentance from the Jews and then baptize the repentant ones.

The transferring of authority from John to Jesus safeguarded the mission of repenting and turning to God. John's message does not suffer diminishment when John leaves and Jesus takes center stage. The twofold message of repentance and believing in Jesus remain preeminent and are never sidelined. John threaded the eye of the needle and that thread once entering the eye remained in place. Believing in Jesus starts with John and is forever the message of Jesus himself.

In addition, the fact that the Son of God came in human form tells us that he came to take charge. He didn't just come, he didn't just whisper in someone's ear, he didn't arrive to merely suggest something with options, or suggest something for a few or for a few chosen ones; he came to take over. He came to occupy. "He is the one, and there is no other." He came, he spoke, and he claimed obedience.

It must be stated and stated emphatically that Jesus was not a peacemaker and that his Father did not send him to perform the duties of a peacemaker. Peacemaking constitutes an effort by an outside party to negotiate a more favorable condition between two parties who are at odds. The peacemaker is the outsider attempting to referee an amicable result for warring parties. The referee possesses no authority to enforce an outcome. He is chosen for the job because he has no personal investment or gain in the outcome and therefore can act objectively for both without preference for either. The peacemaker reconciles two others to themselves not to himself. He is out of the loop. He is a hired facilitator to manage a peaceful outcome.

Another crucial aspect of peacemaking is that in order to achieve a peaceful outcome the two parties at odds have to compromise. Peace comes when two sides each surrender some held demands. The peacemaker suggests compromises to the two sides that create a breakthrough to a settlement for peace. He has no skin in the game. He moves freely outside their conflicts and emotions. Whatever compromises are reached, the peacemaker reaps no direct benefit.

Peacemaking is about two adversaries who are managed by an independent third party with the hope of a peaceful outcome. The problem with this application to Jesus is that Jesus is the principal adversary. He can't be the third party outsider because he is the very one who is agitating and creating the controversy with a second party. He said most emphatically, "Do not suppose that I have come to bring peace to the earth. I did not come to bring peace, but a sword." (Mt.10:34)

The deck of cards Jesus was dealt by his Father did not include peacemaking. He was sent as an adversary to proclaim and demand conformity to him and to his message. Compromise of any kind stood outside the standing orders of his Father. Jesus was not sent to be reconciled to mankind but mankind reconciled to God through his Son. There was only one conformity and it went from man to God. Any and all reconciliation started with the movement of men and women accepting "the One who was sent."

Any comparison of Jesus to a peacemaker is erroneous. Any description of Jesus' life and work on earth to peacemaking is also erroneous. Any fixation on Jesus of delivering peace on earth is even more deeply erroneous. All of these represent a distorted and miss handling of the Jesus of Scripture. It is a fake Jesus who is the invention of individuals who modify Jesus to fit their own moral behavior and emotional needs. And in a PC culture of the 21st century Jesus is more modified than ever.

Technically a peacemaker has no literal authority to exact a peaceful outcome between to rival parties. He is helpless to compel an outcome. He is an intermediary, an ambassador, a facilitator. Jesus was none of the above. When he came to earth he registered in as the Son of God with plenipotentiary authority over all of mankind. He was second to none and first with his Father. He came with full authority to draw all men to his Father, but first to himself. In this capacity his title should appropriately be king, but that is inappropriate because he came not to drag men to his Father but to draw men there.

The very body of Jesus' words and deeds throughout his three years of ministry are on the other side of peace. Peace was never his message or focus. And any thoughts of compromise regarding his message were banished. Jesus did not transport a democracy to earth to have his message second guessed. When the Pharisees tried that they were summarily dismissed; when Peter tried that he was summarily rebuked and condemned.

If Jesus had wanted to establish peace, toning down his message would have been the first step. Compromise in any contested situation becomes a required stratagem. If peace is the goal, then tailoring one's expectations must enter the fray. Peace comes when two sides deliver reductions in their demands. Jesus would have been required to tone down his rhetoric about referring to God as his Father. In spite of his numerous healing miracles, he could not insist that he was the Son of God. That statement carried a self-incrimination of blasphemy. The leading Jews found that intolerable and offensive, and a most serious cause for division. Jesus could not have established peace with the leaders of the Jews if he insisted on implying to himself as "Son of God."

Jesus' fame started with his healings. The gospels narrate that Jesus quickly gained renown when he traveled from village to village and town to town healing everyone who came to him: "Jesus went around to all the towns and villages…, curing every disease and illness." (Mt.9:35) Something very extraordinary had to have launched Jesus into the limelight. Miracles of healing, such as leprosy, as blindness, as lameness and deafness drew crowds in wonder to Jesus, created the introductions Jesus needed to arouse a Nation. In an age where medical science remained uninvented, someone totally healing an afflicted person would receive the welcome of a hero. He was an instant success. In a short period of time people flocked to him, even traveling a day or more to reach him. He was a phenomenon.

But healing was not all that he did. Jesus was not about miracles. He spoke. He had a message. He weaved miracles in between his messages, but above all, he came to deliver his Father's message. And that message becomes an ultimatum: "This is my Beloved Son, listen to him." Peace is not the prevailing thought behind God's declaration. Sounds more like conformity than peace. The Father recognizes Jesus as his official representative and, furthermore, links message and messenger together. Jesus is henceforth simultaneously message and messenger. All of this establishes Jesus as the divine authority on earth with limitless and unconditional power to exact obedience and submission in all things pertaining to human existence.

In fact Jesus spends most of his waking hours in teaching and messaging. He delivers clear decisive instructions to his twelve newly adopted followers: "Whatever town or village you enter, look for a worthy person in it, and stay there until you leave. As you enter a house, wish it peace. If the house is worthy, let your peace come upon it; if not, let your peace return to you. Whoever will not receive you or listen to your words—go outside that house or town and shake the dust from your feet." (Mt.11:11-14)

The topic of peace is neither primary or secondary in Jesus' vocabulary. "Reformation" and "Reconciliation" might be more suitable; however, adherence to God and God's Word would be a better description of Jesus' overall job description. Jesus the "Son of God with a direct message from his Father" rather than Jesus the Peacemaker describes his work and words. He came to deliver God in Person and deliver his Father's messages.

Based on the fact that there is no evidence of peace during Christ's time on earth and there has been no realization of peace after Christ, we can reasonably say that Christ did not confer peace on the world. Jesus played an adversarial role while on earth, seeking out those who listened and accepted his message and condemning those who refused to listen and adhere to his message. For those who refused to listen, he proclaims, "Amen, I say to you, it will be more tolerable for the land of Sodom and Gomorrah on the day of judgment than for that town." (Mt.10:15)

Fast forward to the 20th century and we can confirm that Christ did not leave the mark of peace on the earth. The European continent in spite of its majority Christian heritage during that period suffered the bloodiest period in its history. Adherence to Christ meant nothing in the midst of people who subjected his principles to their own idolatrous injustices and hatred of others. Christ was clearly outnumbered by the monsters who inhabited the world at that time. And for the most part all of them claimed Christianity as their religion of choice.

It is very difficult to read the gospels wherein Christ is the protagonist and not come away with the distinct impression that Jesus flails at those who reject his message. If peace constitutes the theme he is trying to deliver, he fails miserably not only in the outcome but primarily in the effort. People who read that message into the gospels are imposing their own pedagogical interests not Christ's.

When Jesus claims that he is "the way and the truth and the life," he is defending his unique authority on earth and in heaven. Aside from his miracles the only evidence he gives is his claim that he comes with authority from God. God is his defense but God is out of sight. For those Jews not immediately disposed to Jesus because of his works could not possibly be inclined to a peaceable response. They would find his claim objectionable and most likely blasphemous. Indeed for the dedicated educated Jews Jesus established a reputation of a lawless blasphemer. There was anything but a peaceful relationship between him and the Jewish elite. Pharisees and Sadducees opposed him almost universally. He denounced them, and they returned the compliment. Even his miracles ruffled them and incensed them because he chose to perform them in their face on the Sabbath. Almost premeditatedly Jesus chose the Sabbath to elicit a contentious response from the Pharisees. In other words a peaceful exchange was not advanced nor attempted.

When you are dealing with absolutes such as, "I am the way and the truth and the life," there exists no room for dispute or debate, no room for errancy or misconception, and no room for doubt or disbelief. You broadcast a fact that possesses unquestioned validity, and nothing allows the listener to escape from the boldness of the statement. If the listener has not submitted to such an absolute, then more than likely he will leave quickly in silence or remain and become agitated. Certainly a peaceful atmosphere would not ensue. Then add to that an additional absolute: "No one comes to the Father except through me." (J.14:6) For the Jewish Elite this was not received as boldness but as madness. It convinced them that they were dealing with a blasphemer. With this statement there could be no peace.

However, an environment of peace was not what Jesus came to establish. His sojourn on earth was to establish himself as the dominant figure of divinity in the world. He did not exercise this task democratically. Either you accepted him or denied him, and if you denied him there were consequences: "Everyone who acknowledges me before others I will acknowledge before my Heavenly Father. But whoever denies me before others, I will deny before my Heavenly Father." (Mt.10:32-33) If there is any suggestion of peace or accommodation in the words and tone of this ultimatum, it vanishes into thin air.

Jesus' time on earth is distinguished by his claim of absolute authority. He had one commission that came from his Father and he was beholding to no one else. He was self-made, confident, strong of mind and spirit, unflappable in all circumstances, a take-charge attitude with his disciples, fearless in the face of evil and slanderous accusations. Early on in his ministry those who saw and listened to him acknowledged that without any hesitation "he spoke with authority." Above all he sought no advice from anyone. He was not collegial. He had no ghost writers or prompters. He was autocratic without the title of dictator.

Peace was not on Jesus' radar screen. The consolidation of the human race into one happy blended compromising group was additionally off his radar. E Pluribus UNUM was not an affectionate slogan Jesus scripted for mankind or for those immersed in democracy. The only UNUM Jesus confessed and professed was with his Father and those who would accept his message. The only peace that came from Jesus' words was the peace through belief "in the one who was sent." Peace with

God meant adherence to Jesus as the Son of God with one inclusive amendment, "there are no others." If truth had to be sacrificed to peace, truth lost.

When Jesus came two things were settled once and for all: firstly, the mystery of the divinity was released and Jesus was that revelation; secondly, once revealed divinity takes precedence over everyone and everything. That means God rules. His authority prevails. It cannot be contested. And the one appointed to exercise that authority is Jesus Christ. There is no other authority in heaven or on earth, as St. Paul declares: "Because of this, God greatly exalted him and bestowed on him the name that is above every name, that at the name of Jesus every knee should bend, of those in heaven and on earth and under the earth, and every tongue confess that Jesus Christ is Lord..." (Ph.2: 9-11)

Peace becomes a reality when all parties have resolved all their differences and can now share a common time of tranquility. That is not what Jesus came to experience while he performed his ministry on earth. On the contrary, his time on earth produced strife, slander, bodily threats, and finally death on the cross. His words were contentious to the point of calculated hatred. Not only the leading Jews despised his divinity claims, the general public found many of his Eucharistic statements and baptismal claims absurdly false and past the pale of sanity. Jesus spoke with authority but that same authority referenced God as its direct source and this brought out a negative response and a label of blasphemy.

Realistically, how could divinity wrapped in a human form claim obedience from a jealous and recalcitrant humanity that found fault with everything he stated. Jesus challenged the Jewish leaders every step of the way. Not once did Jesus receive any accommodation from the Pharisees or Sadducees. Not only were his words suspect, but his miracles also. Each miracle drove a wedge between them and their complicit subjects causing further questioning of their authority. Each miracle was a heartburn of distaste. And when the miracle occurred on the Sabbath, then instantly guilt and the work of Beelzebub was ascribed to the miracle. Jesus' words and miracles hardened their hearts and the more the words came and miracles happened the more hardened their hearts became. When God "hardened the heart of Pharaoh" it wasn't because of God, it was of Pharaoh resisting each punishment God sent him as a wake up call.

Under these circumstances peace between Jesus and the official Jewish headship was impossible. At a certain point Jesus had to work under cover and stay out of sight. Even when Jesus came out in the open to raise Lazarus, the raising of Lazarus (now four days dead, buried, wrapped in burial clothes, decomposing) sent shock waves of disapproval and disgust in the already harden hearts of many leading Jewish onlookers: "What are we going to do? This man is performing many signs. If we leave him alone, all will believe in him, and the Romans will come and take away our land and our nation." (J.11:47-48)

If peace had been a priority in Jesus' mind, it would have occurred long before. He would have been cautious about referring to himself as the Son of God, constantly referencing God as his Father, performing miracles on the Sabbath, turning over the tables of the money changers at Passover, and accusing the Pharisees of hypocrisy. Too much and too heavy was his method. But Jesus did not come to campaign for approval. His mission was the truth and the truth did not lie in external ritual performances. He chose truth over peace because nothing trumps the Truth. An idolatrous and arrogant nation required the truth.

It would have been completely pointless for Jesus to come and shade the truth in order to provide a semblance of peace.

The previous covenants God had with the Israelites were absolute and unparliamentary. God presented the facts and demanded compliance. With Jesus it is the same. Except Jesus himself is the covenant, not to be exchanged for human mischief and malevolence. What good is peace if it dilutes the truth? What good is truth if it does not emanate from God. If there is anything ever self-evident about truth it is because it emanates from the creator and is therefore incontestable.

If anyone insists on peace on earth, truth will have to be sacrificed. Jesus never accommodated truth for peace. He made it abundantly clear that when truth prevails the map of human relationships becomes disturbed: "Do not think that I have come to bring peace upon the earth, but a sword. For I have come to set a man against his father, a daughter against her mother, and a daughter-in-law against her mother-in-law; and man's enemies will be those of his household." (Mt.10:34-36)

Peace can never be achieved on earth. If we search for the truth and attempt to employ truth in the exercise of justice, peace will be out of reach. If truth is first, then peace will have to wait its turn. Jesus is about the truth, and truth requires one thing—Resolve.

Chapter 5

SYSTEMIC EVIL

WHEN AN EVIL INVADES AN INDIVIDUAL'S MIND and the evil is not extricated, then that particular evil becomes systemic. If that same evil is recognized by a family and the family allows it to persist, then that family has allowed that evil to become systemic. If that same evil appears in a culture and is allowed to prevail, then that evil is systemic. If that very same evil is introduced to a political party and that very evil is adopted and celebrated by that party, then that evil has become deeply systemic. If that same evil is carried into the membership of a large church body and that evil is not condemned and expelled from its members, then that evil has gained acknowledgement from the top tier of that church authority and subsequently its members. When a majority in a state has accepted and endorsed by law an evil, then that evil is intrinsically systemic.

Such has been the case of multiple evils permitted and even celebrated in the United States over the history of the country. Slavery was the starter. In spite of the Declaration of Independence and its attestation of equality for all, equality did not apply to all when the Constitution was signed into law. A pre-existing evil was not denounced and rejected at its commencement. Slavery was systemic and it continued systemic. In spite of the multitude of bible believers and their "loyalty" to Christ, the political elite at the time would not remove the systemic evil in their midst, making the initial claim of "created equal" a sham.

Over the years other evils became systemic. There was segregation and Jim Crow and the infamous KKK. Indian tribes across the West were encamped and exterminated on the basis of economic necessity and advancing migration. Jews were excluded from elite clubs and suburban areas, along with being unacceptable in political parties. Throughout the 19th century and into the 20th century Catholics were summarily suspected of popery and therefore ineligible for political office. And what, pray tell, has really changed in the most recent modern era – "the dogma speaks loudly within you!"

Evil has been around since Adam and Eve. Evil and human nature constitute a systemic relationship. If this were not true, human nature could be absolved of all things monstrous, criminal, and heinous. But such is not the case. Evil quickly flows out of the veins of every average human resident of the earth. It is not a question "of," but a question of "how much." The prosecution of evil becomes an endless chore for the enforcement industry and only the most vile of crimes sees retribution. We pretend virtue and justice while all the time evil ravishes hearts and minds. There is nothing un-systemic about evil. It is a question of eradication rather than a question of something clear and present in human beings. If selfishness is universally present in human beings, so is evil, and that comports to something systemic. We are evilly inclined until proven otherwise.

The evidence of something systemic occurs when that something encompasses the mind and spirit of an individual. Serial evil is not confined to killing. A serial killer destroys the lives of multiple individuals and in doing so his crime is systemic. However, Killing is not the only behavior cited in the Ten Commandments as an evil with systemic characteristics. There is Theft, and Adultery, and Slander, and Greed, and Jealousy. All of these have an infamous history of systemic proportions. One of the most contested evils Jesus dealt with during his three years of his ministry on earth was not serial killing but the evil envisioned in the 8th commandment, namely, "Thou shall Not Bear False Witness." Almost from the very beginning of his ministry Jesus confronted the false witness of the Pharisees. In Jerusalem he faced the Pharisees false accusations almost daily. Anything Jesus did was prosecuted by the Pharisees. His words and his actions, primarily healings, received not only intense scrutiny but zealous condemnation. Jesus was a "watched" man, and subsequently a debased man.

The task Jesus was given was to convey a new message to the Jews regarding his Father's relationship with the Jews, the Chosen Race. The new message encompassed a new covenant. The previous covenant had for all practical purposes expired and Jesus was sent as the bearer of the new covenant. More than once God identified Jesus as his Son: "This is my Beloved Son, in whom I am well pleased." Jesus had a voice of authority and his numerous healings gave ample evidence of his more than human power. Jesus came with purpose and authority to a nation already committed to God and now God was sending a messenger with a new message. This was not a renewal of an old relationship, it was the beginning of something new in which God himself was the center. If the Old Testament introduces God to the world behind a veil, the New Testament introduces God himself in person to the world. Those among the Jewish population who listened objectively to Jesus confessed that he "spoke with authority."

Most importantly Jesus' coming and his message were received by the masses. At times he gathered thousands, even ten thousand, to listen to him. His influence was expansive and electric. In becoming a sensation he subsequently became a danger and a threat. The masses loved him, but the elites despised him. Jesus had bypassed the elites and went directly to the masses. The obvious reason for his avoidance of the religious Jewish elite unfolds in the very reason for his mission. He came to lead the nation out of its bondage to mere Jewish law and its customs. He came for the nation not its leaders. The individual was the focus. not the Jewish nation.

As a consequence, Jesus did not come to coexist, nor did he come to align himself with Jewish ancient practices and rituals, nor did he come to endorse Jewish ethnicity. He was a complete departure from all of that. There is nothing conciliatory in Jesus' manner, behavior, or words with the Jewish leading class. He was as much a foreigner to Jewish customs and habits, either religious or secular, as any Roman was. No rubber stamp of approval for Jewish orthodoxy issued from him. Outside of the Ten Commandments and the acknowledgement and worship of God Jesus kept a huge distance from Jewish authorities and anything strictly Jewish. Jesus came with a new message and a new authority. He came to transition the Jews from an external ritualistic observance to a deeply personal engagement with divinity. He came as a man with divine powers. He came as God with the face of a man but giving evidence of his divine origins. John the Baptist, Jesus' forerunner, kept huge geographical distances from the Jewish hierarchy, and Jesus followed in step.

As expected no one from on top the Jewish hegemony listened to Jesus or accepted him. He became an instant outcast. This was hardly disturbing or unexpected by Jesus. When Jesus called them out for their perfidy regarding him, he accused them of not being Abraham's children. His claim was that Abraham would have listened and accepted him; moreover, he would have celebrated the moment as something expected and awaited and finally occurring. It was Abraham who first received the call from Yahweh to believe in God from afar and Abraham believed; and now it was Jesus calling the Jews to believe in him in person but is rejected. For this very reason Jesus refused to associate them with Abraham, but rather with the devil.

It is vitally important to understand that Jesus was born of a Jewish mother, that he grew up in a Jewish environment, that he read and knew the Torah, but his divinity was not Jewish. His Jewish connections are chronological; his Divine connections are eternal. Jesus did not come to earth because he was Jewish, but because he was divine. God's connection with the Jews starts with Abraham who through his son and further descendants occupy a preferred position in the religious world. However, this position was not indefinitely guaranteed. Somewhere between Abraham and John the Baptist the original attachment of Abraham's descendants with God had fallen to the nadir of their relationship and that required God to then send his personal representative, namely, his Son, to reestablish a deeper and more personal relationship with not only the Jews but all mankind.

From the very beginning Jesus' coming was not intended to be a one nation event. The Jews were first on the list to be visited just as they were first with Abraham. But this was not a one stop event. They had been chosen earlier but their "chosen" status had an expiration date attached to it and that date had come due with the arrival of Jesus. They were chosen once, but not chosen forever.

The core problem within the Jewish leadership was their allegiance to themselves and not to God. The chosen aspect of their calling was that they were first in line to worship and obey God before anything else. Over the centuries this condition in their relationship eroded and finally at the time Jesus appeared it had reached maximum collapse. They were

Jews alright, but not Jews believing and following Abraham's example. They claimed descendancy from Abraham but their claim lacked veracity.

There was a systemic fallout among the leaders of the Jewish religion as it pertains to the very core of the faith covenant enacted between Abraham and God. They had replaced themselves over everything including God. They were blinded to anyone coming from God. John the Baptist attempted to make headway but failed, and Jesus failed as well. There was a systemic collapse among those in charge with regards to things of God and "his" commandments.

The systemic sin Jesus found among the leading Jews was the utter self-importance of those claiming supreme authority in matters religious and spiritual, in matters of law, in matters of culture, in matters of history, in all matters pertaining to belief. They walked the earth as prosecutors not as shepherds. They accused and condemned. They defied and judged any deviancy from their norms. All behavior and belief came under their scrutiny. God himself could not penetrate their self-proclaimed sanctuary. No one escaped and no one exceeded their superiority. They were untouchable.

The ruling class of the Jews had moved away from the divine authority of God. Abraham had become a titular head only, his name used to establish historical relevance to the past and a chance to claim credible authority. But a lot can happen in nearly two thousand years since the coming of Abraham. Once clerical men grasp authority unto themselves, the origin of that authority is whisked away by self promoting inventive minds. There were numerous periods when the God of Abraham was literally shut out of Jewish life, when Jewish kings, both north and south, had abandoned the God of Abraham, Isaac, and Jacob, and had removed the sacred books from daily life and Jewish eyesight. Belief in the divinity had declined, and even disappeared. The clerics had become the center of the Jewish universe. God was invoked but merely as a hammer to enforce their will.

When Jesus came the Kings were gone and in their place were clerics who were keen on observance of the trivia of the law and lean on the spirit of the law. Essentially they were law enforcers and judges. Nothing suited them more than to indict offenders. This is why Jesus became the popular offender. It seems much of what he did was indictable, especially his healings on the Sabbath. Preaching the law and demanding absolute adherence to the law provides a position of dominance to the ones enforcing the law. Such became the reason for the Pharisees position of power. The Pharisees had reached an absolute position of dominance and no one superseded their position. They could convict and execute. Under the guise that they were advocating for "God's Laws," they acquired Carte Blanche to power. God became their excuse for dominance. God was used as a weapon against his own people.

What the Pharisees had lost was the recognition and respect for the divinity and dominance of God. In assuming authority over the Jewish religion and Jewish culture, the Pharisees seized superiority over every aspect of Jewish life, including its privileged relationship with God. There was no separation of church and culture, of earthly versus heavenly; there was one power that spoke autocratically on every level. Anything earthly and anything divine came full circle under the hand of the Pharisees. There was a "systemic prejudice" created by the Pharisees in their favor that led to their complete takeover of all things God, Laws, culture and truth. "Systemic" dramatizes the depth and profundity of this self-acquired arrogance. Nothing and no one surpassed their judgment.

Jesus came and stood in their way. He disproved their authority and their ignorance, along with their impudence and injustice. The Jews were a flock without a shepherd for the simple reason the Pharisees had overrun the covenant of Abraham with their false jurisprudence and power. The systemic nature of Pharisees' evil very likely prompted God to inject his Son at this very time in history in order to reconnect with the Jewish people directly and then onwards to all nations.

What Jesus confronted as he started his ministry in Israel can be correctly labeled tyranny. Those of the ruling class had shoved God out of sight and replaced themselves in his place. God was off their radar. They were the sole authority. John the Baptist, though highly regarded for his integrity and preachings by the masses, was entirely ignored by the Pharisees and, in spite of his universal appeal to the masses of Jews, their leaders credited him with credulity and treated him as an oddball bordering on fanatic. They left him alone merely because he stayed out of their sight.

Jesus, on the other hand, was always in sight, and for a very good reason. His coming constituted an intervention. Over the centuries a crisis had metastasized in the Jewish nation which left the Jewish sheep unguided and untaught. God did not just suddenly invent his Son's incarnation on earth on a whim. The human race starting with the Jews triggered this intervention from the Father. Their systemic disregard for his primary law, "Love God and do good to your neighbor as you would have it done to you," was not center stage and not the focus of the Pharisees. Moreover, and secondly, God wanted a closer relationship established with mankind, and hence his Son was chosen to walk among mankind and establish this new covenant relationship. He came first among the Jews because his Father had already established a relationship with them. It was a natural beginning: "He came to that which was his own..."(J.1:11) Jesus was Jewish because of his Father's prior commitment to Abraham. But with Jesus' coming that covenant was being updated. The term "Chosen" would expand from one nation to many nations, and, finally, "Go into all the world and preach the gospel to all creation." Jesus' divinity would not be limited to the Jews, but expand to every creature on earth: "to all who did receive him, to those who believed in his name, he gave the right to become children of God." (J.1:12) "Chosen" henceforth would apply to all those who would come to believe in the name of Jesus.

The systemic arrogance of the leading Jews led them to condemn Jesus because they were impervious to the spirit. They, the upper echelon, categorically refused his divinity. Blindness was in their hearts and souls. They were shut out from anything spiritual and of God. Their claim of affinity with God was bogus. Nicodemus, one of their upper class, revealed this very ignorance of matters spiritual and Jesus called him out: "You are Israel's teacher..., and you do not understand these things." (J.3:10) For this reason God had taken pity on the masses among the Jews and sent his Son to raise up believers. Jesus reveals this dire condition when he observes: "When he saw the crowds he had pity on them, because they were harassed and helpless, like sheep without a shepherd." (Mt.9:36)

There was a systemic evil pervasive throughout Israel and throughout mankind that prompted God to send his Son to earth. Israel could no longer be relied on to bring the faith of Abraham to his own people or to the world. Only God himself could turn the tide. Jesus was the tide.

Men have always resented God's interference in their lives. God sent Jesus to clarify the fact that God is the only Ruler. Men and mankind are mere surrogates of his authority and rule completely at his mercy. His rulership is absolute and that what you do or fail to do you do to Him. Jesus, without attempting to overrule human dominion on earth, stipulated the rules for behavior and added the severe consequences for non-compliance. His coming and the interjection of his Father's rules were not suggestions, they were ultimatums. They were not intended for optional consumption. Exceptions were ruled out. If you refuse, you are "vomited" from his mouth. God rules, God dominates, God judges. We follow or we lose.

Shepherds exist among us, but shepherds do not necessarily lead on the behalf of God and the One he sent. Whether it is arrogance or self-importance, or lack of spirit and conviction, or fear of rejection, God's word and his laws come weakly proclaimed. The culture with its ever shrieking Media Mouthpieces keeps the Christian Shepherd at bay; the louder they shriek, the softer the Shepherd intones. And that is not Jesus.

Chapter 6

EQUALITY

IN THE DAYS FOLLOWING JESUS' ASCENSION
into heaven the apostles along with several other disciples
of Jesus formed a community in which everything was held
in common. From the account in the Acts of the Apostles it
appears that the rules set forward for the group established
stringent guidelines for behavior. The rule stipulated that everything was held in common, and that rule was obliged under
pain of death. Two violators, namely, Sapphira and Ananias,
were punished for keeping a portion of their property that they
were obliged to surrender to the community. Peter himself
supervised their demise.

The church in its infancy attempted to share everything
together surrendering all private ownership, apparently living
out what Jesus asked the rich man to do: "Go sell everything
and give it to the poor, and then come follow me." Unity of
faith in the early days of Christian life additionally translated
into an effort to unite everyone into one strong, consolidated,
like-minded body of believers. It also offered the group a sense
of safety-in-numbers, given the fact that Jesus was gone and his
death triggered a sequence of persecutions.

However, the sharing in common was short-lived. The
attempt at equality soon suffered under the weight of

individuality and the undeniable propensity for privacy and private property. Beyond living with one other person in a single household, individuals as a whole have never collected together under one roof and shared everything in common. This is asking for more than just sharing, it is asking for equality. You surrender your goods and privacy for the common good. Without the drive to equality, the sharing does not work. The common denominator is equality, the belief that no one has a right to more than what someone else has. In fact, any disparity between individuals who do choose to live a common life leads to jealousy and irascible discontent. Equality in everything without exceptions guarantees a successful and harmonious common life, otherwise the effort is destined for failure.

This early effort at "communism" for Christians survived but a few years beyond Jesus' death. There is no evidence that the early Christian faithful lived a common lifestyle far into the first century. They shared their dwellings for the Eucharist and for teaching, but beyond that they lived separate and distinct lives.

Equality did not measure up to a priority status for Jesus either. His messaging focused on personal behavior not communal arrangements. Jesus talked about the kingdom rather than a commune. When he hired the apostles, there is no sign that he had established a "club" for his itinerant messengers. His relationship with them emphasized steadfast loyalty to him and through him to his Father, along with a resolute insistence on repentance. Jesus was the embodiment of individual and personal obedience to God: "'Who is my mother, and who are my brothers? ...Whoever does the will of my Father in heaven is my brother and sister and mother.'"(Mt.12:47-50)

Jesus had one direction for his loyalty, and that resided in his Father. He came by order of his Father and he yearned to return to his Father, and in the meantime he spent his every waking moment attempting to enlist others to follow him in his footsteps and believe in him and the One who sent him. Loyalty to group style life, to group rules, to group thought, to group equality in everything was rejected by Jesus. Not only was it rejected, but considered destructive and therefore condemned. Group equality places emphasis on likeness in behavior and thought and relationships, and virtually everything else. However, Jesus did not require likeness. Loyalty, yes, but not likeness.

Likeness among human beings presupposes that we can all fit into the same place at the same time with the same needs and same ambitions and same thoughts for the same motives and drives. God did not make us for likeness but for uniqueness. As unique we cannot be locked into an environment of equality where everyone is reduced to singularity of purpose and thought.

Those who profess a profound reliance on equality to level the playing field of life ignore all the pitfalls of "equal everything for everybody." Equality for everyone becomes equality for no one. It is an attempt at the impossible and the absurd. It never happens voluntarily and it is only accomplished by a dictatorship of violence.

The Jesus of the New Testament never called for equality among his followers. He did not come to establish a social order on earth with oneness of property and goods in order to balance the inequities of nature and human nature. On occasion he fed the multitudes, but those events were out of compassion rather than an effort at reorganizing the insufficiencies of a large segment of the population. Never did he initiate a social structure that would benefit a large group of the populace. His efforts at improvement were all devoted to the blind, the lame, the deaf, the lepers, the possessed, and even the dead. These were all individual one-on-one healings. He came and healed body, mind, and spirit, but not once did he invent a new social fabric. Whatever social order existed before Jesus, that social order remained when he left.

Jesus himself demonstrated no equality with God. "Who, being in the very nature of God, did not consider equality with God something to be used to his own advantage..."(Phil. 2:6)

If Jesus had wanted equality he was quite capable of asking and getting that done. Jesus, as God, was equivalent with the Father; however, as the Son, he was not equal with the Father. He deferred everything to the Father—authority, message, and purpose. Jesus came on behalf of his Father and performed as his Father's Surrogate. A display of unity with the Father surpassed any needed claim to equality.

The attainment of equality amongst individuals of any species bespeaks futility. If we are created equal, it is only in our common humanity not our individuality. Our claim to independence in America started with our belief "that all men are created equal." The equality referenced was directed at the individual's right to "life, liberty, and the pursuit of happiness." There was no reference to a collective equality, that everyone must share life, liberty, and the pursuit of happiness in common so that each individual receives and experiences the same degree of those gifts. In America we strive to make these gifts available to everyone equally, but the attainment of those gifts are not reached equally.

The kingdom Jesus spoke about had the title of "Kingdom of Heaven," not a kingdom on earth. Any attempt at an equality of individuals underlies the belief that everyone sharing equally will benefit equally, and that will usher in peace and prosperity for everyone equally.

However, nothing Jesus did or said advanced a kingdom of equality on earth. No such hegemony of universal tranquility existed in Jesus' mind or thoughts. He came into a world of disadvantage and discontent and when he left the world had not changed. He left universal hope but not universal happiness: "Come to me, all you who are weary and burdened, and I will give you rest. Take my yoke upon you and learn from me, for I am gentle and humble in heart, and you will find rest for your souls. For my yoke is easy and my burden light. (Matt.11:28-30)

A hegemony of universal peace and equal fortune for everyone on this earth has never happened and will never happen. As long as there are individual human beings with different ages, ability, intelligence, ambition, ingenuity, good fortune, education, culture, family and faith, and all of the above in various degrees of proficiencies and deficiencies, there will be different outcomes for each person. Equality will never happen. The French Revolution tried and failed and no one will ever create a magic kingdom with equality for all without revolution, and if revolution is tried it will fail also.

Christianity is built on men and women following Jesus Christ faithfully one by one. Faith is personal and never the result of equality. Saints are saints not because of their similarity to each other but because of their personal attachment to Jesus. Any coercion to compel someone to believe in Jesus violates the very essence of faith.

Equality requires compulsory action on the part of the person demanding it. It can never be natural if the person submitting has lost freedom in the process.

Jesus claimed that his words were truth and in that context he insisted that "the truth will set you free." Equality is not an agent of freedom. The concept produces stagnation and dis-in-genuity, something Jesus would not subscribe to. Jesus was a hardworking, dedicated, passionate, no-nonsense individual who had a message from his Father that had to be delivered undiluted to the Israelites and no attempt at a diminishment of that message could be tolerated. Equality in Jesus' context would have required a watered-down version of that message. Equality simply stated requires equivalence in sustenance, shelter, wealth, and THOUGHT. He would have had to become the "Jesus of today," "the Jesus in today's pulpits," "the Jesus who walks on two sides of the road," "the Jesus who is sensitive to others' feelings," basically a Jesus who keeps his mouth shut.

Equality and faith collide. Believing in Jesus is not a collective effort. Faith is not about becoming like others. You do not adapt to what others want. Least of all you do not ascribe to what others think or believe. Faith is unique to every unique individual because it is a unique relationship of you and God. It bears no similarity to anyone else's faith in God. The definition of faith in Jesus may bear a collective meaning, but the relationship with Jesus is singular to the person. Common dogma or creed does not turn you into a "one shoe fits all." The faith of the youngest person can surpass others who are generations older. In faith none of us is equal. There exists no equality amongst faith-in-God believers.

Jesus commended the faith of the centurion who acknowledged Jesus' power without proof. He acknowledged the amazing interests and faith of the Samaritan woman at the well who returned with many others displaying her convictions in Jesus. There is the Syrophoenician woman who begs for help for her daughter in spite of Jesus' resistance. And there is the blind man who cannot see but believes with helpless devotion that Jesus can heal him. Each individual displays a singular dedication to Christ that matches no one else. There is no equality of motive that attracts people to Jesus, and there is no equality of purpose that keeps people attached to Jesus.

Politics reverberates with equality seekers and makers, promising to create a utopia of free benefits for the many—free medicine, free education, free housing, free borders, free Abortions, and sanctuary cities for criminals. It is a government without order and responsibility. It is an attempt to make everyone equal and no one deprived. Everyone is promised utopia. But this is not the message of Jesus Christ. He came to change individuals not societies.

Equality attempts to provide utopia. If everyone is equal, everyone is better. If everyone has the same amounts, no one is cheated. The scale of life and fortune is leveled so that each human being has every necessity but no surplus. This concept sells to a lot of people but places a vice on the innate ambitions of most individuals. Politicians preach the concept but do not live it themselves; they make fortunes, then keep their fortunes, and absolutely never share their fortunes. There is a mote with defensive protections around everyone of their fortresses.

Jesus disengaged himself from any kind of man made utopia. He came in swaddling clothes in Bethlehem and was left naked on the cross in Jerusalem, not exactly a poster child for a utopian success story. He started his "evangelical career" as a middle aged adult and gathered followers who had no proven record of success. If he had envisioned a utopian world, he should have found men with better leadership qualifications. Proven success leads to greater success, something that was missing in the apostles. But Jesus was not looking for this world success. He wanted unproven men who would first believe in him, then follow. He wanted a mixed breed of men, unqualified and un-equalized, who could take his message of another world to other unqualified and non-equalized individuals. Jesus was not a politician who preached a message of false promises for a false world, but a truth sayer who wanted men to believe in him for the sake of another world.

If equality sets its mind on a temporal utopia in this world, it has devised failure. Life is a struggle, not a utopian adventure, and any effort by equality seekers to reverse that reality is doomed. The "American Dream" concept provides an avenue of success for individuals not an absolute guarantee of success for a collective body, hence it is for some not many at once. Jesus, as God, with his divine powers could have taken the masses and made them perpetually comfortable and equal. He could have demoted Herod and Caesar and taught the Pharisees a few lessons about fairness and justice. He could have equalized the entire society for the common good of all. After all if he fed thousands of people on a few occasions, he could have continued these welfare events ad infinitum. The greatest act of equality would have been to heal everyone of lameness, blindness, deafness, and leprosy, and every other unmentioned disease in the scriptures. This would have been the most merciful act of equality he could have performed. But he had none of that. Jesus cured and healed in the thousands but he changed nothing. After he left, humans still suffered disease, still experienced injustice, and still succumbed to death. He radicalized nothing. Human behavior continued unchanged.

The Father commissioned Jesus to announce the Kingdom of Heaven without any heavy regard for the realities of this earth and all its struggles. He left us as we were. We were maimed in the Garden of Eden and nothing will change that until the end of time. Our ship is out to sea and will not return to port until God brings it in. What Jesus did was promise absolutely that our ship will return in the final outcome.

We are travelers without an earthly port, and we are left here as individuals to seek out the Son of God and live among each other as helpers, not equals.

The utopian message Jesus gave us is the one he gave to the rich man who thought he had achieved perfect righteousness in his life: "Go and sell everything and give the money to the poor and then come follow me."

Chapter 7

CONDEMNATION FOR SURE

THE STANDARD RUBRIC ACCORDING TO THE New Testament for judging is a flat "NO." You may not judge, or be judged. Jesus in his own words cautioned and condemned judging others: "Do not judge, or you too will be judged. For in the same way you judge others, you will be judged, and with the measure you use, it will be measured to you." (Mt.7:2)

Judging can get you in trouble. It's a category that belongs to God. It's the exclusive prerogative of God, who sees everything, hears everything, and knows everything. Without being privy to all of the facts in a situation no man can judge another. We are shortsighted and inclined to miss-judging and consequently are incapable and therefore unauthorized to judge anyone else. At best we are superficial in anything we see and know; only God sees in depth. That puts God light years ahead of us who see but don't see, who hear but don't hear, who know but don't know. We may be living in the sunlight but embedded in clouds.

So don't judge, don't condemn, don't point a finger, don't resist, and don't offend and don't object. Stand off and out of the way, God is the only judge. That's nice and comfortable, but it's ridiculous. God is NOT the ONLY Judge. He is the FINAL Judge, but never the only judge. In the interim there are judges everywhere: in the courts, in the homes, in the schools, on the athletic fields, throughout the military apparatus, in private clubs, in every facet of human interplay there is judgment and judges to go along with that judgment. God is not here in person to judge behavior, that is why surrogates abound in every field of human endeavor. Any parent and any teacher judges behavior and performance. And every civilized society must judge criminal behavior. And every religious society judges moral behavior. The world possesses a reservoir of judges.

The Book of Genesis opens with the fall and subsequent judgment of Adam and Eve. Then there's Cain who is judged for his murder of Abel. Next the inhabitants of Babel are judged for their foolish attempt at matching God's supremacy. God then commissions Noah to build a boat for a few chosen so he can summarily dispose of the rest of the human race. In subsequent years every prominent leader of the Jews experiences judgment for mishandling the covenant signed with Abraham and their serious denunciation for idolatry. Judgment from God permeates the Scriptures.

The theme of judgment continues in the New Testament. In this vein Matthew's gospel is most distinguished. Jesus forever makes judgment calls for everyone and anyone who chooses to defy the truth. No one escapes Jesus' critical eye. There is almost an atmosphere of prosecution going on in the gospel. The times are serious and the message more serious. Obviously Jesus did not come to pat people on the back. It is tough love, not a party on the beach. Perhaps not the full wrath of "fire and brimstone," but certainly a shot across the bow. Jesus' theme of judgment endured throughout his ministry.

When a truth is introduced that cannot be miss-handled or overturned, then the preservation of that truth must endure at all costs. The truth that Jesus introduced could suffer no deletions or exemptions. Any rejection of that truth had to meet severe consequences. For this reason Jesus attached judgment to any attempts to resist and reject the truth he brought from his Father. Without exception he rejected the non-conformist and non-believer. His clarity was swift and persistent. "Amen, amen, I say to you, whoever hears my word and believes in the one who sent me has eternal life and will not come to condemnation, but has passed from death to life ." (J.5:24)

When Nicodemus approached him for answers regarding baptism and the necessity of being born again in the spirit, Jesus concluded the conversation with, "Whoever believes in him (referring to himself) will not be condemned, but whoever does not believe has already been condemned, because he has not believed in the name of the only Son of God." (J.3:18)

Similarly John the Baptist on the shores of the Jordan saw Jesus baptizing and testified to the exclusive authority he had from his Father with the demand of full adherence from everyone: "For the one whom God sent speaks the words of God... The Father loves the Son and has given everything over to him. Whoever believes in the Son has eternal life, but whoever disobeys the Son will not see life, but the wrath of God remains upon him."(J.3:34-36)

Truth is not for sale. It commands adherence. Adherence is the natural corollary to truth. Without adherence the truth, a fact, withers into opinion and oblivion. Jesus' announcement that he is the Son of God was not a proclamation suited without an audience. It was designed for consumption. Mankind was the designated consumer: Jews first, then everyone else.

Truth requires acknowledgement. Jesus' entire three years of ministry were devoted to that very activity. He conveyed the truth—about himself and about his Father. He was not subtle about the acknowledgement he expected from his audience. Acknowledgement was required, and if not forthcoming, then there were consequences. Hence the strong judgments that were rendered along with each truth:

"I am the vine, you are the branches. Whoever remains in me and I in him will bear much fruit, because without me you can do nothing. Anyone who does not remain in me will be thrown out like a branch and wither; people will gather them and throw them into a fire and they will be burned. (J.15:3-7)

Truth requires acceptance, and absolute truth requires absolute and unconditional acceptance. The message out of Jesus' mouth allowed no loopholes for escape. Nothing was conditioned or nuanced. From God's prophetic mouth to our listening ears. God speaks, we listen; and that listening requires our participation. The alternative is judgment: "'And this is the testimony: God gave us eternal life, and this life is in his Son. Whoever possesses the Son has life; whoever does not possess the Son of God does not have life.'"(1J.5:11/12) In Jesus' lexicon, "You are either with me or against me."

God is the precondition for life. And God the Father introduced Jesus, who came in the flesh, as the immediate pre-condition for life. "This is my beloved Son in whom I am well pleased. Listen to him." Jesus came to deliver the truth his Father had destined for mankind.

Once truth arrives there follows an impenetrable shield around it. If it stands as truth then it cannot be dislodged. Any adjustment to it becomes a violation. Any distortion of it becomes a lie. Any denial of it becomes anathema. It is universal and obligatory: not for just a few but for everyone.

The consequence of rejecting the truth is judgment. This is why there is an intrinsic connection between truth and judgment. Jesus proclaiming himself as the Son of God with the authority of his Father after volumes of miracles then demanding adherence to this truth does not permit disavowal. Any rejection of the Son automatically inflicts a rejection on the person who denies the Son: "Everyone who acknowledges me before others I will acknowledge before my heavenly Father. But whoever denies me before others, I will deny before my Heavenly Father." (Mt.10:32/33) This seeming harshness of Jesus' judgment of disbelievers justifiably withstands scrutiny because it is consistent with the very essence and demands of truth. Truth is non-negotiable, and coming from God it is irreversible. Jesus' judgments of disbelievers are self-inflicted not imposed by him. Hypocrisy, arrogance, and hatred, all are characteristic of disbelievers. We are all capable of belief and we are all vulnerable to disbelief. However, hatred predisposes one to disbelief as does arrogance and hypocrisy.

Jesus always rewards faith. Whenever Jesus is congratulatory of anyone, it is specifically due to the person's faith. Indeed, Jesus profusely congratulates the believer for his or her faith. The woman who had suffered 12 years with an irremediable blood disease desperately touched but a thread of Jesus' garment in the middle of a vast crowd and she was instantly healed, and Jesus ecstatically exclaimed: "Who touched me?" Then realizing the power of her faith he rewards her by saying, "Courage, Daughter, your faith has saved you."

Faith is the one and only doorway to Jesus. Without that anyone is at a loss. Without it nothing is possible and with it everything is possible. Nicodemus came to Jesus with a puzzling question about being born again asking Jesus if that meant reentering your mother's womb in order to experience this spiritual rebirth. His question was absurd and his explanation even more absurd and Jesus reflects that in his answer: "You are the teacher of Israel and you do not understand this?" Nicodemus, a Sadducee, of an intellectual Jewish religious elite class, knew nothing of the world of the spirit and conflated "being born again" with a physical event. Jesus, frustrated with with him and the entire elite class, told Nicodemus that they do not accept any of his testimony on temporal matters why would they on spiritual ones: "If I tell you about earthly things and you do not believe, how will you believe if I tell you about heavenly things?" (J.3:12) Nicodemus demonstrates how void the religious upper class was on matters of the spirit.

Over and over again Jesus applauded those who operated on the level of faith, especially those who were not Israelites, such as the centurion, a pagan and non-Israelite, who had a surplus of faith. Jesus not only commended him for it but extended severe judgment on all those who had no faith: "Amen, I say to you, in no one in Israel have I found such faith. I say to you, many will come from the east and the west, and will recline with Abraham, Isaac, and Jacob at the banquet in the kingdom of heaven, but the children of the kingdom will be driven out into the outer darkness, where there will be wailing and grinding of teeth."(Mt.8:10-12)

At Jesus' presentation in the temple following his birth, a man named Simeon unexpectedly appears and proclaims a prophetic judgment on the Israelites who were expecting the arrival of a Savior but who rejected the One who did come: "Behold, this child is destined for the fall and rise of many in Israel, and to be a sign that will be contradicted..." (Lk.2:34) Even before Jesus began his ministry, judgment was forecasted on those who would not believe and receive "the One to Come."

Disbelief is persistently accompanied by judgment. As has just been demonstrated Jesus frequently passes judgment on those who don't believe in him. If acceptance of Jesus is vital to eternal life, then believing in him becomes a necessary condition. Anyone who refuses to believe in him is subject to judgment. The gospels provide a consistent narrative by Jesus of praise and admiration for those who believe in him and follow him. When John forecast the coming of the Savior he did so with demonstrative certainty and with exclusions for none: the

Savior's coming required everyone. Jesus, the Shepherd, came for all the sheep of Israel, and subsequently everyone in the universe. Jesus is God of all, not just Christians. The universe and all its peoples belong to him. There is "one Lord, one Faith, one baptism; one God and Father of all, who is over all and through all and in all."(Eph.4:4-6)

Jesus Christ is not the head of a religion, he is head of the universe. His universality extends everywhere without bounds and without limits. Jesus clarified the Godhead. He also rendered all other contenders impotent. With miracles and healings and messaging, and above all with his coming from the dead, he established his and his Father's authority on earth. The truth stands absolute and universal and any denial is apostasy and suffers judgment.

Two things Jesus came for: revelation and judgment. He did not come to excuse and forgive "willy-nilly." Truth has consequences and together they demonstrate the story line of his ministry. When he dispatched his disciples to carry his message from town to town he gave them unconditional authority and that included rejection to the point of "shaking the dust off their feet."

We have seen how the Bible judges individuals and nations for apostasy, and we have seen how Jesus in particular judges those who reject the truth about him and his message. Judgment is an outgrowth of truth. It is not that judgment is a violation of someone else's rights, but a violation of the truth. Anyone who rejects or violates the truth has submitted to judgment. There is an overwhelming demand for judgment when the truth has been shattered. In the one singular defense Jesus gave of himself standing before Pilate was that he was "born" and came into the world, to testify to the truth. "Everyone who belongs to the truth, listens to my voice"(J.18:37) In this statement Jesus clearly indicates that anyone who does not listen to his words does not belong to the truth. It is a judgment by non-association.

Jesus passed on his authority to the apostles and his many other disciples. The same message and the same judgment authority was conferred on them. Logically if Jesus' message was to continue and be preserved, it had to sustain rejection and falsehood, and no better way than by applying judgment to both.

When evil rises in an individual according to scripture, we have a formula to follow. "If your brother sins [against you], go and tell him his fault between you and him alone. If he listens to you, you have won over your brother. If he does not listen, take one or two others along with you, so that 'every fact may be established on the testimony of two or three witnesses.' If he refuses to listen to them, tell the church. If he refuses to listen even to the church, then treat him as you would a Gentile or a tax collector." (Mt.18:15-16)

When evil befalls a society as a whole and is authorized and justified by that society, then it behooves other members of that society to stand firm and cast judgment on those erring and evil members. Judgment should befall them. A majority of citizens do not make evil right. A PC consciousness does not make evil right. A Supreme Court of the Land does not make evil right. Slavery was just such an evil, followed by segregation and Jim Crow and the KuKluxKlan. The magnitude of the judgment and condemnation should match and exceed the evil in question.

The judgment should be loud and intense and without restraint. When life is at stake and human freedom is crushed, then judgment should clamor over all other voices. Short of violence the judgment should resound incessantly so that those committing the evil are reminded every day of their ungodly actions.

To say that "we cannot Judge," or that "only God judges" undoubtedly expresses a feeble moral attitude. It is the statement of a weakling and a coward. If God has invested us with a noble conscience and directed us by faith toward justice and his goodness and truth, then we are obliged to judge and condemn the evil in our midst.

The consequences of not standing up to evil is that evil will prosper and proliferate. It feeds on itself. It clings together and when added to additional forces such as Media and Entertainment and weak church leaders and political agents, the evil solidifies into a monster of unimaginable proportions.

Those who insist that "only God knows what's in someone's heart" are correct but misled by an ineffectual church population that sits in church pews and looks for soft idealistic messages. Jesus was not soft nor idealistic. Everything in his portfolio spoke to the truth with teeth. With Jesus no one had to read between the lines to understand the punchline in the message. Either you were with him or against him. If Jesus had wished to deliver a non-judgmental message, he should have left out all his "Woe" and "Wrath" statements. Hypocrisy, slander, injury of any sort to another human being, and, certainly, killing a human being, were at the top of his wrath list. Anyone who steps outside the boundaries of truth becomes a subject of judgment and condemnation.

With Jesus came the truth; they are synonymous: "And this is the verdict, that the light came into the world, but people preferred darkness to light, because their works were evil. For everyone who does wicked things hates the light and does not come toward the light, so that his works might not be exposed. But whoever loves the truth comes to the light, so that his works may be clearly seen as done by God."(J.3:19-21)

The argument from the naysayers and do-nothings who claim "only" God judges and "only" God knows what's in someone's heart fall short of the actual truth because it is not what is in someone's heart that matters when it comes to truth, it is what is in their MOUTHS. Slander is in the mouth. Lies are in the mouth. Hypocrisy is in the mouth. Treachery is in the mouth also. When Jesus condemned the Pharisees, he did so for what they said not for what they thought. It is the actual commission of an act not the mere thought. Jesus told this parable:

"A man had two sons. He came to the first and said, 'Son, go out and work in the vineyard today.' He said in reply, 'I will not,' but afterwards he changed his mind and went. The man came to the other son and gave the same order. He said in reply, 'Yes, sir,' but did not go." (Mt.21:28-31)

Evil is a staple in humankind. It cheats people, it hates people, it blames innocent people, it segregates people, it even kills and rapes people. Some of it is caught and exposed, but so much of it thrives and thwarts the lives of the innocent. If evil is not judged and condemned, it will destroy. So many times over so many years and centuries mankind has been destroyed because it walked away from judging and condemning evil doers before they masterminded a holocaust. If the mouths of the just do not stand and condemn the evil that confronts them, then the mouths of the evil doers will destroy them. If the just leaders of the people do not confront evil, it will prevail over freedom. If the churches do not condemn the evil that is outside God's truth, then evil will masquerade as the truth.

The truth is a delicate thing. It is everywhere but so easily overrun by lying mouths. Without defenders who will take up arms against a sea of deceit, of slander, of hate, of extortion, of thieving, of rape and murder, then the truth will be an abused orphan. To judge and condemn the evil perpetrator is not an invasion of God's singular jurisdiction but the obligation of all mankind to protect the truth established by God for creation.

If we do not guarantee that protection, we will suffer under the unlimited tyranny of evil.

Truth is fragile, and without the perpetual strength and courageous vigilance of a few strong men it will perish. If the light does not shine on darkness, darkness prevails.

Justice is futile if it is not gaveled into judgment.

Chapter 8

LYING IS A PROFESSION

THE INVENTOR OF LYING IS NONE OTHER THAN the Devil. Lying is his Profession. He started with Adam and Eve in the Garden of Eden and ever since has developed a lengthy resume of lying. Jesus himself experienced first hand the lying strategies of the devil. Throughout the history of mankind lying sits at the top of human pursuits. If you are caught in a corner, so the axiom goes, "lie your way out." Or, "Better to lie than die." Or, when the truth is unavailable, "produce a lie."

Actually, lies are more fashionable than the truth. History exemplifies a proven record of lying. Truth requires research and evidence which require patient study and careful examination. The most problematic matter with truth underlies the honesty applied in obtaining the truth. Truth without honesty becomes half-truth or no truth at all. If honesty is not the starting point for truth, then truth will never emerge. Without honesty truth is DOA.

Jesus is the gatekeeper of truth. In all of his messages and lessons and parables he shared the truth about himself and his Father. It was a truth very few could accept. Telling human beings that your Father is God, that you came from heaven, that your purpose in coming was directed by your Father in heaven, that everyone must listen to you or perish, that you own the truth, must in the end drive a nail in someone's head. To suddenly emerge from Nazareth and claim divine sonship pushes truth not into the limelight but into a raving abyss, which is what his kinsfolk wanted to'do with him when he announced his premier relationship with God. Once Jesus left his hometown after 30 years of silence he became relentless in announcing the truth about himself, his Father, and the world.

Truth even coming from the very mouth of God could not be sustained, let alone accepted. Jesus' attempts overall were futile. He came to the Jewish Nation as the first and primary recipient of his Father's message, but was rejected. He was condemned for lying. More specifically he was called a blasphemer for inventing a lie about himself claiming that he was the Son of God. His truth was overturned by a group of self-righteous religious autocrats who were invested in restrictive religious practices rather than the Spirit of God that abounds everywhere in the world if it is sought after. Evidence upon evidence poured out from Jesus in the form of thousands of healings and other miracles that for some became overwhelming proof of Jesus' authenticity but for so many others that evidence became the work of Beelzebub, the master of lies.

So truth, no matter how revealing it may be, and who the provider is, is ultimately subject to human scrutiny. It has to pass the man-made mustard test. Truth is in our hands—soiled, dirty, malicious, and clawing hands. Jesus had to pass through these hands in order to submit the truth for approval. In the end on the cross he was labeled a liar: "Those passing by reviled him, 'You who would destroy the temple and rebuild it in three day, save yourself, if you are the Son of God, and come down from the cross."(Mk.15:29-30) Moreover, Pilate's inscription on the cross accuses Jesus of his false claims: "The King of the Jews."

In the hands of human handlers truth is held hostage. In a crowd truth suffers too many setbacks, repulses, and outright rejections. There are myriads of eyes, myriads of ears, myriads of brains who will not advocate for its birthright. Truth suffers under the weight of human scrutiny. Arrogant human brain cells repel every evidence of truth for their own personal gain. Jesus was convicted before Pilate not because he didn't tell the truth, but because the lies of the leading Jews posed him as a threat to Caesar. Then before Pilate pronounced sentence over Jesus the leading Jews fearing their lying had failed raised a mob to demand Jesus' death calling for his crucifixion. Their lies determined his death.

Truth is at risk every minute and every hour of every day. Jesus said, "The truth will set you free." What he should have said is, "If you speak the truth, the truth will make you an orphan." If you insist on the truth, you will lose your parents and grandparents and ancestors. That is what he meant when he said, "Someone told him, 'Your mother and your brothers are standing outside, asking to speak with you.' But he said in reply to the one who told him, 'Who is my mother? Who are my brothers?' And stretching out his hand toward his disciples, he said, 'Here are my mother and my brothers. For whoever does the will of my Heavenly Father is my brother, and sister, and mother.'" (Mt.12:47-50)

Martin Luther King, Jr., in the mid 1960s was an orphan. Yes, he had lots of followers and lots of sympathizers, but he suffered tidal waves of hatred and rejection and violence. His safest place was in prison. His declarations of truth about segregation turned the Non-Negotiable South into a frenzy of serious violence and the resistant North into a panic of hatred. Even some of his followers stopped following. Martin was an orphan of the first class; except for his Scriptures, he would have despaired. If ever St. Paul had a reincarnation, it was Martin.

And it was all about the truth he spoke about hatred and seg-regation and violence, and the menace all these were to Black individuals and families. The Liars who denounced Martin were in abundance everywhere in the country. Every profession and every industry, every media, every political party, even most churches, wrote him off as a menace or agitator. He was not only an orphan, but a dangerous orphan. They lied, and for so long the country bought the lie.

The problem is that truth has no parents and no grand-parents and no ancestors. It's an orphan in the hands of fickle, feckless, and self-seeking mankind. Lying is a ready made pro-fession for human consumption. It comes faster, more man-ageable, more easily created, and supported by a multitude of accomplices who think in unison. If hatred is your game, and violence is your intended action, then lying is the first step.

Lying is a way of leveling the playing field you don't like. If winning at all costs is required, then the most convenient approach comes with lying. Without lying Jesus would have survived the indictment of the Jewish leaders, and without lying Jesus would never have been convicted of a crime and subse-quently sentenced to death. The mobs that shouted, "Crucify him, crucify him," outside Pilate's courthouse were bought and paid for by the liars in the Pharisees' party. They had developed a detestation for Jesus that led them to arrest him, charge him with false allegations, then turn him over to Pilate with the libelous claim that he presented a danger to the nation: "Then the whole assembly of them arose and brought him before Pilate. They brought charges against him, saying, 'We found this man misleading our people; he opposes the payment of taxes to Caesar and maintains that he is the Messiah, a King.' Pilate asked him, 'Are you the King of the Jews?' He said to him in reply, 'You say so.' Pilate then addressed the chief priests and crowds, 'I find this man not guilty.' But they were adamant and said, 'He is inciting the people with his teaching throughout all Judea, from Galilee where he began even to here.'"(L.23:2-5)

With lying, destruction is limitless. Lying has no fences, no boundaries, no borders, and no walls. It is found everywhere—in families, in schools, in courts, in medicine, in the military, most supremely in politics, and even in churches. It is a ready-made vernacular for cheaters and deceivers. It is a profession without a degree.

If a prosecutor in a criminal case harbors animus toward a defendant, it is likely that evidence against him will twist in and out of negative, even false, presentations. If lying to prove his case will work, he will. He will call this "strategy," and let the defense attorney uncover the lie. Lying in court is not an injustice, it's a procedure. It's called proving your case, or for the defense it's simply denying an accusation. No one has to tell the truth in court, you just have to convince the jury.

"Innocent until proven guilty," celebrates what we want to believe not what is fact. Anyone giving absolute credence to this oft quoted slogan suffers a naive truth. There is no unproven innocence in a court of law when a licentious prosecutor or defense attorney sandbag an accused with fallacious evidence and convoluted facts. Any lie can appear as a truth when uttered by a corrupt mouth, even if contested by an opposing side. Jesus' defense of his claim of divinity was overturned by a clamorous group of Pharisees who actually did not argue their case against him, but rather demanded compliance from Pilate to execute him. Pilate himself found no criminal guilt in Jesus; he saw through their lies and false statements. However, he was persuaded not by the Pharisees but by the shrieking mob they brought with them that Jesus not Barabbas be put to death. The mob became the jury and Pilate under pressure sentenced Jesus to the cross. Euphemistically this is called public opinion. The Pharisees did not argue their case well with Pilate but they did with the mob. The issues of truth and facts were not pertinent, just enough passion and hatred to incite a riot. The sentenced criminal is exchanged for the innocent healer and teacher.

If we could solve the propensity to lying, the scars and consequences of original sin would rapidly disappear. Every crime comes with a lie. People at times are sentenced to death because of a lie. People are very often slandered due to a lie. People lose family and property because of a lie. Advancements over other people often come because of a lie. Jurisprudence as a rule benefits the best liars.

By far the best examples of the processing of lies occur in the media, where the research and revelation of the truth falls into the hands of dedicated propagandists spending each hour of the day turning out reams of innuendo and slander. Facts taken out of context twist relevance rather than deliver relevance. A constant diet of bias permeates every news report and drowns the story with defamation. News outlets create salacious slants, and dots are connected to dots in order to satisfy editorial political defamation. Someone's destruction is the headline in every deadline. The assumption is that readers want bad news over objective news, that readers (their readers) want dirt not details about the issues. That makes lying an acceptable art form.

Under Caesar and the Pharisees Jesus did not survive back then, and he certainly would not survive today under the hand of a negligible and inconsequential Christianity. The Jews of today would not kill him, but the Christians would. As long as lies prevail in humanity, the Christ of unflinching truth would die today also—not the body, of course, but the message yes. Christianity today has accommodated the lies of society, its money, its politics, its immoral laws, its greedy wealth holders, its monstrous shepherds, its corrupted and fallaciously deceptive political heads. Members of Christian Churches throughout the land believe they can abort babies in the womb and live promiscuously outside of marriage. These are outright lies and negate the Christ of the New Testament. These lies are subversive to Christianity. So called Christian Churches that do not disavow and condemn these practices and those that practice them should have disclaimers on their door fronts: "CAUTION: OUR MESSAGE IS NOT THAT OF JESUS CHRIST; WE JUST USE HIS NAME."

Jesus did not tell a lie about himself and his Father, and what he and his Father wanted. Hence it behooves us not to tell a lie about him. His message is straightforward. It also comes without conditions and excuses. It must not be watered down. Jesus was always on message. He condemned hypocrites. He condemned the money changers in the temple. He condemned Judas for the betrayal of the Son of God. He condemned the "goats." He condemned the man who stored up his wealth. He condemned the rich and the greedy, because sharing is the gospel of Jesus Christ not hoarding. He condemned tax collectors for extorting. He condemned without exception every evil doer and evil thinker. Above all He condemned those who refused to believe in him. His gospel is not a gospel of "take it or leave it," it is a gospel of "take it you must or you lose." Jesus is not an optional prophet, he is a MUST GOD.

The lie that is perpetuated in the churches of Jesus Christ today is the felonious gospel of peace. Let's all just get along. Let's all be together. Let's all be inclusive. Let's all stop shouting. Let's all be nice and compatible. That is not the gospel of Jesus Christ. He did not come to make peace or establish peace if peace means "flow with the crowd." Coexistence never came out of Jesus' mouth. He came to establish the Kingdom of Heaven, not the Kingdom of Peace on earth: "I have come to set the earth on fire, and how I wish it were already blazing!

There is a baptism with which I must be baptized, and how great is my anguish until it is accomplished! Do you think that I have come to establish peace on the earth? No, I tell you, but rather division. From now on a household of five will be divided, three against two and two against three; a father will be divided against his son and a son against his father, a mother against her daughter and a daughter against her mother, a mother-in-law against her daughter-in-law and a daughter-in-law against her mother-in-law." (Lk.12:49-53)

The force of Jesus' message accommodates no compromise. He belonged to no family, no synagogue, no party, no social club, no society of intellects, no band of brothers looking for notoriety. He had no affiliations except his Father. He acknowledged no obligations except his Father's. He owed nothing to anyone. NO ONE was on his list of favorites: No king, no disciple, no friend or family member. No one and nothing intervened in the delivery and execution of his message. His message was safe from human intervention and editing. He and his Father were one and nothing separated him from his Father and his Father's message.

However, in the church pulpits today, as they have in the past, the truth of Jesus' message undergoes suffocation. There is misdirection and vagueness in the message, and there is missing a crucial sense of critical urgency in the message. Jesus was sharp and pushy in his declarations. He did not mince words and he did not merely "encourage" with his words. They are declarative and demanding. It's now, it's not tomorrow. It's today, not later. It's MUST, not MAYBE. Centuries of handling the "Word of God" has declawed it and placed it in a glass cage where you look but never touch or feel. It's perfectly safeguarded in the cage in its original form and you are safe outside because you only have to look and peek at it without direct exposure. The Exposure could be deadly.

The big lie is that Jesus is presumptively all compassion and mercy. He healed, he forgave, he turned the other cheek, he preached love, he suffered false allegations and never returned the compliment, he apologized for sinners and became their defender, he died taking the place of a condemned criminal. The story is that Jesus is love, peace, patience, kindness, joy, long suffering, and endlessly open armed.

Another lie surrounds the belief that Jesus preached coexistence. Today's liberal population preaches coexistence as a dogma that supersedes all matters of disagreement. Its objective is compromise. In matters of weight and intransigence the suggestion is that all parties lay down their swords so that coexistence reigns. Disarm your arguments and let a facade of no contest usher in the appearance of agreement and peace. The Pro-Abortion crowd wants the Pro-Life crowd to lay down its weapons and leave Roe vs Wade alone. But that's not going to happen because the reality of Life at conception must stand and oblige everyone. Jesus did not surrender the truth. He was a man of peace and mercy, but neither one overturned the upholding of the truth. If he had wanted compromise he would have toned down his insistence that he was the Son of God and reassured the Pharisees that he did not want them to think he was a blasphemer; this would have created an atmosphere of peace between them. If Jesus had wanted compromise, he could have and should have stayed away from the Eucharist doctrine, which absolutely severed all chances of coexistence with the Jewish leaders and even many of his followers.

Jesus never had coexistence on his mind. It was not one of the doctrines of required belief. When he preached love at all costs (loving enemies without reserve and doing good to others unconditionally) he did not have coexistence in mind. Coexistence consists in accommodating others in their beliefs and compromising yours with their beliefs. Love is not a compromising agent when it involves truth. Truth requires separation and dislodgement if it is at risk. Love does not amend the truth; rather, it champions the truth. To believe in Jesus requires first and foremost the love of truth, and the first truth is that Jesus is the Son of God with plenipotentiary power in heaven and on earth.

When issues of truth become rejected Jesus tolerates no resistance. His messages accommodate no disbelief. He pushes confrontation. Family and friends disappear—mother, brother, sister, disciple are all gone. The New Testament pages are full of rejection and condemnation: "Whoever is not with me is against me, and whoever does not gather with me scatters." (Mt.12:30)

If coexistence means becoming an "accommodationist," Jesus will instantly disappear from your midst as he did many times when others attempted to confront him or destroy him. He is not "for hire." There is One Lord and Savior of the World and he will not back down. Bi-Partisan does not fit his title or his persistent behavior. If you want neutrality, talk to a minister of pablum. When he revealed that sins against the Son of Man would be forgiven, but any sin against the Holy Spirit would not, he had reference to the "Spirit of Truth." Defiance against the Spirit of Truth enters a place of no return, of no forgiveness. Truth submits to no abdication. If you lie about the truth, you perjure something in reality; if you lie about the Spirit of truth, you perjure against God. God is absolute. In God there are no exceptions to truth.

Love suffers everything except the truth. You can bind someone's wounds, but you don't acquiesce to someone's lies. Placing love and truth in contention is the work of the devil, the most masterful liar. There is a time for love and a time for truth; they are not mutually exclusive but they are not unconditionally inclusive. The work of love offers others comfort, confidence and help, but it does not allow for the disembodiment of truth. Truth emanates from God and touches the very essence of God and therefore will not tolerate dismemberment. Jesus told the devil that there is only ONE to worship and that is his Father.

The One Person Jesus said he was sending to take his place after he left this earth was the Advocate, the Spirit of Truth. He insisted that if his disciples remained in the truth they would remain in his word. Hence, in spite of his leaving, the truth that he brought would remain and continue with the Holy Spirit. His very last prayer of petition to his Father at the Last Supper on behalf of his disciples concluded with a special request: "They do not belong to the world any more than I belong to the world. Consecrate them in the truth. Your word is truth. As you sent me into the world, so I sent them into the world. And I consecrate myself for them, so that they also may be consecrated in truth." (J.17:16-19)

Truth defines Jesus' mission on earth. Love is the environment in which he displayed his healings and miracles, but truth is why he came and what he left.

Chapter 9

THE VERY NARROW GATE

ONE AREA THAT BEFUDDLES CHRISTIANS overall is the statement Jesus made about the "narrow gate." We can assume that the gate in reference stands at the entrance to heaven. What we don't know is how "narrow" is "narrow." Jesus never clarifies the word. It is left to our imagination and assumptions. Hence throughout the ages the word has received a multitude of parsings.

Saints have come and gone who represented a serious and perhaps severe definition of "narrow." St. Francis of Assisi placed a revolutionary interpretation on the word and left behind a life of enormous wealth and privilege. St. Benedict founded his monastic system on a life of complete detachment from the world and ordered his life in two words: "Ora et Labora," Prayer and Work. Perhaps the earliest of monastic founders was St. Anthony the Hermit who left everything and went into the desert fasting daily believing that the gospel called him to prepare now for the next life. His interpretation of "narrow" took him outside of the world to a point of "absolute exclusion." For St. Anthony narrow meant something exceptionally restrictive in the form of denial. Indeed, he went through the gate and shut the gate behind him. From that point on he lived in seclusion with a daily regimen of fasting and praying.

Over the centuries very few Christians have held that view of "narrow." Bishops and popes have lived in palaces and minimally in stately homes with never a thought of "narrowing" their dwelling size. They have and still are adorned with ermine and scarlet at ceremonial times. Christian Churches everywhere build big and better not small and narrower. Christianity is in the world and the world is in Christianity. The signs of richness permeate Christian properties. There is very little that is narrow when surveying the landscape of church assets. We look like everybody else. Nothing narrow seems to be apparent in these surroundings.

Christianity follows the same paths that the rest of the world follows: "if you have it, flaunt it." Even monasteries in the past were constructed with high minded design expectations. It is difficult to restrain human ambition whether preaching capitalism or preaching the gospel. When in the world, it is impossible not to be like the world.

Perhaps the problem is not us, but Jesus. He suggested too much and asked for too much. He set the bar too high. He was counter culture, perhaps counter human fulfillment and counter human ambition. Certainly counter human Aggrandizement. After all he came into a world he had never originally been part of. His world was heaven not earth. He came from a world-of-order into a world virtually out-of-order. There was deprivation and there was excess. There was slavery and domination, as well as the lavish environment of a Herod.

Did Jesus come to balance these two extremes? Did he come to bring order in a world laden with injustice and imbalances? Those who had always wanted more always seem to use the people who had nothing to begin with. If you have an advantage, you employ the advantage. People on top use the people at the bottom. Jesus saw all this and seldom examined the cause and nearly never advised a remedy. His healings were to individuals and his message was to the individual. His arrival on earth would not effect a socio-economic change to benefit the people at the bottom. He was not about changing the top tier of society, or making radical shifts in political authority, or reorganizing the underprivileged. The message through him from his Father was a change of heart. He came for the individual not the world. Everything he did was confined to individuals, not society at large, and it all related to tomorrow not today. In spite of his ad hoc healings, the direction of his activities and message dramatized a life far beyond this earth. Tomorrow engaged him not today. He came from the eternal and that is what he talked about.

Building a kingdom on earth was sheer folly to Jesus. "Less" was the measure of sanity for him. Storehouses and warehouses and amassing and accumulating garnered considerable criticism from Jesus: "Look at the birds of the air; they do not sow or reap or store away in barns, yet your Heavenly Father feeds them." (Mt.6:26) This simple incontestable observation from nature about God's providence should instantly shame the listener who demands more assurance of tomorrow's necessities.

The Kingdom of his Father was forever on his mind. Jesus came from there and ever yearned to return. His principal objective was to invite and lead others to that place no one had been but would gladly welcome if they believed in him. The New Testament refers to that Kingdom 162 times, not an insignificant number for something entirely invisible and only believable by faith.

Jesus was consumed in convincing others, starting with disciples, that the Kingdom of his Father is forever and the only one to fully subscribe to. Earth is for starters not for finishing.

At every turn Jesus spent his time introducing others to his Father and referring to the place where his Father dwelt. In the only prayer Jesus left for us he singles out the Father first and foremost and his Father's dwelling place: "Our Father Who art in heaven...". These were the twin attractions Jesus brought to mankind. He was sold on his Father and likewise heaven. He wanted the world to know, not so much his lineage, but his devotion to his Father and his place of origin and the place of his return.

In the middle of the "Our Father," Jesus adds: "Thy Kingdom come, thy will be done, on earth as it is in Heaven." Jesus' constant wish draws the Kingdom of his Father closer to mankind. His singular wish is that it come sooner than later. In fact he declares that the Kingdom of God is at hand. It is in that context that earth becomes secondary and of less concern. It's not forever, not everlasting, not final. "Temporary" dictates a conditional approach to all activities on earth. Whatever is of earth is unequivocally transient. We are merely sojourning in a land of certain uncertainties. Jesus never loses sight of that reality.

If the earth is passing away and we along with it (indeed, we are first to pass, then the earth), it requires an enormous admission that any attempt to stock up on earth's treasures defies all of the reality surrounding us. We were given dominion over the earth, but that dominion is not absolute and extremely short lived. If, however, Jesus is the lead man in all of this human existence, then something terribly drastic has to occur to slow down our surge toward relentless dominion. God conferred dominion on us for necessities but not dominion for domination. No human being has the right of domination. We can say without divine misrepresentation that the Creator endowed us with "life and liberty and the pursuit of happiness," but never domination. We can also say with self-evident proof that God never conferred the right of domination to any human being with regards to property and people. In Genesis "dominion" means order and in the New Testament it means "sharing."

Anyone who comes to Jesus must adopt the same mind set and same behavioral practices of Jesus. To claim affinity to Jesus requires unflinching affinity to his message. How often he said, "Whoever loves me will keep my word, and my Father will love him, and we will come to him and make our dwelling with him." (J.14:23) Or, "If you love me, you will keep my commandments." And, "Amen, amen, I say to you, whoever believes in me will do the works that I do..." Words and works go hand in hand. If you believe in something, you do something.

Jesus' words are works. Jesus himself is "The Word Made Flesh," who came and lived among us. He is many words and simultaneously many works; one follows the other. And one word he announced over and over again was "Believe in me." This refrain becomes an all consuming enterprise. This enterprise is Himself, his Father, and the Kingdom of Heaven, all of which comprise tomorrow but today is the beginning. If you believe in Him then Today is Tomorrow and Tomorrow is Today, for the Kingdom of Heaven is already present. By Jesus coming to earth, the two are blended.

In Jesus' lexicon today is about waiting and anticipating, not about gathering and collecting then storing up for tomorrow. "Tomorrow will take care of itself," he said. But we have stopped believing in Jesus' doctrine about today and about tomorrow.

We are surely made for tomorrow, but not on this earth. Today is only today, it's not tomorrow. Tomorrow is completely in God's hands: "Therefore I tell you, do not worry about your life and what you will eat, or about your body and what you will wear. For life is more than food and the body more than clothing. Notice the ravens: they do not sow or reap; they have neither storehouse nor barn, yet God feeds them. How much more important are you than birds! Can any of you by worrying add a moment to your life-span? If even the smallest things are beyond your control, why are you anxious about the rest?

Notice how the flowers grow. They do not toil or spin. But I tell you, not even Solomon in all his splendor was dressed like one of them. If God so clothes the grass in the field that grows today and is thrown into the oven tomorrow, will he not much more provide for you, O you of little faith?" (L.12:22-28)

However, we are not built for waiting and long range planning; we suffer time impatiently. Who can wait for the promised Kingdom not knowing when it is coming and what it looks like. Going from caterpillar to butterfly is a known reality, but going from death to resurrection is beyond human calculation. In the interim we have to eat and cover ourselves and care for our offspring.

Saving and storing become staple procedures for people on an uncertain journey. For that reason we store out of fear of the future and its vicissitudes. Quite natural and quite right. Jesus condones that action. We provide for today and its necessity. Jesus fed the multitudes several times with baskets left in surplus. He helped Peter and John catch a mother load of fish on Lake Geneserath. He turned an abundance of water into wine at Cana with no restraint on the quantity. There is no ambiguity in Jesus' intent about providing for today as opposed to storing up for tomorrow. It is the excesses of goods and rewards created by men to exceed today's needs and endlessly provide for tomorrow that receives unbound resistance and criticism from Jesus. We prove ourselves unworthy of his promises for tomorrow if we today cannot live in a zone of moderation.

The man in the Parable of the Rich Man, who stored his goods in barns then later in warehouses, is the example of someone who stores and hoards believing that he has overcome all the dangers and risks of life, yet that very night is taken by a sudden death. There are no safe places. We live today, tomorrow is for someone else. That is why hoarding and amassing run diametrically against Jesus' doctrine of creating and sharing and living without excess.

Excess thunders against Jesus' conspicuous examples and messages about living carefully and meagerly today for a Tomorrow in the Kingdom of his Father. The one name that Jesus requires of everyone on earth is that of Steward. We are not Kings, or Lords, or Princes, or Titled Bosses of many sorts, but simply Stewards of this small kingdom on earth. Steward is the ONE Title that fits all of mankind, and fits it equally. At the Last Supper Jesus wrapped an apron around him and washed the feet of his disciples, to manifest to them that he was their servant and they should be the same to others. On earth his lesser title was Son of Man, not Son of God, another example of his persistent example of his servanthood on earth. We are stewards as mothers, as fathers, as sisters and brothers, as family and friends, neighbors, employers, doctors, politicians, presidents and kings. It's the one title that fits all without distinction and all with obligation. No master is better than his servant, and no servant is better than his master.

As servants an incumbency of caring is required in all undertakings, which extends to time, energy, devotion and resources. If you have, you give. If you have in abundance, you give in abundance. There are no restrictions to the stewardship required. Stewardship has no boundaries and no fence posts. It is boundless. Jesus' prevailing predicate is: if received freely, give freely. To hold in reserve earth's resources condemns the holder. The earth is of God, belongs to God, was meticulously created by God and is minusculely maintained by God. When it comes to earth we are interlopers not entrepreneurs.

Ingenuity and intelligence do not release the holder of boundless abundance from sharing that abundance with others. To believe that "what is mine is mine" constitutes perjury. In a court of New Testament law an indictment would be issued to the holder of that belief. There is no "mine" in mine. The "mine" is God's. Starting with conception your "mine" is God's. Following that moment in time whatever "mine" that we are and become also emanates from God. To assert that "mine is mine" blatantly defies the truth of God in existence. "He is everything and he is in everything." God is existence and existence is God. Nothing exists outside the creative hand of God.

Nothing we have came from us. We were gifted in every way. "Recipient" is our authentic name. Ability and talents are God generated, and uniqueness follows in line. We arrived from nowhere and we shall return to nowhere, until God recalls us. Whatever personal credits we possess have their origin in God. Likewise, whatever external possessions we acquired arose from God's generosity. All titles to possessions belong to God. He is the Grand Title Holder. The legal titles we keep in safes are easily disposed of with a match; they represent what we use not what is absolute ownership. God is the authentic Possessor.

Ownership presents a false narrative to the title holder: "It's mine," "It's no one else's;" "It's only for Me." If I have 110 warehouses of goods, they are all mine. If I have 11 houses, they are all mine. If I have 3 jet planes, they are mine. If I have 76 cars in storage, they are mine. If I have 6 yachts in harbor, they are mine. If I have one gold mine and two silver mines, they are mine. And there are 85 paintings by renowned artists, they are mine too. All these are mine.

"But God said to him, 'You fool, this night your life will be demanded of you; and the things you have prepared, to whom will they belong?'" (L.12:20)

Wealth breeds self-sufficiency and self-importance and self-adulation. Worse yet, it breeds power. Surrounded by wealth and possessions transfers an imperious belief in oneself. It creates a plenipotentiary and condescending posture.

Castles make you impregnable and wealth makes you Olympian. Nothing seems insurmountable.

Worst of all wealth and possessions separate you from others. You start to move in a different crowd. You have access to restricted clubs. Friends from the past are dislodged because they no longer "fit in." People with money are attracted to each other: they have similar houses, cars and toys; similar private schools for their kids; similar vacation habits; similar expense accounts and similar buying habits. The world becomes a different place. A new life opens and an old one is shut out. The world of "haves" limits association with the "have nots."

Riches transform the mind and spirit. Wealth does a makeover on the human consciousness. You begin to see things not people. The world is filled with objects of obtainable joy, delight, satisfaction, aggrandizement, and power. There is the underlying affirmation of entitlement conferred on those who come to riches, an entitlement that adheres like glue. Possessions lead to possessed. You can't let go. They become part of you; they are you. Who are you without them?

For Jesus it was different. Once he came out of Nazareth he became immersed with people. In the beginning there were a few healings, but within a short time he was healing in the hundreds and thousands. He became available to every person of infirmity and disease. People from all of Israel came to him. And each encounter brought them in contact with his message. He did not seek out the rich for companionship, nor did he seek out the Jewish elite for affirmation; some came on their own like Zaccheus and Nicodemus but his flock were the masses.

Jesus stayed with the masses who were eager to listen to him. He fed the masses and had pity on them because they had few resources and no shepherd: "He went around all of Galilee, teaching in their synagogues, proclaiming the gospel of the kingdom, and curing every disease and illness among the people. His fame spread to all of Syria, and they brought to him all who were sick with various diseases and racked with pain, those who were possessed, lunatics, and paralytics, and he cured them. And great crowds from Galilee, Decapolis, Jerusalem, and Judea, and from beyond the Jordan followed him." (Mt.4:23-25).

When Jesus told the rich young man, who came to see Him for spiritual guidance and to advance his personal life, to relinquish his possessions, he walked away defeated because he could not possibly comply with Jesus' demand. To relinquish all that he possessed suddenly voided his interest in Jesus. When Jesus asked him for his many, many possessions, he walked away "saddened," or was it a case of self-pity. He simply wanted Jesus to affirm and reward his past religious practices, referring to the commandments ("All of these I have observed from my youth"). He trusted Jesus for the right answer, believing in his authenticity like everyone else, but was reduced to impotency when Jesus told him, "'If you wish to be perfect, go, sell what you have and give to the poor, and you will have treasure in heaven. Then come, follow me.'" (Mt.19:21)

Possessions are obsessions. Once acquired, never dispatched. We acquire them and identify with them. We become them and they become us. Though we are born naked and die naked, we seldom learn detachment from things that burden and distract from God and his Kingdom. We wear them like makeup.

Jesus was adamant about unrestrained attachments and for a very good reason. The closer we are to goods, the farther we are from others' needs. It's always about us and not our neighbor. Possessions pin us down. There's cost, maintenance, security, insurance, undying focus, all associated with possessions. There's little time for others. There's little time to be Mary if Martha is constantly talking.

We are a country of great wealth. We are a Nation of people with enormous individual wealth—a wealth that is held tightly and not gingerly shared. Even the very wealthy who become noted philanthropists do so through foundations which deliver funds under their name brand and which allow them continuing control of the wealth without surrendering control of the wealth. This is not exactly what Jesus called for when he tells individuals to "sell what you have and give to the poor." There is nothing absolute or final in this sort of rationed charity. Jesus' almsgiving meant finally severing all ties to the possessions. Jesus wanted complete renouncement of the wealth, not a slight of hand approach. For so many individuals with millions and, yes, billions, who do not empty their coffers unconditionally for the benefit of the poor, the needy, the very less fortunate, the water deprived, the sick, the jobless, the addicted, will reap the scorn laid out in the gospels. Just think how many thousands of children with cleft mouth conditions could be instantly made whole with just 1% of someone's shameless wealth.

To believe that what is yours is absolutely YOURS is the most foolish fiction ever designed for human consumption. Nothing is absolutely yours, and nothing is even conditionally yours. You are a USER. On this earth no one earns ownership. You are a caretaker of God's largesse. The only title holder is God. The only ownership conferred on human beings is the careful management of the creator's goods. Even on a secular level according to the Declaration of Independence we are granted "life, liberty, and the pursuit of happiness," by our creator; no mention of an omnipotent ownership of the earth and its possessions.

This is why any resistance to selling everything and giving it to the least of the least runs counter to the Jesus doctrine of, "Do unto others as you would have them do unto you." Jesus came to straighten us out, to clarify our obligations, to examine our lives, to testify to the truth according to God the Father not mankind, and to demonstrate how the Good Samaritan behaves at all times. We all participate in creation, and for those who possess more of it, it is incumbent on them to share it with others. This is not almsgiving, it is required reciprocity according to Jesus.

"You Fool, this very day your life will be taken from you!"

Chapter 10

WHICH JESUS?

BEFORE THE PROTESTANT REFORMATION JESUS was pretty much confined to the Catholic Church. If you espoused a belief in Christ you belonged to a Catholic parish somewhere (and the Greek Orthodox Church). For Christianity anything prior to the 1500s was pretty much the domain of the Catholic Church. There were rumblings and disagreements, and departures, with and for those who chose to challenge the authorities of the Roman Catholic Church, but overall Christianity had its home in the Catholic Church.

Anything related to Sacraments, Angels, devils, sin, last judgment, justification by faith, marriage, resurrection, blasphemy, followed the formulas and definitions of the Catholic Church. This included Sacred Scripture and all of its interpretations. The church ruled on everything. There was an all encompassing, one authority for every matter relating to Jesus and life in general. European life celebrated or suffered the will of the Church. Then at the beginning of the 16th century the lid blew off the pot.

The dominance the church had prior to Martin Luther, Henry VIII, John Calvin, John Knox, and many others, was gone in a fortnight. It was a storm that changed the church of Jesus Christ forever. You no longer had to be an originalist. You did not have to be tied tightly to the sacraments. You need not have had to conform to Canon Law. Apostolic succession for priestly ordination became unnecessary.

Scripture became the focus and primary sacrament, which then came in an intelligible vernacular language that all could read and interpret for themselves. Jesus' story was out in the open for anyone and all to read. And they did. Jesus' life and messages were unveiled, along with Paul's. Church vestments and adornments and statuary lost importance along with indulgences and so many other rituals.

For many it was a cleansing. Church authority came under attack and was undone. The chair of Peter lost its legs and the occupant was summarily dispatched. New religious leaders arose and grew in abundance. There was no longer one head. The church of Jesus Christ became multi-headed. Beliefs also became multi-numbered. Sacraments were deluded and minimized, often reduced to just one. Dogma was left in the hands of a group of church elders.

In time the church of Jesus Christ multiplied and multiplied over and over again. Its popularity encouraged any rank and file individual to hang a shingle on a door front and call itself the "First Church of Jesus Christ," or the "Church of the Resurrection," or the "Church of the Reborn," or the "Disciples of Christ" Church.

The gospel of Jesus Christ avails itself of innovation. It promotes individuality. If you hear Christ, you just may believe in him. And if you believe in him, you just might start promoting him. You don't need a lot of dogma to understand Jesus. He's down to earth and in your face. Once Jesus gets into your veins, the next step easily becomes discipleship. His stuff is so common sense that sharing it becomes a compulsion.

When the walls came tumbling down in the 16th century, a variety of religious replacements occurred throughout

Europe. Several nations had their own national brand. France, Germany and England were the most distinctive. Princes and kings became their sponsors and sometimes enforcers. Their fundamental authority was the scripture. Out of the freshly translated pages of the New Testament came their declaration of freedom and religious authorization. Jesus spoke volumes of independence in these pages: justified by faith, predestined by God, baptism is all you need, Eucharist is symbol not substance of Jesus, forgiveness is in the heart not in absolution.

After some 400 years of unleashed Christianity we now have over 32,000 different Christian Churches in the United States of America. There is little common doctrine among any of them. Of course Jesus Christ is the celebrated figurehead of most of them, with his call for love and decency among all of mankind, but beyond that the similarities fade rapidly.

In November of 1517 Martin Luther pinned his 95 theses on the cathedral of Wittenberg and ever since then Christian Churches have published their own theses on door fronts. There is a wide menu of beliefs and practices promoted by each one. On every level of human activity and endeavor these Churches vary in degree of support and acceptance, or resistance and rejection. There is no scriptural doctrine from the New Testament that is held with tenacity by many of these churches. Where there was once uniformity on issues of marriage, divorce, homosexuality, and Abortion, there is none today. Each church abides by its own inclinations. Even the Catholic Church with its commanding pontifical head does not have uniformity of belief among members on these issues. For a church that pronounced condemnation on infractions of every kind on human behavior, ranging from the most serious that incurred the awful judgment of mortal sin down to the least that incurred the judgment of venial sin, today nothing is too offensive and damning that requires church censure. The

Churches have become useless moral arbiters in a world of moral decrepitude.

The Churches have lost all consequential authority over moral issues. They are left in charge of ceremonial events such as marriages and baptisms and funerals, with religious marriages in decline. Defining and scrutinizing the ethical value of human behavior has been lifted from church leaders and taken hostage by a gang of thugs in Hollywood, the Media of all sordid sorts, and the Democrat Party. They have been burning bridges and pushing envelopes for the past many generations. There is nothing above them and nothing below them; they have a complete field of freedom to dash morality to shreds and a limitless potential to devastate anyone who stands in their way. They present their turpitude as morality and their slander as justice. Their arrogance surpasses that of the Devil's.

Churches do not preach right and wrong any more. They preach Jesus the Good Samaritan, and "love one another," and almsgiving for the needy, and "let's all get along," and "forgive your fellowman," and "peace is better than war." It used to be that if you didn't go to church on Sunday you were going to Hell; if you had sex outside of marriage you were going to Hell; if you were living with someone unmarried you were living in mortal sin; if you killed a baby in the womb you committed murder and living in mortal sin and going to Hell; if you had sex with the same sex you were under pain of mortal sin and going to Hell; if you saw a movie rated in the "C" category you had to confess a mortal sin. Mortal sin was deadly and was applied liberally to many objectionable behaviors. In fact if you were a male of young years, you were probably in a perpetual state of mortal sin because "lusting" for women was a steady occupation. The church had its hands all over you way back then.

The Liberal establishments talk forever and feverishly about global warming and its negative effects on the environment while the moral climate of the country and perhaps the world is sinking deeper and deeper into a Sodom and Gomorrah existence. The global temperature is vitally more important than the moral climate. It used to be that all behavior was parsed toward the negative side of life; now the parsing of behavior is done to avoid any connotation of objectionable. Ever since Liberaldom has sequestered moral behavior, it has been placed in an "All is Privacy" zone. All behavior is automatically considered a "private" matter. In fact, your conduct is private until proven public and indictable, and then, only then, with multiple videos and witnesses, unless you have a Liberal Media and Liberal court system that will shadow your crime.

Liberal thinking and bias have taken a hold in churches and synagogues in the country. They do not operate independently of the strong armed Media. What is preached in the pulpit is what has been delivered on the screen. Christian Churches throughout the land are not 100% Pro-Life. They are not 50% Pro-Life. It is more likely 30%. The sanctity of life that is absolute doctrine in the pages of the New Testament is not the doctrine of the American Church pulpits. If Jesus were to return tomorrow and show up on the doorsteps of a majority of churches he would take a rope, wind it in a whip, then tear down the crosses that falsely represent his name.

It is safe to say that the words and messages of Jesus are not preached in Churches and pulpits today. If they were, there would be few Churches and fewer pulpits. Jesus himself moved from town to town delivering his Father's message as long as it was received. If not received, he left and shook the dust of that town off his feet. In the last 400 years the increased volume of Christian Churches has not added clarity or intensity to Jesus and his message. We might have expected that to be the case, but unfortunately the passage of time and the proliferation of Churches has not added to the intensity of Jesus' message. Jesus has not been solidified nor his message better defined. If anything, it has suffered diminution and dilution, with emphasis on the latter.

The doctrine of Jesus Christ is not a take-what-you-like doctrine and leave the rest. On the contrary, it is a take-it-all-you-must doctrine. Jesus leaves if you don't take it in its entirety. It's all or nothing. Jesus once defined the entry to his Father's kingdom as a "narrow gate." Another time he used the imagery of a needle and getting into the kingdom was as difficult as getting through the eye of a needle. If imagery serves as a graphic image for the reality, then one has to conclude that following Jesus is not for sight seers and the devious.

The reinvented churches of Jesus Christ follow no established teaching from the past. Albeit they ally themselves with the scriptures, they have no connection with the past and with tested traditions. They are entirely innovative and self-reliant. Relying on the New Testament for facts and truths does not give one the final and complete body of evidence about Jesus. Jesus is bigger than scriptures. He is the head of the church and as such is undefinable. He is in between the lines of scripture, and he surpasses scripture. He is in the heart and mind; he is in the earth and all its functions. He is not a mere piece of doctrine.

Churches and Church authorities have been reading scripture for ages and have not defined Christ. He's not a book or book of words. He's not a phrase or group of phrases, nor in a single word like "Love." The vernacular brings him closer, but is not a perfect exposé of his magnitude. The scriptures merely open the door to his infinite personality. Perhaps this explains his ability to invite volumes of people into his life without much intervention from humankind. People have come to Jesus for centuries with superficial support from others. Jesus can do it himself. He did it in the beginning, he still does it today. He is the man for all ages, all nations, and all people. God sent him into our world to bring divinity into reality and it will never depart again. Divinity is at the core of our existence and Jesus brought it here. We are defined by it and we are attracted to it, hence our attraction to Jesus.

You cannot lock Jesus up. No one owns him. He is for everyone and for all times. "He was in the beginning with God. All things came to be through him, and without him nothing came to be. What came to be through him was life, and this life was the light of the human race... He was in the world, and the world came to be through him, but the world did not know him. He came to what was his own, but his own people did not accept him. But to those who did accept him he gave power to become children of God, to those who believe in his name, who were born not by natural generation nor by human choice nor by man's decision but by God." (J.1:2-4;10-13)

Without dogma, without doctrine, without scriptures, without preachers, Jesus still comes into the world proclaiming his Father's presence to all mankind. His visibility is profound. He is invisible only to those who do not believe. And once you do believe he is profoundly present. His cross is everywhere and it confirms his presence. He is omnipresent.

No one can erase divinity from our lives. No evil, no devil, no atheism, no arrogance or disbelief can displace Jesus, Creator and Savior. Knowingly or unknowingly we are touched by his magical presence. You simply cannot remove the creator out of creation.

Hence those who come to Jesus and believe in him without any in depth and profound understanding come with intrinsic intuitions that only the Spirit has initiated. If we are born of the creator, then his fingerprints are on us. The fingerprints of

Jesus in particular become labeled on our minds. This explains why those who followed the reformation did so with some divine guidance. Human beings crave a Savior, and for many Jesus is the obvious one. The offspring of the reformation did not require a lengthy discipleship to discern Jesus' validity in their lives. Jesus by mere mention of his name has remarkable results. Paul heard Jesus on the road to Damascus and was forever indebted to him. This explains the many and sundry church groups and institutions that profess Jesus as the "One."

What becomes disconcerting in the world we practice our beliefs is that so many Christian Churches throughout the country lose the values and character of Christ by what they espouse. They adapt to a message that is of the world, not found in the archives of the Spirit. They become disciples of the culture not of the Lord. Whatever the culture favors is where they go.

Segregation, for instance, used to be a solid cultural fixture that was adhered to by all white Christian denominations without exception. North or South it did not matter. Segregation was the rule of the land. It was ritual, it was the law. No one messed with those boundaries. All white Christian Churches without exception were segregated and resisted any change. This practice persisted for a century, and beyond. Whites did not mix with Blacks in any arena, and that included the White Churches. This placed Blacks at a social and economic disadvantage forcing them into poverty and disenfranchisement in everything American. While the White church pulpits preached love and compassion according to the gospel of Jesus Christ nothing was done about the deplorable treatment of the Black members of the human race in their same cities. Apparently the love message of Jesus did not apply to Blacks in America. Whites attended all White churches on

Sunday and then throughout the week persecuted and lynched Blacks. The pulpits remained silent about this scourge.

The Churches were and are copycats of the culture. They reflect the attitude of their paying membership. If they want them back, they have to. The Jesus of the gospels did not favor any culture, nor any race, nor any Nation, nor his Jewish faith. He was always ready to shake the dust off his feet. His gospel was not "FOR SALE." His gospel did not favor anyone except his Father. He preached the truth, and the truth is not human friendly. It is God Friendly.

What the churches of the past and the present avoid is confrontation with the prominent viewpoint of the day. They accommodate not confront. However so much of what Jesus did was precisely confrontational. Taking a whip against money changers expressed confrontation. Healing a leper on the Sabbath was confrontational. Offering Forgiveness to a sinner was confrontational. When Jesus presented himself as the "Bread of Life," he was disturbingly confrontational. You might say Jesus earned the name of "Jesus Confrontational." Jesus did not turn the other cheek when the truth was at stake. He held fast and never walked away.

The truth has few friends. Unfortunately, too often it recuses itself in difficult circumstances. We are very used to non-confrontational gospel preaching. We are only comfortable with non-confrontational conservatives who never offend and always take "the slings and arrows of outrageous fortune." But Jesus did not. He stood his ground and recited the truth. He spoke as a man with the divine truth that he brought with him from his Father. However, as was to be expected, truth does not survive long in a culture of deceit and slander.

Martin Luther King, Jr. spoke every bit the truth and landed multiple times in jail until finally he was killed for the truth he espoused. It was not just the truth he spoke, it was truth that demanded change. Truth that leads to change is what frightens the enemies of truth. As soon as the truth threatens change the landscape turns bellicose. Jesus found that out throughout his ministry. Speak the truth and you are a target. You are Beelzebub, you are a Blasphemer, you are an enemy of the Nation, you are worse than Barrabas. That's why the country's Christian pulpits are soft on truth. That's why the Democrat Party cannot speak the truth any longer, because it has been commandeered by anti-religious, socialist, pro-Abortion powerful proponents who have solidified with the Media who will not stop short of absolute victory. Truth attracts enemies, who do not debate but destroy with a vengeance.

The Church pulpits for the foreseeable future will continue to preach the gospel of the culture not the gospel of Jesus Christ. Truth emboldens evil. Speak a word the ruling class does not want to hear and you will pay the consequences. The Media has become the ruling class of the culture and they tolerate no deviancy from their power. In the past it provided news and information, now it governs with lies, falsehood, panic and slander. Jesus warned us of their wrath: "'Beware of false prophets, who come to you in sheep's clothing, but underneath are ravenous wolves.'" (Mt.7:15).

The churches today stay safely inside the perimeters allowed by the ruling class. Whatever is preached is preached according to the script handed to them by the ruling class, not by the script defining Jesus. Their mouths are bathed in fluff and congeniality, not the originality and integrity expressed by Jesus.

When Jesus was transfigured before Peter, James, and John, the Father in heaven uttered these words:

"This is my Beloved Son, listen to him." (Mk.9:7)

Chapter 11

Born From Above

Nicodemus, the Sadducee, visited Jesus at night to further be enlightened about being "born from above." Nicodemus was deeply puzzled. His suggestion that a person would have to be born again of a woman was demonstrably rebuffed by Jesus: "You are the teacher of Israel and you do not understand this?" It appears that anything of a spiritual nature was over his head. Nicodemus respected Jesus for his "signs" but was completely befuddled about the origin of rebirth in the spirit. His confusion suggests that he could not reach out of the physical realm into a completely spiritual realm for a solution.

John the Baptist throughout his public career baptized with water in the Jordan. His baptism constituted repentance. He broadcasted that his baptism would be superseded by another, greater than he, whose sandal strap he was unworthy to tie, and this "another" would baptize with the "holy Spirit and fire." It was the action of the Holy Spirit that caused one to be "born from above." It certainly was not the water being poured nor would it be the one pouring water on someone. Those are accidental agents to the event. The primary agent is the Holy Spirit. If you are born from above, then all causality for this movement must come from above. Nothing from below can initiate that move. If water were the acting agent, then John could have done it.

Jesus clarified the matter for us when he claimed, "What is born of flesh is flesh and what is born of spirit is spirit. Do not be amazed that I told you, 'You must be born from above.'" (J.3:6) Being born again is not a physical act but a spiritual act. Hence no going back in the womb. No earthly activity could affect this change. No extraordinary event from worldside could turn a physical into a metaphysical makeover. There is only one source for spirit, and that is from above. And since Jesus was from above he started the "born from above" movement that happens at baptism, as John attested.

However, it appears that the physical, mechanical action of the pouring of water and the recitation of the formula of words automatically elicits the "born from above" event. It happens quickly and instantly. But it also appears that nothing from above is involved. It all happens from down below. The minister of baptism does the water and words (simultaneously) with the intention of baptizing someone. There is no visible intervention from above. There is no miracle, there is no divine cloud descending and declaring that a monumental event has occurred, as when Jesus was baptized and the heavens opened and a voice from heaven called out and declared that, "This is my Beloved Son, with whom I am well pleased."

The being "Born from Above" in baptism has no consequential visible "spiritual" signs associated with it. It is documented and ledgered based on the calendar day and time it occurs, and the participants involved. No one knows if the Spirit from above showed up. In Jesus' case the Father showed up and confirmed his Son's authority, but for all others who experience baptism the "born from above" experience is hidden and/or concealed. The assumption is that at baptism the spirit does show up. We are "born again." There simply is no confirmation of that. We are left stranded on our own.

In the end the one and only element that assures us we have been born again is faith. The spirit is introduced through faith. Faith and spirit walk hand and hand. Spirit is born through faith, not mere water. You can have a hundred baptisms, but without faith there is little or no spirit. Though we are born for faith, it is never a guarantee, and without it there is no guarantee of spirit. Faith is the only gateway to spirit. It is exclusively dependent on faith, something that appears to come out of nowhere. This is how Jesus tried to describe the coming of the Spirit to Nicodemus: "The wind blows where it wills, and you can hear the sound it makes, but you do not know where it comes from or where it goes; so it is with everyone who is born of the spirit." (J.3:8)

Again, without faith there can be no entry into spirit; the essential key that unlocks the gate to Spirit is faith. Jesus further tries to explain this rather simple mystery to Nicodemus, "If I tell you about earthly things and you do not believe, how will you believe if I tell you about heavenly things?" (J.3:12) Any talk about Spirit, about "born from above," about eternal life, about God the Father, Angels and the Kingdom, have their origin in faith. We are confined and consigned to faith. It is our ticket to Jesus and "born again" and eternity. It sidelines everything else and surpasses everything else.

One special ingredient of faith is a receptive mind and heart. As Jesus explained many times to listeners who came to him that faith begins with openness: "I give praise to you, Father, Lord of heaven and earth, for although you have hidden these things from the wise and the learned you have revealed them to the childlike." (Mt.11:25). Nothing comes by reason of the intellect if Spirit is the topic of interest, and everything of the Spirit becomes available if faith is the reason for the interest.

Faith drives its own power and directs the occupant deeper and deeper toward the object of faith.

Faith does not require reason for its existence and intensity. Moreover, it has an ability to sweep the individual off its feet to reach beyond earth to the heavens. Faith has the amazing ability to carry us off and outside the earth to a place never seen before but inviting and for real. Faith helps us travel beyond our frailty to a resting place with God. Jesus teaches anyone who will listen to the vision to witness that faith. Through faith we adopt not only his vision but the motivation for his vision. Accepting someone's charismatic vision comes with a deafening faith and relentless zeal. Faith is not just a blinding propulsion but an ecstatic attraction.

Nicodemus only saw and respected Jesus for his signs and his teachings. He struggled to reach a level of faith that carried him over to believe in Jesus. He was an outsider looking in but never coming in. That was too much of a leap. He was much moved by his miracles and admired his words but was checkmated by his Judaic culture. After a life dedicated to Jewish rule and practice he could not adopt Jesus as his leader. Admiration yes, faith no. That is expressly why Nicodemus wanted a physical resolution to "born from above," so he could join the Jesus crowd but not lose his status and longstanding commitment to the Jewish religion. That would allow him to have one foot in each camp: Jesus for his miracles and words and Judaism for its cultural comforts.

Baptism with water does not guarantee a life of faith. It's a ritual, it's recorded, it includes membership in the Christian Church, it may even provide for a washing away of Original Sin, but it does not carry faith with it. They are not synonymous. The lives of so many people, especially past world dictators, demonstrate how far afield they were from living a life of faith in God. There is a serious injustice committed in believing that baptism and faith, which translates into being "born from above," are automatically linked. Perhaps the baptismal seed was planted, but it fell on arid rocky ground and died. Or perhaps it is because many are called but few chosen. Or perhaps it is due to the fact that "the wind blows...but you do not know where it comes from or where it goes." It wasn't blowing in Nicodemus' direction. He was drawn to Jesus but not drawn to his Spirit.

We have a similar situation with the "Young Rich Man," who certainly felt inclined to Jesus, who had equal respect for Jesus as did Nicodemus, but who lost interest as soon as he was told of the conditions. In his case, it was not separation from his Judaic religious roots that kept him away from a new birth in spirit, but his possessions. Being born from above does not constitute a position of status but a lifestyle of "selling what you have and giving it to the poor" according to Jesus. Enrollment in a Christian Church does not transfer automatically into "born from above."

Jesus' conversation with Nicodemus was a turning point for the Jewish religion. Formerly everything centered on circumcision as the primary commitment to God. The covenant by circumcision tied the male Jews to God and this flowed down to the entire nation. By circumcision you became locked into an alliance with the God of Abraham, Isaac, and Jacob and became focused on ritual performances and burnt offerings prescribed in Leviticus and added to by the Pharisees. Jesus came and introduced a new alliance with God that did not distinguish male from female but applied to all equally. John the Baptist had already introduced the practice and gave notice that "another "would come and continue the practice with "spirit and fire." Jesus did just that using baptism as a means of teaching that all had to be born from above. It was this teaching that brought Nicodemus to Jesus on the shores of the Jordan and ask, "How can a man be born again?" The question reveals that union with God starts from above not from below. We are linked by the spirit not by the flesh. Baptism, spiritual birth, supplanted circumcision, a physical alignment with God.

What Nicodemus, but not alone, did not understand was that Jesus came to introduce a new covenant with the Jews and the world. Circumcision was for Jews only and as such became a national characteristic. Jews were circumcised, Greeks were not. God demanded circumcision of Abraham as a sign of loyalty to him. Circumcision meant you were linked to Yahweh: people and God were joined at the hip. It was a national event. There was a blood relationship between God and the Jews. He gave them land and in return they gave him exclusive loyalty. The only problem with this relationship occurred years later when that loyalty went South and they were perfidious.

Jesus exclusively entered the world to establish a new covenant with the Jews: "I was sent only to the lost sheep of Israel." (Mt.15:24). Its primary characteristic was spiritual: each human being coming into the spirit. It was personal and spiritual, each human being coming into the spirit, male and female. Circumcision was a covenant for the nation, not for the individual; the individual was secondary. You were a soldier in an army bound to a commanding officer. With Baptism you were uplifted to something outside the realm of flesh and temporality. Each person now becomes "born from above." Baptism washes the individual, removes a sinful nature, and opens it to God's Spirit. John himself emphasized the role the Spirit will play in baptism: "The man on whom you see the Spirit come down and remain is the one who will baptize with the Holy Spirit." (J.1:33).

The only caveat in this discourse comes when we expect water and spirit to coalesce just because baptismal water is poured on someone's body. Evidence shows that they do not. To "Be born from Above" is not dependent on water, it is dependent on faith. Jesus declares that baptism by water and the Holy Spirit are absolutely necessary for entrance into heaven, however, he never excluded a receptive faith as a preliminary step. Absent faith, absent Spirit. He once joined water and Spirit as a requirement for heaven, but more than once he singled out "born of the Spirit" without mention of water as companion.

In our Christian observance of baptism we assume that the mixing of water and words produces the "born from above" effect. However, we must insist that it is an "assumption," not a fact. If this is a spiritual event, then the acting power is in Heaven not on earth. God provides access and rebirth, not us. Sacraments are "signs," not facts. Reality is in the provider, not the seeker. How many times Jesus said, "Your faith has saved you." Things work on a spiritual level when and if faith is front and foremost. Almost everything Jesus accomplished for others started with their faith, and the fact followed: the lepers , the lame man, the woman with a blood condition, Jairus and his daughter, Martha and Mary and Lazarus, the Centurion and his servant, Bartimaeus. It seems faith is always a precondition to a miracle and all things spiritual.

If sacraments are about things of the spirit, then how can they be approached or received without the necessary element of belief? Essentially they are faith driven and faith made. Everything surrounding them is invisible and everything they effect is invisible. "Born from Above" is invisible, forgiveness is invisible, the fiery tongues of the Holy Spirit are invisible, the Eucharist is invisible, the imposition of hands (the Spirit) at ordination is invisible. It's a world of invisible things and outcomes. What makes it work is belief. Without it all these disappear. They all come from God and He is Invisible Personified. Miracles have visible outcomes but they come from an invisible

113

source. The invisible is always behind the visible. If we are indebted to God for all that he does, that makes us believers personified. "Born from above" only happens to believers.

The world and all that is in it comes from an invisible source. Visible identifies a product not a power. Whatever is seen comes from a source unseen. Nothing we touch is self-made. It's becoming and re-becoming tells us something about the non-Becomer. More importantly, the one and only visible source that brought us closest to the One Invisible Source was Jesus: "He was in the beginning with God. All things came to be through him, and without him nothing came to be." (J.1:2-3). Once this is ingrained in one's head (through faith), then nothing of a visible form makes sense unless it references the One Invisible Source. The earth and all that is in it gives insurmountable evidence of its Creator. We and all the earth are the blessings of the Infinite, Invisible Power called God, who sent his Son for our confirmation and our jubilation: "This is my Beloved Son, Listen to Him."

To be "Born from Above" takes us out and beyond the finite. Finite we must have, but infinite is our destiny. The closer you are to the mere visible, the closer you are to finitude and the particular and a single atom, whereas our capacity is both earth and space. Food and shelter we must have and provide for, however, both of these once satisfied surrender us to a higher more urgent calling inside that brings us to an infinitude of immense proportions. Our essential experience is a spiritual experience. To be human raises us to a level of Angels and perhaps beyond. "Born from Above" is not a religious state; on the contrary, it is a human state at the very root of the constitution of our consciousness.

Jesus elaborated on the distinction between earth and heaven: "What is born of the flesh is flesh, and what is born of the spirit is spirit." His words do not constitute a threat as much as they provide an emphasis on the spirit. But, threat or no threat, the demand for a rebirth in the spirit is absolute: "Very truly I tell you, no one can see the kingdom of God unless they are born again?

(J.3:3)

Chapter 12

GOD'S VISION

THE CREATION OF THE WORLD WAS SORT OF AN experiment by God, given the fact that creation is a host of constantly changing conditions, growing things, evolving species, and nothing staying static. Then put in the mix the creation of man, then woman, adding free will, and emotions, topping it all off with freedom and individuality, plus ambition and self-satisfaction. This becomes a bigger experiment than perhaps he had expected. Certainly we can all agree that the experiment did not work in the Garden of Eden, the very first setting for this experiment.

Within a short period God declared the experiment in the Garden with man a failure, followed by a number of punishments and his banishment from the Garden. In subsequent years God witnessed his experiment continue down the road of failure. After Cain and Abel, there was the flood, then Tower of Babel, then Jacob and his sons, followed by Moses, only to be surpassed by David and his sons and the whole cast of David's descendants, who failed and surpassed each other in perfidy and vicious crimes.

Any first time reader and observer of the story and unfolding of creation in the Old Testament would have to conclude that the author and creator in the background took on more than he could handle. A 99% failure rate suggests he made a mistake. In creating something that consistently failed, not just personally and interpersonally, but against the person of its origin, God surrendered himself to endless humiliation and embarrassment.

The problem lies in God's experiment to allow man dominion over the earth. After he created everything including man, he gave him charge of everything in the Garden. This was a relatively easy task only dealing with other creatures of lesser stature and without challenging ambitions. It is after the Fall and the subsequent creation of other human beings that dominion became a life threatening problem. Abel's death concedes that point.

God's intention in giving dominion to man was, firstly, to share his authority with mankind over the care of the world, and, secondly, to execute order on earth. God had to enjoin the human species to supervise and govern itself for the simple reason that he had given it free will and a consciousness that somewhat matched his. If he had merely dropped programmable instincts into the human species, he would not have had to pass on self-governance to mankind. But given the fact that man matched God in free and conscious personhood, he had to extend rulership to man over man. Also Given the disparities in human beings—age, gender, physical and mental abilities—he had to extend supervisory responsibility to mankind. His experiment simply required that men and women stand in place of him.

God's experiment started with one big assumption: that man would conduct himself like God. If we are made like him, we behave like him; and if we behave like him, we govern like him. His intention was to see the creature matching an orderly and peaceful realm as his own. However, in a short period of time the earth resembled a place called Mt. Olympus where the gods, because of their reckless behavior, overtook the earth and governed ruthlessly and criminally. This was not God's desired goal. However, reality is reality and his expectations though lofty did not match mankind's capacity for a just and righteous governance.

When God turned the earth over to mankind, his primary vision for the exercise of authority was leadership. That's a big word. It has nothing to do with coercion and everything to do with drawing people into a vision that befits their lives now and hereafter. If our here is also for tomorrow, then tomorrow has to be brought into the equation of how it benefits us today. Leadership must have a comprehensive vision of life. It includes God and never loses sight of God in its performance. So many of the Old Testament authorities lost sight of their essential role of seeing "God as Primary" and in their dalliance self-destructed. Leadership is not a one stop shop viewing everything from the necessities and interests of today.

What is a leader without a vision? What is a dog without a nose, or an elephant without a trunk? Lost. One could not smell himself to food and the other could not feed himself. A leader without a vision is doomed. Saul was picked by the Jews as their first king because they could not wait for God to make his pick. It was forced on Saul. He had no vision. He ruled aimlessly and once David arrived and became enhanced in military fame he grew jealous and sought vigorously to destroy him. David had a vision and as king destroyed his enemies and United Israel for the first time.

There have been all kinds of historical leaders in the past with vision. All the dictators of the 20th century had grandiose visions, most of which included murdering millions of innocent people. There are others who, not so murderous, lived lives of munificent royalty and stole the goods and services of their people. Others simply enslaved others to profit for themselves.

Others with military victories in their heads drove hundreds of thousands of men to their deaths. All these leaders who wasted and destroyed lives acted outside of God's vision. Their diabolical acts demonstrated their contempt for God and his vision for this world.

God's vision starts with one primary principle, and that is "to love God and take care of your neighbor as yourself." This vision covers all of the Old Testament and all of the New. The only difference is that Jesus, in the New Testament, expands on what the second part of that vision means. This all may on the surface appear simplistic, however, it is the rock solid foundation of our existence as human beings and as recipients of God's gift of life on earth. We are not here for ourselves, we are here for each other. If God gives, we must give. This fact is displayed every day with every rising of the sun and every fruit that ripens on a tree. We are here to grow and then to share. Growing for the sake of only ONE is not the divine vision. If the earth belongs to God, then its "Bounty" also belongs first to him. He is the primary giver, no one else.

Whoever follows in the footsteps of this vision God has established at the beginning is doing the will of God. His vision trumps every other vision and every other ambition. Nothing is superior to or can override his vision. We are products of the Creator and hence, and therefore, and forever, we are captives of his vision and his order. Creation gives abundant evidence of his generosity and for us who inhabit this (HIS) creation the same principle must be upheld and applied. His generosity becomes our generosity. Any deviation becomes a derelict action. Anyone choosing to violate this one essential self-evident fact selects his own destruction. It is a case of clear and simple logic that nothing belongs to anyone in abundance, but everything belongs to everyone for survival.

An amazing acknowledgement was witnessed at the time of the signing of the Declaration of Independence, stating that "We hold these truths to be self-evident, that all men are created equal, that they are endowed by their Creator with certain unalienable Rights, that among these are Life, Liberty and the pursuit of Happiness." For certain God would have endorsed this declaration for its clarity and its meaningfulness. This one-of-a-kind proclamation identifies that each human being is entitled to the very basics God provides on earth and that no where in this declaration does it mention any exclusions. However, we know from the history of the United States that this Declaration did not always include everyone.

God's vision allows for no exclusions. Life becomes precious and endowable from the time of conception until the very last breath. What Jesus brings forward in the Gospels over and above mere equality of entitlement of the basics is the require-ment on the part of leadership to promote and execute the delivery of Life, Liberty and Happiness to all equally. Those who lead, lead for all, not for themselves. We are all passengers on the same journey.

The precise direction leadership must follow was demon-strated by Jesus. Servanthood is the name. Throughout his ministry Jesus performed as a servant. Not just at the washing of the disciples' feet, but at every turn his concern reached out to all those in need. He was consumed with the care of others—feeding them, healing them, teaching and instructing, and raising them from the dead. In that role he was the leader personified. He was a man for all men and women. The gospels describe in detail almost daily, sometimes hourly, his involve-ment with the needs of people. He was a medic par excellence, a consoler, a forgiver, an arbitrator, a moralist, a fisher of men, fish finder, chef at the seashore, and above all a preacher and teacher with authority.

In spite of centuries of the gospels being preached to millions of the inhabitants of Europe and in spite of the title of Holy Roman Empire, history bears witness to the fact that Jesus' brand of leadership was never adopted by its leaders. "Servants" there were few, if any, who occupied the seats of authority in Europe. Kings there were in abundance, but not servants. Pope's also in abundance, but "few" servants. It's a tough role to fill once you gain authority. Human beings rapidly rush to an authoritarian position once in power. Human nature adopts "control" as the primary methodology of authority. Leadership is sidelined. Then if by chance control does not produce the desired effect, the next step is compulsion. Next after that is threat, then enforcement, then imprisonment. In tyrannical authorities death is the final solution. Once a position of authority is acquired the requirement of leadership wanes and vanishes. Who needs leadership when power is in your hands.

Power and leadership are not Siamese twins. Power applies force mentally and physically. Power acts as law and abrogates the law. It is above the law. Leadership, on the other hand, operates neither above the law or beneath the law, it reaches beyond the law. Jesus said he did not come to destroy the law but to perfect it. Multiple times his leadership travelled beyond the law to heal the seriously diseased and handicapped even on the Sabbath. Leadership requires charisma and fortitude, not threats and force. Power exists for itself not for another. Leadership is for others. Performing as a servant constantly draws you to the needs of others. Jesus embodied that attitude in his teachings and actions. With all the power in the world at his fingertips he forwent any use of it. At his arrest in Gethsemane Jesus rebuked Peter for drawing his sword: "Do you think that I cannot call upon my Father and he will not provide me at this moment with more than twelve legions of Angels?" (Mt.26:53)

One of the lingering curses of the Fall is the temptation to rule over other people. "My way or the highway," exemplifies the symptomatic attitude of power. In general power drugs the ego and shortens the use of reason. It's not that power corrupts; rather, the truth is that power is corrupt. The exercise of power in the midst of a human relationship or activity demonstrates the selfish and petty weakness of the one wielding power. With human beings you lead with ideas, not herd them with a stick. Power suffocates and strangles the human spirit; it does not fit into any Christian ethic. And yet Christians have wielded power no differently than anyone else. Inquisitions and holocausts were executed under the auspices of Christians.

When history is examined and out comes the brutal consequences of power in the world, such as slavery, genocide, bloody wars, segregation, plus all the heinous dictatorships, one can readily understand the enormous danger in power. Jesus condemned the exercise of power. It corrupts the one using it and destroys the person it's used against. Without exception there has never existed a "benevolent" dictator. The two are mutually exclusive and a self-evident oxymoron.

During Jesus' ministry the leading local dictator was Herod. Having ruthlessly beheaded John the Baptist, he was not exactly benevolent, though considerably more benevolent that his father, Herod the Great, who easily matched the devil himself in treachery. Both had enormous power and no scruples. Jesus once called him a fox. (Now that was benevolent.) He is the one person in all of the gospels Jesus never shared a word with. Perhaps that is a judgment in itself. He was an adulterer and murderer who killed the one man who proclaimed the coming of the Light of the world. Jesus would have nothing to do with him. Others whom he observed and objected to he spoke words of criticism, but Herod nothing. Even the devil received responses from Jesus. Not Herod. His silence speaks to the depths of Herod's evil life of power.

There is something synonymous about power and the commission of evil. Power begets evil and evil is the offspring of power. For all of history this has been borne out. Those who seek power invariably commit evil. One does not exist without the other. On a small scale or large scale power destroys character and virtue and allows the occupant free reign to destroy others. In any capacity of power the one holding the whip can and will subjugate another with whatever means available. Those with mighty means will destroy absolutely and those with words will destroy slanderously. God's justice will sit like the weight of Everest on their heads. There can be no escape from that wrath. God made each one of us subjects of his to be respected and lifted up by others, never to be subjugated by the hand or mouth of another of earth's "mere subjects." We are all here at the pleasure of God, not at the disposal of the self-appointed mini and major dictators that abound on earth.

During his ministry Jesus confronted many factions who wanted nothing more than to destroy him. Their death threats were framed by how much Jesus threatened their power. The Pharisees in particular reacted aggressively because Jesus charged them with hypocrisy. Their religious claims to authority were fundamentally power based not God based. There was scarcely anything religious in their actions except their preachings, "For they preach but they do not practice." Jesus provided limitless condemnation against the Pharisees for their lives of deceit and vice and corruption. The title of Rabbi was a name of distinction directed at controlling the pocket books of ordinary Jews. Their titles and power subdued every aspect of Jewish lives and Jesus clearly outlined their crimes: "Woe to you Scribes and Pharisees...," "Woe to you Blind Guides...," "Woe to you, Scholars of the Law..." (Mt.23; Lk.11)

Jesus eliminated all titles. You were not to be called "Rabbi," nor "father," nor "Master." Brothers and servants we are all. His fear was that someone would grab the front row seat, then assume that he is first. His fear was that some one of us would assume power and overlord it over others. Only absolute servanthood set well with Jesus' mind, not absolute power. When James and John wanted special seating in heaven, Jesus abruptly responded, "'You know that those who are regarded as rulers of the Gentiles lord it over them, and their high officials exercise authority over them. Not so with you. Instead, whoever wants to become great among you must become your servant, and whoever wants to be first must be slave of all. For even the Son of Man did not come to be served, but to serve, and give his life as a ransom for many.'" (Mt.10:42-45)

In Jesus' lexicon of most egregious evils power over others constitutes the greatest and gravest of crimes. The only reason Jesus was accused of blasphemy occurred because the Pharisees sensed he was a threat to their power. Then the final reason he was sentenced to death is because the Pharisees pushed the mob to frighten Pilate into issuing the sentence of execution because they wanted him gone. As long as he was out of the way their power was intact; only Caesar was left to stand over them, and he cared nothing about their internal beliefs and practices.

Jesus wanted nothing to do with power. It was antithetical to all that he did and preached. From beginning to end Jesus demonstrated in the gospels the rank absurdity power is and the utter disgust he had for power and for power seekers. When he entered into his ministry Satan was the first to demand power from him, and in the Halls of Pilate's court at the end of his ministry the Sanhedrin tumultuously demanded all his authority be destroyed. Evil exists in the universe for one reason—men want power in order to destroy others, which is the ultimate antithesis of God's commandment to "Love your neighbor as yourself."

We are subjects of God exclusively, not the subjects of other created subjects. Any man who thinks he has power over others is the mightiest of Fools ever to live on earth. In the end he will reap the hand of God's power. "Woe to you, scribes and Pharisees... You serpents, you brood of vipers, how can you flee from the judgment of Gehenna?" (Mt.23:33)

Chapter 13

OUT OF EDEN

IN THE VERY BEGINNING THERE WAS NOTHING. Then suddenly by the word of God there appeared light, then heavens and earth, then sea separated from earth, then trees and grass, then creatures large and small, then finally man in His Image. But that was not enough. God created a companion called woman. He set them together in order to make more. God's image would be multiplied tens times, a hundred times, a thousand times across the earth. And so God enjoined these two together forever in one union and they cling to each other, "and the two of them become one body." And this we call marriage.

To be sure marriage is a phenomenon of unspeakable proportions. No human being could have invented it. Even for God it becomes unquestionably a road to be traveled only by the greatest optimist. To invent a system whereby two human beings of polar opposite genders, of seismic emotional makeups, of untested virtue, of physical sizes unequal, coming from cultures and religions in strife, with separate and tortuous expectations, with never pre-approved maturity, are brought together as one for their good and the good of others is a road too far. Either God had a morbid sense of humor or he enjoyed civil war.

Marriage had never received a testing period. It had never passed the lab test of endurance. It had a pre-dated expiration date on it before it started. God ignored all that and placed his stamp of approval on it. When he dispatched them from the Garden of Eden he simply ordered them to "increase and multiply." He included no instruction manuals for the marriage experiment. Years and years of experiments have been conducted and still there are no conclusive results. Some have succeeded, many have failed, and many more have simply survived.

No matter what the failure rate is, the experiment is richly desired by a high percentage of the population. It's a state still Idolized by all ages. For some reason the opposite sexes appeal to each other in spite of enormous personal and individual hurdles. Perhaps a key to understanding why it remains an attraction to multitudes is precisely because it is idolized. The dream outweighs the reality, but no matter what happens the dream stays alive. "If it's not good today, maybe it'll be better tomorrow." Hope is the magic ingredient of success. "It'll come, just give it time."

God designed this experiment by installing a magnetic quality in the sexes for the purpose of instant matching. People who have never met before, who have come from long distances, who have come out of socially opposite environments, educated and less educated, suddenly meet and the world and all its noise disappears except for them. It's a physical event and the force of nature locks in these two people like a vice. It happens in a flash; it happens without intellectual investigation; it happens and it cannot be stopped. Usually emotion is the primordial driving component, but in this case it lags behind a built in "lock-on" mechanism in the eyes of the beholder. It is a case of "I see it, I like it. And I want it." No questions asked.

This experiment of two bodies suddenly colliding then matching includes or is preceded by one other factor, and that is availability. Availability opens the door to new horizons and bold adventures. Without availability there are no new attractions. Other interests and preoccupations will avert one's attention from something new. Timing is essential to seeing and then matching up with someone else. Seeing something in a very particular moment first demands the ability to look. If your gaze is elsewhere, there is no focus. Enchantment begins with availability. You can only see what you are drawn to, but drawn at the precise moment. Why does someone see something in a crowd of one thousand that no one else sees? You were not even looking, but you were open and available. And that is the fortune or your Achilles heel.

God's experiment fundamentally starts at a physical level. The eye opens the door to delight. In an instant it draws us into the environment of another human being who from all appearances could very likely promise a lifetime of sheer happiness. Before words are spoken and glances mutually exchanged this conviction takes hold and grows. God does not allow us a lengthy screening process. Overmuch scrutiny may dampen the attraction and nullify the process. The less we know the better our chance for an encounter and then deepened interest. Too much advance knowledge could and easily would cancel the attraction. Too many details up front entangle the instantaneity of the attraction. God keeps us away from details and allows the pure magnetism of the physical work eagerly and forcefully.

After all, this divine experiment accomplishes a specific divine process, that of increasing and multiplying the species. If God had wanted mere companionship for Adam he could have easily created a companion of similar makeup, one who provided friendship and support with no physical attraction. Physical attraction and companionship need not concur within a relationship. In marriage the two are inevitable, but in time the former wanes and the latter remains. God wanted a specific process to unfold, namely, procreation. The species mattered. He wanted longevity in the species and the only way to achieve that goal was to create a complementary but different sex. And, furthermore, he wanted a guarantee that his design would occur, hence magnetism in the polarized sexes. In a setting of opposite sexes, the occupants of either side become somewhat too entirely helpless in avoiding contact. The impulse to migrate to the opposite sex is not an option but a compulsion.

What we call romance is the magnetic gravity one sex feels toward the other. We are designed for physical reproduction and that is specifically accomplished through sexual attraction. Minus that attraction none of us would move out of our fortresses and allow compatibility free reign.

Reproduction in marriage becomes the focal point of the relationship. Sex is short lived even if the couple is sexually active in the beginning. Marriage is not a bordello. It's an industry designed by God for the continuation of the species. Once marriage starts the normal overlying activity in the relationship is the creation of children. Even for those who postpone children the overlying concern is the avoidance of pregnancy, which means less sex, and for those who do not want children, then the preoccupation every month becomes a huge task of dodging the reproductive cycle and reducing sexual activity.

The historical successor to marriage is family and that emphatically entails children. Children become the consummated bond of the two people entering into marriage. "It is a consummation devoutly to be wished." Children become the one necessary common goal to which all activity in the marriage is directed. Progeny prevails over all other demands. It governs their lives, absorbs their lives, sometimes overtakes their lives, and overall blesses their lives. Goals, activities, expectations, center around children. We follow their needs and provide for their needs. Eventually we become their bystanders.

When God initiated the world and created Adam and Eve, his intention included the creation of mankind at large. Adam and Eve were the catalysts to start this process. Within seconds of their creation "God Blessed them and said to them, 'Be fruitful and increase in number...'" There was no disconnect between Adam and Eve's creation and his command to "multiply over the earth." They were created for themselves and for others simultaneously. They were forerunners with a mission. Their companionship was important but never exclusive of their mission. Their companionship was necessary for them to better serve their offspring. How many times the scriptures indicate that "If you obey God's commands, you will be blessed in your children."

The sexual nature that God placed in the human being serves essentially a reproductive function. In other creatures the sexual nature is governed by a time clock. A once-a-year mating season or thereabouts determines the reproductive process. It is controlled absolutely. Human beings, however, do not have that sort of limited and fixed season for reproduction. It's open season all year around. Men attract women and women attract men without shut downs. They meander in and out of singular attractions at a single whim. In former times (before the sexual revolution) men attracted a woman to marry. The culture and, above all, religious tenets did not permit sexual activity outside of marriage. Courting was an official practice supervised by parents with timelines and approved activities. But those days have long passed and now we have a culture without religious restrictions that allows sexual activity for anyone at any time as long as consent is given.

Today sexual activity is deemed a normal exercise not a reserved privilege for those who are married. Consent is the only requirement. Hollywood and TV shows advertise sex as a normal pastime for men and women. They have taken the normal attraction of the sexes and turned it into an official nighttime pastime. After hours is for adult beverages and sex. It's a Bordello life. Any viewing of TV shows, once only for "family" ears, has become licensed sex sport. The language is explicit, the environment is explicit, the clothing (or lack of) is explicit, and the actions are explicit. When Adam and Eve realized they were naked in the Garden they immediately covered themselves out of a sense of shame. Today "getting naked" has become a normal shameless profession for this culture.

The culture (a conglomerate of media giants of all sorts along with the movie industry and universities plus all the innumerable pleasure seekers, even churches) defines every aspect of life. It keeps morality at bay. It has taken sexual behavior and practices out of a moral context and reduced it to a purely private matter. In general whatever we do sexually is no one's business but our own. Sex between a man and a woman, both consenting, has no moral consequences. Performed before marriage, inside of marriage (adultery), with no marriage in sight, or with marriage an impossibility, sex has no moral hammer to apply to it. Hence there has developed a sense of normality portrayed on the screen regarding sexual behavior. It fits in anywhere. It's like chewing gum or taking a walk. If two unmarried people have dinner together, sex follows; if you meet someone at a party, sex follows; if there is a pleasant encounter at a store outlet, sex follows; if two people are having a conversation together, the next minute they're having sex. It seems sex is always a "natural" follow up wherever there are men and women. Sex pops up so frequently in the culture as portrayed in the movies that one wonders if there is anything else but sex.

What the culture has achieved is a Bordello "morality." It's not right or wrong, it's simply right. What used to happen in towns in the Wild West before law and decency showed up has now become the norm for this country and beyond. What God created in Genesis has been thwarted by a new world view of sex. The direct connection between sex and procreation has been dismantled and shoved aside and finally disposed of. God ordained man and woman to be one in spirit and the flesh for the sake of themselves and a third party. That is no longer sustainable. The new world order of sex according to this culture has jettisoned marriage and procreation entirely. But there is more. It has also jettisoned companionship from sex. Sex is self-serving. It does not require a supporting cast. It serves one master. It does not require companionship short term or long term from anyone. Multiple companions are fine.

As a result of this tumult of redefining sex in life, marriage and procreation have shrunken. The Churches have not stood up to this redefinition of the essential function of sex. Everyone knows what the truth is but everyone is put in their place by a shrill Media and Culture. Sex is a right, sex is private, sex is none of your business, so the argument goes. When you hear that over and over again repeated in mountain high decibels you just give up. The cacophonous Democrats with their Media supporters take to the airways and shame conservatives for butting in. It's not about morality, it's about me, and me is private. So Get Out Of The Way and Shut Up.

The Churches of America are fundamentally scripture based. Most limit sacraments to baptism. Scripture is what they advertise and preach. But it is not a "hard" preaching. The message is soft and generally related to "love your neighbor," "compassion," "forgiveness," "hope not despair," "pray for peace," "God loves you," "keep God's laws and you will prosper." God's world is not preached. God's world is kept out of view. God's world is too harsh and too rigorous. It's for ascetics and celibates and rebels, not average human beings who mind their own business and just want to get along. There are no John the Baptists, no Pauls, no Peters, no Preachers who Dare, and certainly no Jesus Christs. Martin Luther King, Jr., was an exception among American preachers. The gospel is selectively preached, only what the culture will bear.

So we preach the CULTURE SCRIPTURES, not the Church Scriptures. Any acceptable moral argument has to pass through the eye of the culture and its approval boards operated by Media owners, Democrat power makers, University administrators, and willing Church leaders. Morality today is defined by Liberals of all persuasions and backgrounds, including church leaders and officials who make and control policy. Political practice and law is especially defined by them. It's a dictatorship both political and moral. Hence whatever issues from the mouths of preachers has to have been filtered through the Liberal dictatorship boards. No one preaches outside this board. Knowingly or unknowingly no one preaches beyond their boundaries. They set the rules and limits. Hence preaching a sexuality that belongs exclusively to marriage does not fit the Liberal boards' rules, and certainly preaching a sexuality that belongs exclusively to procreation is considered contemptible and ridiculous. That preaching occurred 60 years ago but is now out of style and date. You are branded an Apostate if you dare.

The Old and New Testaments Of God demonstrate that God designed sex for procreation not recreation. But the Liberal Testament of today rejects any intrusion of the scriptures in its lifestyle and behavior. It declares itself exempt, as it does from whatever law displeases it. Borders, babies, and anything "fossil fuels" are unacceptable and non negotiable. Whatever they declare taboo becomes ostracized. Their system gives them full authority to declare something evil in spite of an overwhelming reality to the contrary. They sit as lawmakers and judges over all matters. Their mentors reside in Hollywood and universities and big and small businesses that control ideas and propaganda.

However, God who created sex designed it for a specific goal. Because He designed it, he therefore exclusively determines its purpose. According to the scriptures God created male and female and commanded them to "increase and multiply." That sounds like procreation, something with a consequence and a product. He set forward a task, something to be accomplished and achieved. "Be fruitful and increase in number; fill the earth and subdue it." In the same context He added another task, that of taking dominion over the earth: "Rule over the fish in the sea and the birds in the sky and over every living creature that moves on the ground." At that moment in time God was in the business of creating a world with creatures of all sorts and commissioning them to specific functions. Sex was not left out and not left for grabs. The obvious takeaway from these first moments of creation is that we exist at the pleasure of God; our bodies exist at the pleasure of God; all our bodily functions exist at the pleasure of God. He gave us a sex life in order to create life.

The culture of Liberal propagandists preaches a different doctrine: "We have bodies; they belong to us; we will use them as we please; no one tells us what we have to do with our bodies; stay out of our bodies." They have exempted themselves from the obligations of God and scriptures and history. There are no tie downs for Liberals. Any commandment circulated by God is off limits for them. They may claim they believe in God but the nature of "their" God is unrecognizable. Something from Mt. Olympus perhaps, but not from the recognizable Scriptures.

When sex becomes a recreational sport, something adverse happens to the person engaging in it. When it becomes an after dinner sport with no consequences for the male, the male abandons respect and responsibility to the one he is having sex with. He engages sexually in an act that by its essential nature has consequences; however, he is impregnating someone with a portion of himself that he will take no responsibility for.

Intercourse is more than a sexual act. It is a life act. "Increase and multiply" is a life act. Every species on planet earth does not know that but does it by command. The command was given by God. The only difference for the human species is that in advance of doing it, it knows it. When you plant a seed in the ground and you get a vegetable or fruit, it is there because God ordained it. It is not an accident. It is not magic. It is God's ordained hand at work. If something life giving is serious, it requires serious handling.

Once separation between sex and procreation occurs, an avenue of unbridled sex is opened. Sex is frozen outside of marriage and morality. It acquires a life of its own. Names don't count, places don't count, only bodies count. It becomes an end in itself— sex for mere gratification. If power corrupts, and absolute power corrupts absolutely, then sexual deviancy corrupts, and unbridled sex corrupts absolutely. God created sex and added desire, but he did not create deviancy.

When men are allowed to reign freely in sexual matters without the strict guidelines and prohibitions of morality, then a feral atmosphere is established. Animals in the wild are feral because they gather and run in packs led by a dominant member who rules their behavior. Men who run in packs, as in gangs and clubs, create their own rules for behavior submitting to any and all forms of deviant and criminal behaviors. They become feral in that they run outside the domestic norms of society and pose a threat to safety. Similarly men who adopt the sexual behaviors of the culture at large that ignores the morality God has established in sexual matters make themselves feral. The culture substitutes for the pack, or gang, but in substance the behavior becomes feral. If the conduct is inherently immoral, the individual is not excused from depravity. Men who act sexually without moral borders yet impregnate women and abandon them and the offspring to a life of poverty and struggle are feral in every instance. Feral animals are guided naturally by instinct, men are guided by a superior morality that culture cannot exempt itself from or ignore.

The difference between commandment and culture is the same as between God and mammon. You can serve one or the other, but you cannot serve both. The culture follows the most prevailing forces in the society. As for instance prior to 1863 the South had adopted the practice of slavery and its culture had not only permitted its physical abuses and violent deaths but condoned and celebrated its practices. Culture is not a moral guiding force. It pales and staggers in the midst of justice and morality. The true voice of justice and morality is in the hands of a very few, not society at large. John the Baptist stood very much alone. Martin Luther King was also very much alone. Jesus was abandoned by all. And all three were killed. When morality finds its voice, the voice is soon silenced.

Ignored or defiled, God's commandment still stands. Sexuality came out of the Garden of Eden for the purpose of procreation, not a renegade society of sexual deviants who practice sex for recreation and then abandon all consequences to society. Jesus may forgive adultery but he does not sanction sin. Although the culture does both, there remains only one commandment, "Thou shall not commit Adultery."

We are living in a culture without sexual borders. There is idolatry in celebrity and idolatry in money, and simultaneously idolatry in all matters sexual. The culture adopts what is in the raw instincts of men, not in the steady mind of God.

Lastly, marriage is such a complexity of issues: two individuals of mutually unknown paths, of distinct ethnicities, of uncommon faiths, of buried idiosyncrasies, of uncertain emotional levels, of two genders often in contention, are brought under the umbrella of marriage by God to bear and rear his children, "for better for worse, for richer for poorer, in sickness and in health, til death do us part," is an amazing experiment. For ordinary men it is conceptually inconceivable. For God, however, it was apparently conceivably conceptual.

Chapter 14

SOLA WHAT?

IT IS BELIEVED THAT PRIESTHOOD AMONG Christians was Instituted at the Last Supper. Not all Christians practice that belief nor do they believe in priesthood. It is tightly observed in the Catholic Church but limitedly anywhere else. Jesus is referred to as a priest in Hebrews but not in the gospels.

The establishment of the priesthood among Christians did not have an official inauguration date. Jesus' words at the Last Supper, "Do this in memory of me," somewhat mysteriously invoke the creation of a priesthood. His request and demand that they repeat the Eucharist again and again does not simultaneously establish a special group for that task, except that the group hearing that message were handpicked and appointed to deliver his messages to the world.

Like so many other developments in the Christian world, the priesthood was evolutionary. The Scriptures themselves were evolutionary, starting some fifteen years after Jesus' crucifixion and continuing to near the end of the first century and not finally authorized as such until the end of the fourth century. The practices of the Eucharist were evolutionary occurring in homes for decades. Paul himself is part of the evolution, Jesus picking him posthumously some six or so years afterwards probably because he realized that Peter and the others lacked the stamina and energy to carry his message to the Gentiles. Also, very early on the apostles attempted life in common, but that evolutionary part of Jesus' command "to sell everything and come follow him" failed in practice. The term "Christian" became an identifying title only many years later. We, who believe and cherish Jesus, are part of the evolution. Each one can share and spread his magnitude.

Evolution stands tall in the development of Christianity. Nothing happened automatically and autocratically inside its walls. And to be noted in the beginning there were no walls, no structures. Christianity suffered through its development along with the many who believed and suffered persecution and death for subscribing to Jesus. Jesus himself, the reason for Christianity, underwent an evolution. From the time of his death those who gathered and followed him developed a variety of titles and definitions of him, some actually becoming dogmas of faith. He is "Son of God," "coequal with the Father," "two natures," "one person, divine," "one of two others in the trinity," "begotten not made," "came in time but existing from before time." Not until the early 4th century, in the Nicene Creed, did we have a uniform statement of Christian belief, this nearly 300 years after Jesus left the earth. Jesus himself left no script to follow except his spoken words and his healing actions. However, he did send the Holy Spirit for instruction and inspiration, but, of course, not everyone heard the Spirit in the same way.

In an evolutionary process the development that occurs happens gradually, over time. Something starts and something is tested. Something begins and something is past on. Each time it's past on, it is tested and authenticated. Jesus started something when he came in Person and manifested his Father's will. That something was gathered—his words, his messaging, his commands, his directives, his healings and all his actions, plus the character and depth of emotion in his behavior—then placed into writing called the Scriptures. Along side that "something" came the words and messaging and performances of those who had heard and watched Jesus and then began to execute his directives and intentions in their own lives. These after-the-fact actions become the living out of Jesus' words and actions. This starts the evolutionary process carrying us through the first century into the second and on. It all starts with Jesus then unfolds with and through those who follow him. Each person coming to and believing in Jesus is part of the evolutionary process of Christianity. As participants we bring something and leave something. As participants we can also change something and redefine something.

The defining and identifying of Jesus in the subsequent years after his death is what took place. Those who followed after Jesus lived what he said and what he wanted. In living that message they began to define the message. "Who is Jesus," "What did he say," "How did he say it," "Who did he say it to," "What did he do and to whom," are only the beginnings of constant inquiry into a man who claimed he was God. As Jesus' words were lived his life unraveled into written words and living actions. Those who were closest to Jesus during his ministry were depended upon to lead everyone in an evolving understanding and continuation of Jesus "in the flesh." In the early pages of the Acts of the Apostles the earliest evidence of this evolution is on display with Peter taking front stage. He gives a confident and powerful witness to Jesus and his message. Peter, the denier of Jesus, now stands out to lead others in their affirmation of Jesus. The 28 chapters of the Acts of the Apostles span approximately 30 years of the unfolding and living out of Jesus after his death, the first evidence we have of the evolution and development of Christianity. The gospels narrate Jesus as he enters into his ministry and carries through to his death and resurrection, which is a mere three years, then the Acts brings us forward another nearly two generations. The Acts proves that Jesus was not a short-term attraction. Indeed it defines in much detail the effect Jesus had on others especially those most closely associated with him. Jesus came and he was here to stay.

What is vitally necessary to understand is that this evolution from Jesus to the future could only transpire with the imprint of his person and words on the lives of others. Jesus did not leave a written word about himself, He left HIMSELF. Secondly, he left himself to Specific Others. He chose Twelve Others in a very deliberate fashion. They were called individually, their names spelled out in the gospels, and they followed and lived with Jesus for three years through many healings and miracles and messages and finally his death and resurrection. They were inundated with his Person. No one escaped his charisma except Judas. When Jesus left they were the direct descendants of something that had never happened before and would never happen again.

One very important stimulus Jesus, the Man, left on the Twelve after his resurrection was his continued presence for forty days afterwards. Jesus was now the Resurrected Man. Seeing and hearing him brought conviction and confidence to their faith. During those days he became the man-God he claimed to be. He continued to teach and lead them as one who had overcome everything, even death. His power extended beyond death. Any lingering doubt in their faith would have been dispelled in those many appearances after his resurrection. He brought them past his death and raised their level of commitment by staying and face-timing with them.

The day Jesus left is the day the evolution started. The twelve he handpicked stayed together locked up together for a period of time waiting for the promise of the Spirit. Once that event occurred the twelve issued forth to live and deliver not only the message but most supremely the Person of Jesus Christ. Jesus was not a religion, he was a PERSON. He was not an idea, or great event, he was a PERSON. God is not a category or philosophy, a theology or event, or dogma or cult. God is PERSON. The first twelve who came and followed him admired Jesus for what he did and said but above all they admired him for himself. Jesus captured their souls. To be a Jew devoted in every way to its past and deep traditions and ethnic and religious history then one day become struck by a man who dares to call himself the Son of God did not happen because of an idea, but the Person. Miracles were the first attraction, but the final and lasting attraction was Jesus, the MAN.

When the initial Twelve left the room after Pentecost, there was no structure in place and no manual of instructions. They had but one command: "'All authority in heaven and on earth has been given to me. Go, therefore, and make disciples of all nations, baptizing them in the name of the Father, and of the Son, and of the Holy Spirit, teaching them all that I have commanded you. And behold, I am with you always, until the end of time.'" (Mt.28:19-20)

The first to surface and take charge was Peter. Immediately following the event of Pentecost during which those receiving the Holy Spirit began speaking in numerous different tongues that amazed and puzzled a large crowd gathered outside, "Peter stood up with the eleven" and explained to the crowd that Jesus was the power behind this event. Acts of the Apostles singles out Peter as the spokesman but in conjunction with the other apostles. They are an official collegial group.

Following Pentecost Peter and the apostles along with numerous converts began living in common and sharing everything with those in need. Their practice was to devote "themselves to the Apostles' teaching and to fellowship, and to the breaking of bread and to prayer."(Acts.2:42) These are the first glimpses of what took place immediately after Pentecost and who is playing a prominent role in leadership and teaching plus the prominence of the breaking of the bread: "Every day they devoted themselves to meeting together in the temple area and to breaking bread in their homes." (Acts.2:46)

In subsequent days Peter establishes a prominent role among the Apostles. His leadership is in evidence throughout the early chapters of the Acts. This early evolution of the church displays the power of Jesus' Person, his teachings, his commands, his promises and predictions, and above all the evidence of his presence in those who followed, "I am with you always, until the end of time." Their early communal life kept them together and focused on the mission. Peter and John are singled out together in several events in the Acts but the apostles as a unit are clearly included. They operate as a unified body speaking one message and winning over many to Jesus.

At one point all of the apostles, after having been warned about speaking in public on behalf of Jesus, are arrested for their disobedience and jailed. When they are brought before the chief priest and Sanhedrin, "Peter and the other apostles replied: 'We must obey God rather than human beings!'" (Acts.5:29). Their singular voice adds strength to their common conviction and above all displays the uniformity of their group as believers and leaders. They think in unison, believe in unison, and act in unison. Their strength is in numbers. Peter does the speaking but he speaks the message of the group. Peter also stands out among the apostles having exceptional gifts of healing: "Thus they even carried the sick out into the streets and laid them out on cots and mats so that when Peter came by, at least his shadow might fall on one or another of them." (Acts.5:15) Unquestionably Peter is the leader among leaders.

This evolutionary description of the early days and very early years after Jesus' departure depicts a consolidated group of believers who eagerly and forcefully and fearlessly spread the life and meaning of Jesus to the many Jews who were receptive to their message and were baptized. The twelve apostles together were the catalyst behind every action taken on behalf of their faith in Jesus. Not one, but all contribute, with Peter in the lead.

The Apostles continued their successful advancements into the Jewish population until Stephen, one of the first deacons and most outstanding for his zeal and preaching, came under the heavy hand of jealous Jewish leaders for alleged blasphemy. After he was condemned and martyred a severe persecution broke out against christians. Here is where Paul enters the storyline and instead of carrying out his commission to capture and torture Christians in Damascus, he himself is met by Jesus and forever becomes the lead Apostle to the Gentiles.

By this time we know who the leaders are and who holds special consideration among those leaders. We also know that they are all committed to preaching the necessity of Jesus to the Jews, followed by baptism for those who join them in their faith. Along with preaching they meet daily for prayer and the breaking of bread, the very symbol and substance of Jesus himself. The apostles follow every directive Jesus outlined for them: preach salvation through Jesus' name, baptize in his name, and sharing his presence through the breaking of bread. This becomes the substance of the evolutionary Christian Church. All of this occurs at the hands of the Apostles with the major help from the Holy Spirit.

Jesus' coming to earth and establishing himself among us for our eternal salvation is transferred to a dozen men to pass his gift onto others. These men, along with Paul, the one chosen later by Jesus Christ but no less an Apostle, are the forerunners of the Church. They are the ones who brought the gifts of baptism and Eucharist and repentance into the early evolving church. Each one of these gifts is central to Christianity. Jesus gave us all three of them. All three were past on to the initial twelve. The twelve, minus Judas, were given his authority: "The eleven disciples went to Galilee, to the mountain Jesus had ordered them. When they saw him, they worshipped, but they doubted. Then Jesus approached and said to them, 'All power in heaven and on earth has been given to me. Go, therefore, and make disciples of all nations, baptizing them in the name of the Father, and of the Son, and of the Holy Spirit, teaching them to observe all that I have commanded you.'" (Mt.28; 16-20)

With that commission Jesus established the leadership class in the Christian Church. The apostles were the direct recipients of Jesus' authority, having been personally chosen by him, having firsthand knowledge of his message, having experienced his power of healing and miracles, having witnessed the divinity behind the Man, then having been given authority over his gifts of Baptism and Eucharist. If Jesus is priest, then they too were priests. The succession falls to them.

This commission does not cease with the Apostles. As they received, they concurrently received the power to delegate the same power to others. We see that happening with Matthias who was picked to replace Judas. Peter called for a vote after two names were submitted and a prayer invoked with Matthias being selected. This was a collegial vote that dramatizes Peter as leader, the other apostles as participants, and further authority being delegated to another person worthy of the calling. This is the first demonstration of power being transferred after Jesus' departure. Matthias was now counted as an Apostle.

For centuries now the center of the evolution of the Christian faith has been the priesthood. The bishops are there but at a distance, and the pope is there but even farther away. In the midst of everything has been the priesthood. The sacraments, the key elements of Christian practice, are carried out by the priesthood. Church and priest have been inseparable.

From early beginnings the priesthood, in its representations and misrepresentations, in its dedication and disloyalty, kept the flow of Christianity moving through the ages. The church was locked up in the priesthood and the priesthood was locked up in its sacraments, its rituals, its top leadership, and its language. There was one language for the church and only one language for the scriptures, Latin. This unified the church throughout every country: One faith, one baptism, one Lord and Father, and "one Language." Latin also kept the scriptures locked up in the church and the only minister of the scriptures was the priesthood, from priest to pope. The church faithful had slight participation.

But this closed scripture lockdown began to change in the 15th century. Translations in various vernaculars began to appear. Martin Luther's break gained instant support which followed with his own translation of the scriptures. Suddenly an explosion of discontent and reform took place with the production of numerous other translations of the scriptures. In less than fifty years the priesthood had undergone a convulsive fallout with the churches falling into the hands of the state (England and Germany)and in other cases in the hands of innovative leaders (Zwingli, Calvin, Knox).

At this point the Church of Rome had lost its comprehensive authority over European Christianity. Prior to the Reformation the Catholic Church held unchallenged authority in matters related to Jesus and all matters of religion. Christianity was locked up by Rome. Technically speaking any and all European State Leaders, including kings, were subjects of Rome. The churches in Europe were administered by priests and bishops and these were directly beholding to Rome. Once the Reformation began automatic affiliation with

Rome ended. Bishops and priests in England and Germany and Scotland became the subjects of their respective government heads. In France the country was ready for selective separation from Rome which gave John Calvin an open door to his new found reformation theology.

All in all the reformers made rapid headway away from Rome and into a variety of newly formed Christian congregations. Almost all of the reformers were priests who distanced themselves from the abuses coming from Rome. Once past the confines of Rome the early reformers left two major portions of Catholic life, first, the priesthood, second, the Eucharist. After first questioning the real presence in the Eucharist, it was no huge step to the complete abandonment of the Eucharist. Once the Eucharist was dispatched, priesthood followed.

In many ways the Reformers departures went much beyond the abuses in the church; their attention was drawn to both dogmatic and speculative issues. In support of their theological quests and declarations they employed the authority of the scriptures. Scripture rapidly became the go-to-source for the answers they sought. If a question required authentication, scripture was a must read. With the scriptures now in the vernacular and the printing press invented and alive throughout Europe, they were available for all to see, and subsequently to oversee.

The misleading factor in all of these reforming efforts was the fact that scripture arrived through the regular evolutionary life of the church. Scripture in fact was a part of the evolutionary life of the church. It was one of the primary products of that evolution. It started approximately 15 years after Jesus left the earth and it concluded in the mid nineties of the first century. It did not become the authentic "New Testament" as we know it until the end of the fourth century. Scripture was an outgrowth of this evolution. It details the early evolutionary life of the church and itself is part of that evolution. It was not the beginning of Christianity; Christianity began before scripture. The apostles and the lives they lived were its beginning. Scripture was an outgrowth of their activity and their faith with the enormous guidance and assistance of the Holy Spirit.

Scripture is predated by many facts. One fact is the Apostles. They were called by Jesus and performed alongside Jesus and were the direct and appointed descendants of Jesus. He gave them authority directly and Peter as leader. Scripture reveals these facts to us but THEY (the Apostles primarily) created scripture and the facts inside scripture. Without them there is no scripture nor any continuation of Jesus on earth. Jesus does not come to us without his successors. Scripture gives us a list of facts AFTER they happened, not before. If there is no Peter and no eleven, there is no Christianity following Jesus nor in the 21st century. We are the descendants of the descendants of Jesus. Jesus is first, then the Apostles, then their disciples, then their disciples and many more, then us, with scripture coming after the Apostles.

If scripture as "sola" stands as the essential and only starting point for Christianity, then it is bogus because it does not come from the hand of Jesus. To ignore everything else in the first century, and also later, regarding scripture is an historical misrepresentation. Even if Jesus had personally written the scriptures then directly delivered them to Peter for transmission, those writings would not constitute a "sola" position in Christianity. Those scriptures would have to be placed along side and inside the historical environment and conditions in which they were written. Anyone who knew Jesus and talked to him and witnessed his work would be part of the scriptures that were presented. There is no absolute "sola" when it comes to the human Jesus. He is bigger than scripture and Christianity itself is bigger than all the scriptures.

Jesus told his apostles and future descendants they would receive the Holy Spirit, he did not say they would be the recipients of Scripture. The "SOLA" in Christianity is the Holy Spirit, not scripture. Hence Sola Scriptura is an absurdity and a misconstruction of the facts. Jesus is first, then the apostles, then their direct delegated descendants, such as Matthias, then on and on and on, and all of us who believe in the ONE who was sent from the Father. Jesus did not intend us to read scripture in order to get to heaven. Even scripture does not say that.

Chapter 15

THE REAL SOLA

NOW THAT SCRIPTURE HAS BEEN OUT OF THE bag (Latin) for centuries and has been acclaimed as "SOLA" Scriptura for many believers, meaning we have one source and one authority to go to for all things Christian, why are we still confused about the message of Jesus? If scripture is the answer, why are there so many meanderings about the message? Furthermore, if Jesus is sufficient for us in Scripture, why did John say at the very end of his gospel, "There are also many other things that Jesus did, but if these were to be described individually, I do not think the whole world would contain the books that would be written." (J.21:25) Coming from an eyewitness as John was, this leaves us with a lot to pause about the thoroughness of "Sola Scriptura."

One major reason for the claim of the exclusive Oneness of authenticity of "Sola" in scripture is the divine source of its origin. The Holy Spirit is the recognized inspiration for all of scripture and his authority is unquestioned. When you have a thoroughbred as the Holy Spirit, there are no questions asked. If the Holy Spirit said it, case closed. However, in one of Jesus' last discourses with the twelve, he said that the Holy Spirit would come and stay in his place.

Apparently in spite of the Spirit's coming not everything would be locked down once and for all: "If you love me, you will keep my commandments. And I will ask the Father, and he will give you another Advocate to be with you always, the Spirit of truth,..." (J.15:15-17). Jesus indicated that the Holy Spirit would come and take up "residence" with the Apostles and be with them "always."

One has to assume that Jesus meant that the Holy Spirit would come and occupy space with them as guide and teacher, not once, not twice, but always. Moreover, one has to believe that the Spirit's residency would apply not only to the Apostles in their lifetime, but to those following in their footsteps also, leaders and believers both. Hence the Spirit's residency would span an eternity on earth. It would apply to all things related to Jesus and his mission, all things written and spoken, all things spiritual and physical. Scripture would be "one" of those inspired moments. But there would be others and more if Jesus truly meant "always."

If "Sola" is really and exclusively "sola" in scripture, then every word Jesus uttered should be taken literally and without interpretation. Interjecting a human analysis or exegesis should be outlawed because this could jeopardize the authenticity of the Holy Spirit's message. Nothing should intervene in the words used and stated in the scripture if the purity of the divine action producing them is to be maintained. In other words leave the text alone and deliver only the words. Even an attempt at originalism is not permitted. Any tampering would be a crime against the Holy Spirit, an unforgivable sin. Logically if insistence on scripture is the foundational document for Christianity, then it follows that the document may not undergo human interpretation.

For example, if you attempt to define what the word "heaven" means without words from scripture, you are deviating from the sworn text. The same follows for the word "Hell," likewise resurrection, or damnation, or justification and faith, and above all the Spirit. You cannot put words in the Holy Spirit's mouth. Sola Scriptura has to abide by its own making, that scripture is the only authority and that authority must, therefore, stand on its own and as it is. No human hand or mind can add or subtract, or attempt a revelation regarding its meaning. Epiphanies don't count either.

If this "Don't Touch" policy were followed stringently, the Reformers would have had little to say and less to do. If the scriptures were left intact, they would have been required to abandon any interpretation of scripture. However, over the centuries since the Reformation the scriptures have had many visits and revisits by the original Reformers and then by the many that have followed them. The Protestant Churches have never shied away from adding and commenting on the scriptures. Interpretations and commentaries have grown in abundance over the ages and have never ceased.

Initially Martin Luther wanted reform from the authorities of Rome who were marketing indulgences for money in return for the "automatic" removal of any guilt due to sin. This explicitly constituted a quid pro quo— "Your money for getting out of purgatory." His 95 theses were all about the obscene selling of grace for the immediate release of someone, regardless of true contrition, from the penalty of sin. Martin Luther argued his case through the aid and authority of scripture. He also argued that if the pope possessed the power to absolve someone's guilt due to sin, he could accomplish that without the requirement of a paid-for indulgence. The pope did not back down and Martin Luther, with the aid, protection, and support of the German princes, resisted and solidified his cause. With that the door to the Protestant Reformation was open.

In the subsequent years just after the beginnings of the Reformation the Catholic makeup of Europe changed drastically. Germany, England, Switzerland, Scotland, parts of France, portions of Scandinavia, along with the Netherlands, all departed from the Holy Roman Empire and its Church. They all subscribed to the absolute authority of scripture ("sola scriptura"), first and only, leaving Rome to tend to itself. Scripture became the bedrock of their new found confession. This was not a new religion, it was their way to escape the financial and theological tyranny of Rome. Rome was at fault, but it would not confess and change its money-based theology about indulgences.

The coming of "Sola Scriptura" was somewhat of an accident, just as was Martin's departure from the Roman Catholic Church. None of this was planned ahead. Martin Luther did not start out with the fixed proclamation that scripture was the solitary authority for all things Jesus. It happened over time as the forces on the pope's side dug in and the supporting forces on his side further dug in and gave support. Having grown up in the church and having been educated as a cleric and risen in the ranks of a professorship at the University of Wittenberg, plus placed as Dean of its theology department, Martin knew well that tradition was the companion of scripture in the arsenal of the church's reliance on authority. Scripture "and" tradition were linked together like Siamese twins. The only problem at times with this scenario is that scripture had a silent voice and tradition, which was a living entity, had a loud and commanding voice. In fact, unless scripture had a defender, it had no voice at all. Indeed, with the assistance of church law tradition waffled around scripture and kept scripture's voice locked up, with the added fact that scripture had been somewhat locked up for ages in the church language of Latin.

Martin's bridge to scripture itself, however, was not an accident. As a doctor of theology he knew it well. In his 95 theses he had references to it five times, and much of the document reflected the thoughts and messaging and directives of the scriptures. The truths of Jesus' teachings were captured in his 95 Theses, not falsely, but accurately, and they refuted in detail the "money-for-indulgence" program the pope was conducting. The pope had his "infallible" authority and diadem and Martin had the scriptures. Thus a climactic moment in Reformation history was born. The two sides entrenched and the two sides never relented. The pope used his papal authority and Martin drove himself deep into the safety and security of scripture, with the critical promotion and protection of the German prince of Saxony and numerous supporters. The rest is history. The pope excommunicated Martin, and Martin then went on to write his way into Lutheranism.

But the rest of the story is about how the other Reformers took hold of the"Sola Scriptura" argument and carried it into their fledgling church groups for even greater development. It has become the one linchpin that binds all Protestants sects together. Casting aside Rome meant adopting Scripture as the founding piece of their beliefs. Why Rome when you have the gift of the Holy Scriptures, the very embodiment of Jesus himself "walking and talking and healing and rising from the dead. There is plenty of Jesus in scripture to satisfy one's faith without anything else. If you have nothing else but the scripture, you have an enormous blessing. If you were a castaway on an island with but one book that happened to be the scripture, you would be in the presence of the greatest treasure. With but the scripture in a prison cell, you are not alone and abandoned: "I will be with you always even to the end of time."

The word "Sola" was used by the Reformers in reference to authority, meaning "One" Authority. It gave them deliverance from the pope and his authority. With scripture alone they could move ahead with their particular outlooks on theological matters. Scripture was a safe and authentic doorway out of the church of the past into a new and unfolding future. The Churches that started at the time of the Reformation were only a few of the many thousands that would follow all because scripture, specifically the New Testament, gave its blessing to a pathway of freedom for Christians.

Sola means "alone," or "one, but it also means "free." The message of Jesus cannot be locked down and put away in anyone's storehouse. It belongs to the world and to everyone in it. It is a message to all mankind: "I am the way and the truth and the life. No one comes to the Father except through me." (J.14:6) What gives scripture the unique "Sola" argument is not because the Reformers declared scripture a "Sola" document in their departure from Rome but because in itself it stands alone as a calling from God to the individual about his life now and forever. It is about a living man preaching a living message to a living individual about living a right life for ultimately living in eternity. The gospels are an invitation to eternity by a man who lived to go beyond death. And Jesus in scripture opens his arms to anyone who believes in him.

There is a certain sense of intimacy between Jesus and his Father and the reader in the gospels. Jesus is front and center throughout the pages. His language is personal and clear. No interpreter is required. He works healings on volumes of people, without distinction or reservations or requirements. His message is universal—not Jewish, not male or female, not for intellectuals, not for kings and potentates, but every individual human being on earth. He came to one race—the human race and all mankind is included.

Scripture is not a theological book. It is a book about a man you fall in love with: his honesty, his simplicity, his demand for truth and justice, his quickness to forgive, his unreserved respect for men and women, his steadfastness for the message from his Father, his innumerable individual healings, and in spite of being divine his humility. His story draws and his message conspicuously compels. He is "The Lamb of God Who takes away the sins of the world." He is beyond identification. He is in the scriptures and he is more than the scriptures. As John said at the end of his gospel, there is not enough room in the world to contain what Jesus did on this earth.

What the original "Sola" of the Reformers attempted to do was to make scripture the one and only and exclusive authority for all things in Christianity. It was a doctrine. Their claim of "Sola" bolstered and substantiated their break from Rome and their subsequent theologies. It was a "separation Sola" that allowed them freedom from an overbearing and corrupt papal authority and at the same time create new credible religious foundations for themselves.

However, in essence, the scriptures of Jesus Christ are a different "Sola" Document. They are not about endorsing a particular doctrine, but about opening a door to a man who claims he came from God, then once you are in them you discover he "IS GOD." "For God so loved the world that he gave his one and only Son, that who ever believes in him shall not perish but have eternal life." (J.3:16)

The real "Sola" is believing in Jesus Christ. In fact, the only "Sola" in "Sola" is Jesus. He is not a doctrine, not a church, not somebody's favorite translation of the Bible. The most beneficial effect of reading the gospels is developing a relationship with Jesus, not providing a religious sectarian establishment its authority so it can prove it is right. The scriptures are an introduction to Jesus and his message for all mankind. It was not intended to justify a particular group's religious existence.

A further essential point about the real "Sola" in scripture is that it contains ONE voice, that is, Jesus' voice. The Churches throughout the world that subscribe to the scriptures do not all address this one voice, nor do they speak this one voice. There is a distinct separation from that one voice based on what they preach, or there is an avoidance of that voice based on what they prefer. For instance, how can a Christian Church not preach life in the womb is of God from its beginning as Jesus himself was? How can a Christian Church with the scriptures sitting on its lap not preach that God created "male and female" and joined them together, not some other gender combination? How can a Christian Church preach prosperity above all other attainments? How can a Christian Church ignore and disregard the Last Supper's call to "Do this in memory of me?" How can a Christian Church that preaches Christ for all have avowed slavery and segregation? How could a Christian Church with the sacred scriptures in its veins have preached the redemption of the penalty of sin for an exchange of money?

When Jesus lived we heard one voice—HIS. In the scriptures there is still but one voice. There is still "one Lord, one Faith, one Baptism, one God and Father of all, who is over all and through all and in all." Today there is still but one "Sola," and that is Jesus, but that "Sola" is bigger than any scripture or scriptures because it includes a Spirit that carries His message out and beyond any written confines. Without the Spirit we cannot find the scriptures and without the Spirit we will never find His voice, and as a consequence we will never find the true "Sola."

When Scripture becomes Spirit then the real "Sola" will reveal itself. "Unless I go away, the Advocate will not come to you; but if I go, I will send him to you... But when he, the Spirit of truth, comes, he will guide you into all the truth. He will not speak on his own; he will speak only what he hears, and he will tell you what is yet to come. He will glorify me because it is from me that he will receive what he will make known to you." (J.16:7; 13-14). If we take Jesus at his own words, then the "Real Sola" is the Holy Spirit.

The scriptures are a written document, but they are not a dead word. If the spirit, which is the maker and inspiration behind scripture, abounds as Jesus promised and then provided, then the word is alive. If we insist, however, that scripture is the final word, that everything is finished and final in the written document, then Jesus' Advocate is dead. That means Jesus came, worked and died, then left, and is gone.

However, there is no final Sola in "Sola." Indeed, in the end there is no "Sola." There is ONLY SPIRIT. Nothing of Spirit is contained in a single text. When the Angel came to Mary to announce Jesus' coming, he said, "The Holy Spirit will come upon you, and the power of the Most High will overshadow you." And that is how it happened when Jesus came. Suddenly out of nowhere the Spirit came and everything was changed.

The Spirit has the final word and he is always coming: "And I will ask the Father, and he will give you another advocate to help you and be with you forever—the Spirit of truth. The world cannot accept him, because it neither sees him nor knows him. But you know him, for he lives with you and will be in you. (J.14:16-17)

With the Spirit nothing is final.

Chapter 16

THE IMPERATIVES

LIFE IS LOADED WITH IMPERATIVES. IN FACT, we are driven and directed by imperatives. They are inescapable. Many are physical, others emotional and psychological, still others intellectual and financial, then there are those that are spiritual and religious. Without imperatives life would border on aimlessness and inanity. Survival and activity originate with imperatives.

Indeed, imperatives rule our physical lives. Food, reproduction, activity are the consequences of natural, instinctive, and hormonal demands. The body commands obedience to its directives regardless of our conscious volition. Mother Nature will not allow resistance. We live according to her formulas. Without her we would be awash in chaos. There is nothing less human or demeaning in this arrangement. Our conscious nature does not suffer diminishment because of our less autonomous behaviors.

The same is true of our other levels of life, those that affect us emotionally, intellectually, and psychologically. Emotions and intellect operate in a conscious framework, but not without underlying imperatives. Nothing is accomplished without imperatives. An emotion is an imperative, and intellectual pursuits are equally imperatives. "Life, liberty, and the pursuit of happiness" come naturally because they fit into the imperative narrative.

Befittingly, God is also an imperative. He is not self-invented. Although we arrive at God through consciousness we do so with instincts that draw us to and near God through already provided telepathies. He is not an outsider waiting for "us" to find him and draw him in. On the contrary we are the "outsiders" being drawn in.

We have been under the spell of imperatives all our lives, some conscious, others unconscious. The physical ones are usually front and center and, therefore, drive us the most. These are generally manageable, as long as they are guided with moderation. The less manageable and more unpredictable ones are the emotional ones that often fling us in opposite directions and cascade from nowhere. They are a blessing and a blemish without warning. The most invisible and clandestine imperatives live in our hearts and minds and spirits. They subsist quietly in a place we cannot see and only surface at intervals of emergency and stress. They are the ones that defy definition. Jesus said, "The wind blows wherever it pleases. You hear its sound, but you cannot tell where it comes from or where it is going. So it is with everyone born of the spirit." (J.3:8)

The imperatives that come from above are as powerful as the imperatives of our physical nature. Believing in something from above equals anything that arises in our appetites. There is a parallel between matter and spirit. What matters is not matter, but spirit. The driving force behind matter is spirit. Wherever there is matter, Spirit was there first and in abundance. Spirit precedes all life: "Now the earth was formless and empty, darkness was over the surface of the deep, and the Spirit of God was hovering over the waters." (Gen.1:2)

The one imperative that is superior to all other imperatives and that drives all of life and sustains it is goodness. This, of course, matches God himself. Earth is not a bad place, it is a good place. Above everything and beyond everything goodness reigns in abundance everywhere. If it is of God, it is good. Earth is not an evil place, it is merely filled with contesting interests, and too often detestable.

On every level we see goodness on display throughout every living moment of the day. Life would be totally unbearable if goodness first and foremost did not carry the day. It is a prerequisite. Evil is an accident for the most part, only premeditated by a few who have defied God and his rule for life. Anne Frank once wrote, "I still believe, in spite of everything, that people are truly good at heart." Goodness persists beyond all measures and all upheavals. It will surpass all exceptions.

Goodness is a preoccupation for God. Evidence of this is in creation. Everything and everywhere displays this fact. If God is perfection, then when God deals out life he necessarily deals out goodness perfectly. There are "imperfections," that is for sure, but existence as we see it is an enormously generous perfection. Everything God does is a derivative of this imperative of goodness. As creation unfolds God is seen delivering this innate imperative. It starts with the Trinity, where goodness does not reside in singulars but in multiples. One becomes three where the divine imperative of goodness is exercised and exemplified. When God commanded Adam and Eve "to increase and multiply," he extended his imperative of goodness on earth. Goodness multiplies. Goodness shares. Goodness extends beyond itself. God and his goodness are exceedingly un-narcissistic.

That same imperative of goodness is instilled in human nature. We want good, we wish good, and we extend good. There is an indwelling of desire to share and spread the bounty of life to others. In spite of the challenges and discomfort and pains of labor in childbirth, for instance, a woman will bear the pregnancy and delivery of a baby so "that a child is born." Innately she believes the child replicates the image of God, demonstrates the power of his creativity, and furthers his goodness in the world. She participates in that goodness with him. There are heroes everywhere at every level who give and sacrifice for the good of others. They respond to the divine call in all of us to "Do unto others as we would have them do to us."

The imperative of goodness built into our nature comes not as an option, but a command. To deviate from that commanding imperative abandons a central principle of Jesus' teaching: "whatever you do for the least of these." Jesus went beyond suggesting goodness was an option for mankind to the point of declaring it an ultimatum. Shedding ourselves and our possessions appears at the top of the list of Jesus' references to goodness. When he pointed out to the Rich Young Man, who called Jesus "Good Teacher," he simply clarified the fact that God in his essence is good and the rest of us are "becoming good," and that we "become" good by selling what we have and giving it to the least of these.

In Jesus' lexicon goodness is not a theory, or philosophy, or mere virtue. It is a practice, a behavior, a way of life. It becomes who we are. It drives our thought processes and our outlooks. Nothing else really matters. Helping the less fortunate becomes who we are. We are not kings and princes; we are not CEOs and capitalists; we are not rich and famous; we are not republicans and democrats; we are not keepers and takers. We become who Jesus was—a healer and giver. Nothing less.

The "narrow gate" and the "eye of the needle" are not about becoming poor, they are about delivering to others who have the least in the world. "Keeping" runs contrary to Jesus' doctrine of "giving." Creation could not exist unless "giving" were not the compulsion behind its quintessence. Every movement of creation is outward, never inward. Every Spring nature rushes forward out of the death of winter to deliver a new and renewed gift to life. If it were not for God's goodness, none of us would be here.

Apparently the apostles very well understood Jesus' message of sharing because in the days following Pentecost they began living a communal life that required absolute surrendering of property and giving everything to the group. There were no exceptions. They understood the necessity of giving as opposed to possessing. They had learned from the Master that only God is the Possessor and his possessions are all shared. No one else is a "possessor."

To believe that you or anyone is a "possessor" falls in the category of rank idolatry. To believe that you or anyone has title to any object on this earth does not fall into the category of dilution, but into impudent imbecility. Among humans there is no jurisdiction over the earth. There is divine sovereignty and there is none other. The temporal dominion we have been allotted applies to service not possession. You do not own, you use. We were born as users and we will die as users— naked born and naked buried, you came with nothing and you leave with nothing. We are all borrowers of God. No matter the amount you claim you "own," the mortgagor is God. He never surrenders the title. When you die, he collects the property in full. It would behoove the borrower to release as much as possible before he dies so that God cannot point a finger and claim, "You did not give to the least of these."

Ownership conveys the illusion of power. This is why power assumes it owns everything and as a consequence can destroy everything. If you own, you command and dispatch. You develop a god-like authority believing that all power rests in you. Power quickly overrules goodness. Rumor has it that goodness is for the faint-hearted and weak. The universal principle of goodness, "love your neighbor as yourself," disappears in the ash heap. With absolute power comes absolute authority to make or break everything in your grasp, and then grasp at more without limits. Power settles on one method for control, and that is destruction. If you destroy, you conquer and own. Death and slaughter are part and parcel of that methodology.

Power and evil share the same environment. Power begets evil, and evil begets power; they are consorts. One cannot exist without the other. They equally detest goodness. Anyone who seeks the destruction of another human being, whether in word or action, is aligned with the devil. Power and evil by way of destruction are the incessant diabolical overlords of this earthly life. Malicious men have menaced the earth throughout the history of mankind and goodness continues to suffer at their hand. Evil men prosper until good men arise and annihilate them, but always it follows after much executed destruction.

In spite of everything, the everlasting imperative established by God is goodness. No matter the degree of evil or the volume of evil, goodness thrives in nature and human nature. God's hand and his fingerprints still prevail in the minds and hearts of men and women. The reason why goodness too often suffers at the hand of evil is because it creates and unleashes weapons of death, whereas goodness thrives only with the invisible tools of peace and love. Evil men fashion evil tools, commit evil deeds, and overtake other good men, until good men return the gesture. The misfortune is that the gesture is so long in coming.

Goodness has no ownership, no possessions, no attachments. If it is the imperative God placed in the original human heart, then it seeks not to gather for itself but to share the bounty of God with others. Anyone who offers his own life for another surrenders the ultimate attachment he has in life. Jesus did and many others have followed, though, not everyone will or should.

What goodness God asks of us is anything and everything we have been blessed with. There are no limitations and no reservations. Time, money, treasures are all candidates. The more of any of these, the more the obligation. Goodness received is goodness given. There are no exceptions. We are not possessors, we are recipients then transmitters. Every rich man is a qualifier for transmitting wealth and every very rich man is a super qualifier, and any man holding enormous wealth is an infinite qualifier. All of these are under an imperative by Christ to give to the many needy in the world. The single incumbent right they have is the stewardship of their wealth. If they have received infinitely, they in turn are obliged to transfer that wealth infinitely. Withholding God's largesse constitutes a failure in returning that largesse to others. Taking something that comes from the earth, that comes from the world God created, that evolved from thousands of years of human and divine invention and intervention, that did not start with one man today gathering up billions of dollars and assets with one profitable idea, then locking it all up in his safe, is a sinister conclusion. What if those billions from that one magic idea included the sweat and hardship of peasants, or the tragic lives of slaves, does that constitute a self-made accomplishment?"

The goodness of God that comes through the life, liberty, and pursuit of happiness, provided by God is not to be squandered on one person for one person's power display and comfort, but for the help and support of others with less life, less liberty and much less pursuit of happiness. The disciples Jesus gathered, namely the twelve, were not of the wealthy class who were encumbered with managing their properties and assets and riches, but from the lesser among men who were unchained to wealth and position and could allow the counter culture ideas of Jesus to take root in their minds. Christianity does not espouse wealth, does not engender gathering as opposed to dispensing, does not spend a lifetime in the pursuit of "happiness." The happiness of this earth is a dissatisfying pursuit of endless pleasures that can never satisfy the human spirit that God imprinted with his underlying commission of "Good will to all men."

When looking at the citizens of the Christian Churches throughout the United States and having evidence of the wealth possessed by so many of these members that is locked up in their vaults, one wonders about our understanding of the integrity of Jesus' message to the Rich Young Man.

His advice to the young man was not about prosperity, and similarly it was not vague. The specificity in the advice was shocking: "go, sell all that you have and give to the poor, and you will have treasure in heaven; and come, follow me." This was not a recommendation, but an imperative for goodness if he wanted to be perfect like the Heavenly Father.

Jesus did not bring a weak message from his Father. He did not act democratically. He did not take a vote. He did not bring options. His messages were precise and inclusive of imperatives. Riches were not on the list. Possessions were not his focus. Amassing was specifically off his list. Hoarding was a death wish: "You fool, this very night your life will be demanded from you. Then who will get what you have prepared for yourself?"

Jesus gave no fake messages to the world. He never compromised the truth. However, Christianity is full of fake messages because those living it have conceded Jesus' real message. Christianity is what it is today because it surrenders to the mob of the culture, because it lets the swamp of perverse beliefs walk inside the churches and occupy a seat next to those struggling to believe in the authentic message, and because we have groups and political parties and media that together propagate utter lies and falsehoods about life in the womb, about marriage between a man and a woman, and all the while push slander on news broadcasts and advertise sexual immorality. The world of Fake and Fraud and infamy is suffered, not condemned, by the churches with crosses on their entry doors.

If you believe in Jesus, you believe in a divine Teacher. As testified in the gospels, "He spoke with authority." When you listen to Jesus, you do so to follow, not reconstruct the message or cut and paste the message. When he is listened to, you hear on every page a litany of Imperatives for life in God's pathway. The essential pathway is goodness as an action, not a theory. And one primary action is the delivery of our lives over to the good and betterment of others. At the Last Supper one of Jesus' final acts was to wash the feet of the Apostles. The gesture was followed with an explanation and a command: "If I, therefore, the master and teacher, have washed your feet, you ought to wash one another's feet. I have given you a model to follow, so that as I have done for you, you should also do. Amen, amen, I say to you, no slave is greater than his master nor any messenger greater than the one who sent him." (J.13:14-16)

If Christianity were preached as it is written in the gospels, Jesus' message would be lived with greater integrity and intensity. His authority would be spread authentically without revision and accommodation. Jesus did not come to make peace. He came from his Father as a last resort to demand goodness from all of mankind. He healed the sick, he raised the dead, he forgave sinners, and he condemned evil. Today Jesus' words would condemn the baby serial killers, the drug assassins, the political slanderers, the entourage of media vultures, the Wall Street money changers, the capitalists who store money away from the needy, and those who would destroy the precise words and the accurate meaning of the truths that come from the Son of God.

Chapter 17

ACCOMMODATION
(SELLING OUT GOD'S LAWS)

CHRISTIANITY TODAY AND FOR MANY GENER-
ations has stooped to accommodation. Jesus preached the truth
and spoke coherently and without trepidation about the truth
he brought from his Father. Hesitation and accommodation
lost any leverage in his spoken words. He conferred with no
one but his Father. He deliberated with no one but his Father.
He requested no evaluation from anyone but his Father. His
authority was plenipotentiary. When he spoke, he stood as one
speaking for someone else who possessed uncontested authority,
namely, his Father.

Jesus did not attempt to reconstruct his Father's words. He
spoke them "trippingly on the tongue" as he heard them from
his Father. Jesus was the dutiful messenger not the author of
the message. In many ways this preserved him from attack as
to the fundamentals of the message. If the message comes from
elsewhere, and that "elsewhere" is beyond question, then the
message requires obedience and compliance, without modifica-
tion. Jesus could not adjust the message. When Moses received
the Ten Commandments they came prepackaged in two stone

tablets. Moses could not revise the wording on the tablets. He was merely the delivery agent.

What is always amazing is that in spite of the fact that the scriptures we subscribe to in following Jesus are inspired by the Holy Spirit, the adherence to them varies from group to group and person to person. If the Holy Spirit breathed his inspiration into them, why is it that so much has been changed by men over many years and centuries. If the word is "inspired," why so much wrangling about the very substance of its meaning? If the word, for instance, is "baptism," why restrict it to adults only; children who are properly educated will advance in faith and come to aspire to believe in Jesus. If the word is "faith," why squabble over "faith without works" as opposed to "faith with works," when if faith is real then works will of necessity follow, because faith without works is an inexpressive faith.

If the word is "Eucharist," why not take the 6th chapter of John as it is written and abide by its pronouncements. If the gospels are inspired, why are we "un-inspiring" them?

Christianity universally claims that the Holy Book is inspired, yet for a book that is inspired it runs the gamut of diverging inspirations. From church to church, from preacher to preacher, the book changes meaning and demand. With over 32,000 Christian Churches in America one might expect some diversity, but not the disunity of message that exists in current Christianity. No one church any longer claims preeminence among all the churches. This was the claim of the Catholic Church within recent history but that claim is hushed today. No one has the front seat any longer; we are all in a gathering of Christians trying to evangelize without anyone in the superior position.

In former days the Catholic Church held command over the behavior of its members declaring certain behaviors mortal sin. There were no exceptions. Mortal sin drove you into hell and as a consequence it demanded and commanded attention and avoidance of what was considered evil and condemnable. Not attending Sunday Mass constituted a mortal sin, likewise adultery and any intimate sexual behaviors outside of marriage. Serious theft fell into the category of mortal sin, and a myriad of criminal actions, including slander, against another person, were all deadly sins that were punishable with damnation. Murder and suicide were mortal sins, and any killing of innocent life. Top on the list of murder was Abortion. There was no confusion about the crime. Everyone knew that the womb conceived babies, not no-bodies.

The Catholic Church identified the truth and demanded adherence to it under pain of sin. That included all matters related to moral behavior and dogmatic beliefs. After Vatican II the hand on the steering wheel was relaxed. We had to become ecumenical and more sensitive and open to the human condition, which meant becoming more culturally embedded and dominated. The new policy became "Fit in." "Let's look like a forgiving church not condemning church." "Jesus condemned sin but forgave the sinner." "Let's just all get along."

In the meantime, Hollywood and its power brokers began taking over the airwaves. What was seen on the screen was what was already reflected in life and very soon the screen began endorsing and advancing that life in full color and uncensored. The screen became the moral barometer for sex, marriage, religion, and justice. To their aid came the news media that at one early point in their history prided itself on the search for truth in reporting, but soon turned itself into a mob for falsehood and slander. News was no longer the order of the day. If you were on the wrong side of their political bias, you were pilloried out of existence. As a weapon of mass destruction, they used their airwaves for mass disinformation. The lies were no longer nuanced, they were bold, audacious and full of vitriol. This is how same/sex/marriage moved out the DOMA doctrine of the 90s. This is how the Ten Commandments became objectionable and removed from courthouses. This is how the swamp government (once long ago the national government) spied and lied about innocent citizens they disagreed with, then destroyed their rights and existence. This is how Abortion became a right and the baby lost its primordial rights.

This takeover by so many malignant mouths in the Media has neutered the political and religious leaders on the Right. If you are persecuted by an angry crowd of self-appointed mud slingers, your first reaction is to take cover and stay out of the sight. You keep your face and message away from those with clubs and knives for fear of annihilation. In order to maintain a voice you soften the message and never point fingers. The message is diverted to something else or the message is muted, and overall it is modified to fit into the ruling class of the airwaves who dominate with determined hate and vengeance.

Jesus was not a pushover. He came, he conquered, and he won. He is still here. Not completely intact as he once was when he spoke for himself. His message keeps vacillating with the times and with the messengers, but he is still here. Only so much Jesus is allowed in the public arena now. If his message sticks to purely religious days and anniversaries, there is generous acceptance, but if his message interferes with the ruling class of the airwaves then he is pronounced illegitimate and out of place. Jesus no longer belongs in the public arena even if an issue of morality is top billing. Jesus is for Christmas and Easter, otherwise he is out of place, and perhaps those days are numbered also.

The ruling class of the media has placed a moratorium on "Church" morality and has disavowed any application in the public sector. They have created a divide between "church" morality and "public" morality. Whatever you do that your church sanctions does not spill over into the public arena. The first amendment of the Constitution gives full respect to the establishment of religion without any preference for any one religion, but the errant media has rewritten that protection clause to instead mean "Separation" of Church and State in an absolute sense. Hence today any norms of morality once prescribed and upheld universally with church influence are now unbinding for the general public. Church and state are divided absolutely and any morality demands by church entities follow the same lines of absolute separation. You may not conflict church values and "public values," or take church values and place them into the public domain.

Moreover, the Media Ruling Class has also successfully separated political rulings from church rulings. Once an issue has been placed into politics, church bodies lose their exclusive franchise on the issue. And once that happens the fictional separation of church and state applies and the matter in question becomes solely the prerogative of the state, whose mouthpiece is the Media. The DOMA doctrine that respected the singular position of a man and a woman in marriage was declared null and void by the Obama Whitehouse and that ended quickly and virtually overnight the church's singularly upheld position on marriage. Once the political state declares its preeminence in a matter, the church loses its foothold and is forced to back off. No matter the gravity of the issue, the state once it arrests authority unto itself, the church retreats to irrelevance.

The Media Ruling Class has superimposed politics above and beyond any other authority, including God. You do not talk God in politics. You do not bring God into the Citadel of the United States. God is Religion and Religion is forbidden in the United States Citadel of America. The State is "separate" from Religion and operates outside of Religion in order to preserve its superiority and allegiance to no one except itself. The Congress of the United States plus the Whitehouse, plus the Supreme Court, have jurisdiction over people without any consideration for God or his ideas, even though we obtained ALL of our rights from the Creator when King George III was expelled from these United States. But that was almost 250 years ago before the Great Enlightenment occurred as a result of the Liberal takeover of 95% of the Media. The Media is now owned and operated by a Liberal hegemony that executes its will of lies and slander as any red dictatorship has done. The Red Liberal Media Ruling Class has decreed that there are two things to be defeated at all costs—God's ideas and Conservative ideas.

With the Media Ruling Class having now established this dissection of church and state, and the Democrat Party having become the face and beneficiary of this dissection, and the Media and the Democrat Party having installed millions of their minions in the government bureaucracies, they now control the very mechanics of this government. The Media runs the show. The Democrat Party delivers the message but the essential message comes from on high, from the Media and its Despots.

There is no Democrat who can think on his own. Once a Democrat you are bought and paid for by the party, and the party bought and paid for by the Media Mob. The only oxygen you breathe comes from the Party and the Media. The only morality you can profess issues from the Democrat Party. Evil is only what they say it is. Similarly good is only what is defined by the party and, primarily, the Media. Once a member of the party you profess the morality and religion of the party. When they declare adultery is a private matter, then it is private. When marriage is declared anything but between a man and a woman, then it is so. When slander is employed to destroy an opponent, then it becomes a mere political tactic. When Democrat officials use their public power to illegally take down a member of the opposite party, that is called "winning the game." If a complete falsehood is used to advance their storyline, that's Party strategy. If the ballot box is overtaken by squads of Democrat thuds and thieves to steal an election, that's not terrorism and treason, that's gamesmanship. Evil has taken front stage and no other morality will upstage it.

If you are a member of the Democrat Party, upon entering the door you must surrender all tenets of whatever religious faith you hold. Your beliefs and your morality are suspended while a member of the party and a follower of the Media Ruling Class. There are no exceptions to the rule. Those democrats who profess and uphold the policies of the party and simultaneously claim some sort of allegiance and membership in a Christian Church are blatantly schizophrenic: they vote for Abortion, and additionally support and vote for partial birth Abortion, but insist they are pro-life.

The Christians who are members of the Democrat Party, and they are in the majority, have surrendered all Christian morality to the atheistic and corrupt doctrine of the Democrat Party. A party that once associated itself with the working class and espoused high civil principles has become the party of no principles, no values, no morality, and reduced to a party of slander as its frontline policy and winning strategy.

Joe Biden, who is currently the face of the Democrat party, dramatizes the absurdity of the Democrat position. Joe Biden professes two opposing doctrines of morality. As a Democrat he professes a belief in the murder of babies in the womb even up to the time of birth. He not only professes it, he has voted for it and would vote again if required. For Forty-Seven years he has publicly and unabashedly proclaimed his commitment over and over again to anything Abortion, including now the abolishment of the Hyde Amendment, plus defunding the Little Sisters of the Poor for their restrictions on Abortion. He is a committed Democrat with no exceptions to Abortion.

Moreover, if Joe Biden becomes president of the United States, he will become the highest ranking political leader in the country and the world and simultaneously he will become chief officer of the Democrat Party. He will wear two hats: one as president of the United States and one as Leader of the Democrat Party Platform. As head of the Democrat Party he will oversee the Democrat Party in its determined dedication and execution of the Unborn. He will become the chief mouthpiece of anything and everything in their Abortion agenda. He will become the chief proponent for the Killing of the Unborn.

At the same time Joe Biden professes to be an upstanding Catholic who upholds pro-life principles. His claim is that he is "pro-life in private." With this position he feels protected from Church scrutiny and condemnation. He attends Mass on Sunday and receives the Eucharist and there is no outcry from the principals of the Catholic Church about his diametrically opposite positions on Abortion. On the contrary, he has been coddled by the Princely members of the Catholic Church and for that reason considers himself untouchable. He has managed to escape ecclesiastical limelight and remain in virtual obscurity. He has been kept off the Church's radar, either by his own maneuvers or the Church's "hands off position." For Forty-Seven years there has been no kickback from those in the highest ranking levels of the Church who weekly preach the commandments and the undeniable truths of morality, one of which is that the Killing of the Unborn in the Womb is an unequivocally "intrinsically evil act."

If there is any conclusion to be drawn from any or all of this travesty of the moral depravity on the part of Democrats and the moral delinquency of the Church, it is that the Church, not just the Catholic Church but the Christian Churches throughout the country, have accommodated and allowed the Democrats and their Media Mouthpieces to literally destroy without remorse the lives of the Unborn. As a frightening consequence, it is therefore safe to say that Joe Biden, along with Andrew Cuomo, Nancy Pelosi, Dick Durbin, and a host of other lesser Catholic/Christian politicians, have defiantly and obstreperously taken over one of the most sacred categories of Christian morality—the very life of the Unborn in the Womb. By omission the Churches have surrendered their duty and authority to condemn and reject, personally and individually, the perpetrators of the Killing of the Unborn. For this reason the professed Churches of Jesus no longer hold first and preeminent moral authority in standing against an "intrinsically evil act." The culture and the Media and the Democrats have silenced their voice.

After Herod marched into Bethlehem and slaughtered hundreds of babies looking for the new born divine king, we hear a lament from the pages of Jeremiah:

> "A Voice was heard in Ramah,
> sobbing and loud lamentation;
> Rachel weeping for her children,
> and she would not be consoled,
> Since they were no more." (Mt.2:18)

For forty-seven years a deptavity of monumental moral proportions has defined a major political party of these United States of America and no church entity of magnitude has stood front and center to condemn these villains to their face. Instead they are allowed to enter church sanctuaries on Sundays and pray like the Hypocrites Jesus called his wrath on: "Woe to you snakes and vipers!" YOU WHO KILLED THE UNBORN SLEEPING IN THEIR MOTHERS' WOMBS!

Chapter 18

A Relationship, Not A Membership

When Jesus stopped along the shore of Lake Genezerath to talk to Peter and Andrew, the two brothers had no idea where that initial conversation would lead them. Then, shortly after, he approached James and John, another pair of brothers, and had a similar conversation. They were all fishermen very devoted to their profession. They had no ambition for another way of life. But that all changed when Jesus showed up and made an offer they could not refuse.

The offer he made them was not a better job, with better pay, with easier hours, with lots of benefits. No. The offer was himself: "Come follow me," he said. Pretty preposterous when you think about it. He was offering them nothing monetary or power driven. There was no status attached to the offer either. Nothing of earthly compensation would advance them by following him, yet the gospel says they dropped everything and followed him. They followed him, the MAN.

When you meet someone who appears bigger and better than life, and simply amazing, you jump to conclusions. We are inclined toward people of distinction, and knowledge, and privilege, and celebrity. For the most part Jesus was none of the above. He was an attractive individual, but with no pedigree; he had a commanding personality, but no celebrated distinctions.

It is nearly impossible to read the gospels and not come away with the impression that Jesus was a person who spoke well, performed beyond expectations, and did marvelous things for others. There is a sincerity and seriousness about Jesus in the pages of the gospels that draws people to become his followers. He is real and genuine, never overbearing, dedicated to principle, indefatigably consistent, universal in his mercy and love, voluminous in healing the sick, exceedingly critical of false and ungodly behavior, and forever indebted to his Father who had sent him. If there was ever a person one would drop to his knee for, it is Jesus. And Peter and the others did just that. They left everything to follow a man who spoke like no other human being.

There was a sterling quality about Jesus that permeated his persona and actions. That quality was simplicity. Not just in appearance, but everything. Simplicity in his looks. Simplicity in his words. Simplicity in his miracles. Simplicity in his teachings and parables. The logic and common sense expressed in his dealings with the Pharisees exemplifies simplicity. The forbearance he exhibited before Herod, a crime ridden man, when Jesus never uttered one word in reply to this "fox," speaks untold degrees of his simplicity—his silence defied the other man's crime. When you can reduce all of the commandments down to "love God and your neighbor as yourself," you have condensed the essence of human life into the simplest common denominator. Above all there is enormous simplicity in being able to confront evil at its doorstep and not melt into "political correctness"—he told Peter to "get behind me Satan"; Judas was someone who "better if he had never been born"; and "who are my mother and brother? The one who does the will of my Father in heaven." But the very foundation of Jesus' simplicity lies in his singular devotion and allegiance to his Father: He came for his Father, he spoke for his Father, he healed on behalf of his Father, and he died by the will of his Father. Jesus, the very essence of divine mystery, far surpasses all men in his utter simplicity. He is much known, and yet completely unknowable. He is someone tangible, yet remains out of reach. He draws people with unflinching conviction, and yet remains an invisible reality.

One thing Jesus was not was a man of obfuscation. What you saw is what you got. He ran circles around the Pharisees just using simple reasoning: when accused of casting out Beelzebub with Beelzebub Jesus replied, "then Satan is casting out Satan," how absurd is that. With Jesus you got the unexpected as the expected. He never wavered from his purpose. Three years of righting a wrong was all he needed. Any more time spent on earth would have deluded the focus and intensity of his work. Leadership lasts but a short while. And if that leadership delivers the truth without reservations it will last even a shorter while. In a world of power seeking liars, truth cannot suffer long "the slings and arrows of outrageous fortune."

Without a doubt Jesus attracted followers during his quick three years in Galilee. It was the person, his words, and his works. The followers he chose to work alongside him were all from the working class. There were none among the immediate disciples who were renowned leaders, gifted speakers, proven and dedicated religious professionals. All of them came from the second and third tier of society who had no formal skills in Hebrew and the Jewish traditions. They were Jews who believed without any theological preferences or prejudices. They came to Jesus as Jews with an open mind and heart who could receive a message not yet heard. They carried no baggage. There was no ideology driving their individual lives. God for them was more generic than dogmatic. Abraham and Moses were national leaders rather than sectarian theologians. The apostles were teachable and receptive to a new narrative, perhaps even a new covenant.

There is hardly any argument against the fact that Jesus was an Iconoclast. He did not come to confirm the practices of the Pharisees. He did not come to overlook human behavior. Many of the traditions of the past were suddenly put in question. Certain practices and emphases of the Jews were quickly questioned and examined for veracity. So much of practicing Judaism focused on externals and left out God's immanence in the process. Jesus came to fill an inadequacy in the lives of the Jewish nation. They believed in the One True God, but they subordinated his presence to their man made rules and ordinances. Jesus came and fractured those artificial regulations. That made him a law breaker and outcast.

Above all, Jesus came to clarify and establish himself and his Father's authority over mankind: "All power in heaven and on earth has been given to me." (Mt.28:18) He did not come as a weakling or compromiser. The Father sent his Son to rekindle the relationship he had started with Abraham, then furthered with Moses and the Israelites, then gave them David to govern them, then lost control with David's descendants. After generations and numerous kingships of apostasy and idolatry by the Jewish leaders Jesus came to pick up the lost sheep of Israel to return them to his Father. That was his purpose and mission, but he never completed that task. Only some followers Jesus found among the Jews came to link themselves with his message and understand his coming. As he left the earth he commissioned them to go into the world and baptize everyone in the name of all three persons in the Trinity, something radically new in the Jewish religious lexicon.

The one primary aspect of Jesus' coming to earth was to establish his relationship with mankind, which preeminently started with his Father and the Spirit. Jesus was about relationships, not about the law. In everything he did it amounted to starting a relationship or deepening a relationship. Every time he healed, every time he forgave, every time he raised someone from the dead, he was about relationships. "For God so loved the world that he gave his one and only Son, that whoever believes in him shall not perish but have eternal life." (J.3:16) The Father sent his son to reopen a relationship with mankind. "No one has ever seen God, but the one and only Son, who is himself God and is in closest relationship with the Father, has made him known." (J.1:18)

When Jesus called Peter and Andrew, then James and John, he called them into a deeply committed relationship. When Philip brought Nathanael to Jesus, Jesus quickly established an instantaneous relationship with Nathanael by revealing his whereabouts when Philip called him underneath the fig tree. The enormous crowds that gathered around Jesus when he spoke could relate to Jesus because of his words and the authority of the man who was speaking. Zecheus suddenly found a relationship with Jesus by climbing a tree. Lazarus, Martha and Mary were in a deep personal relationship with Jesus and never wavered. Mary Magdalene had her own gifted relationship with him. Every healing of a disease in those he cured opened up a grateful relationship with Jesus. Anyone who came to Jesus with openness ended up in a relationship with him. When he purposely encountered the woman at the well, he opened a relationship with her by asking for a drink and in spite of her attempt to close the door on the conversation by shoving in race and gender disqualifications. Jesus revealed something personal in her life that brought her and many townsfolk to his side.

If "religion" has any significance and relevance at all it is about one thing, and that is a relationship with God. It is not about a particular dogma or declared tenet of faith, but about relating oneself to God, the creator of all life and the essence of goodness in all of life's expressions. If Jesus exemplifies one thing to his disciples and to all of us, it is his devotion and intense relationship with his Father. John's gospel narrative of the Last Supper narrative gives us a glimpse of the intensity and intricacy of his relationship with his Father and, of course, with the Holy Spirit. We are privy to the makings and mystery of the Trinity—Three are One, and One is Three because of an unfathomable relationship in the Trinity.

Wherever Jesus is, it is about a relationship. Faith is a relationship. Love is a relationship. Baptism opens the door to a relationship with God. Eucharist is a relationship of a most personal kind with Jesus. Repentance and forgiveness re-establish the relationship if it is broken. Sin brakes the relationship. Dogma does not create a relationship. Theology is not a relationship. These are intellectual pursuits. You can be a theologian and skip a relationship with God, just as you can be married and skip a relationship with a spouse. What Jesus called for with indefatigable insistence was a demand that he was the one sent by his Father to draw all men and women to himself: "And I, when I am lifted up from the earth, will draw all men to myself." (J.12:32). His final prayer at the Last Supper centered on the relationship he had established with his disciples and that, once he left, they would be protected from the evil one.

Everything that is Christian, everything that speaks of Christ, addresses a relationship. If you believe in God, you are married to God. If you believe in Jesus, you are married to Jesus (He is the Bridegroom). You are locked in a relationship. Baptism initiates that relationship and a conscious faith activates it. Eucharist perpetuates that relationship. Jesus came in person to deliver a personal message from his Father that the essential way of reaching the Father's home was through a personal commitment and relationship with his Son: "For my Father's will is that whoever looks to the Son and believes in him shall have eternal life, and I will raise them up at the last day." (J.6:40) It is person to person in Christianity. There are no brokers, no prophets, no middlemen, no dogmas, no referees between Jesus and the follower. Once you enter the relationship, you have entered into a mystery that only God can code or decode. It is not a religion, it is a relationship without a writ of divorce. Jesus dominates the relationship. "All those the Father gives me will come to me, and whoever comes to me I will never drive away. For I have come down from heaven not to do my will but to do the will of him who sent me. And this is the will of him who sent me, that I shall lose none of all those he has given me, but raise them up on the last day." (J.6:37-39)

When Jesus gathered followers and disciples, some of whom became apostles, he was gathering believers not mere followers. Believing is an active, conscious, and persistent preoccupation that one cannot live without and can never be separated from. It becomes something indelible in the mind and therefore in consciousness. It surpasses language and creeds. It is bigger than any "Summa Theologica." It has no basis in reason, yet it exceeds all reason. And no reasoning can create it. "I believe because I believe," is completely irrational, and yet it is totally authentic. You can take the belief out of the person, but you cannot take the person out of the belief. When someone truly believes in Jesus, that belief is inexpugnable. Death becomes more compatible than disbelief.

When Jesus called the 12 Apostles, he called them to follow him. His purpose was to transform the entire world with them and through them. He knew what he was turning over to them but had no idea what and how they would accomplish the task. He himself did not create the rules. He established the mission and the raison d'etre of the mission, but he did not establish the means and methods. This was left to the Apostles, who at first stumbled around making slow progress in Jerusalem and elsewhere in Israel until Paul was abruptly ushered in to reach out to the Gentiles. During the time immediately before Paul, however, there was a state of "Political Correctness" in play. Jews who had converted to Christ still expected everyone, even the occasional Gentile, to adapt to Jewish customs and habits. Becoming a Christian did not exempt anyone from the Jewish culture and rituals. It was simply a case of "adding Christ" without excluding Judaism. Jewish Christians still practiced as Jews and they expected non-Jews to practice similarly.

In subsequent years and in the following centuries Christianity often fell into the Political Correctness of its surroundings. It was not simply a matter of "giving to Caesar what is Caesar's and to God what is God's," but it became a matter of adapting to and adopting Caesar's lifestyle, outlooks, conditions and power, with the result that Caesar and God became less distinguishable. Unfortunately, if God looks more like Caesar, then what happens to Jesus' message? Jesus then becomes weakened and overruled by Caesar. Jesus' independence suffers intrusion and ultimately disillusion. But the Jesus of the first century never lost his independence in facing Pilate, Herod, the Pharisees, the mobs who would make him king, not townsfolk, nor Peter. There was no Political Correctness in Jesus' bones. Reading the gospels, in particular Matthew's gospel, one grows in the conviction that Jesus gave no indulgence to anyone else and preserved his absolute independence over everyone without exception. Only once did he exercise a seeming apology to Mary at the occasion of Lazarus' death due to his late arrival, but his late arrival was scripted "for the glory of God" when he raised Lazarus to life.

Over and over again history unfolds the utter dependence the Christian Church has on the culture and its leading proponents. The culture speaks and the church listens. It used to be that the Church spoke and some of the culture listened, but now it is the culture speaking and overruling everyone and everything, in spite of its often utter detachment from reality and the truth. Those who have nothing to say, and those who have lies to advance, speak the loudest because they are driven by a shameless moral disengagement. Every oddity and single minority becomes a ruling majority and every majority becomes an outcast dictatorship. The major media and social media have subordinated morality and religion to a backroom closet where expressions and ideas are kept quiet and private. Prayer, religion and theology are kept out of reach and off topic. Jesus is okay for baptisms, weddings, and funerals. Any topic once moral has been overtaken by the political crowd where anything of a moral consideration and assessment is deemed outdated and unconstitutional. The babbling rabble have taken over the microphone and stage.

As a consequence those with moral authority and credentials have stood aside. Those dedicated to bringing the unsullied word of God to the sheepfold have folded for reasons of Political Correctness, or group suppression, or worries about expulsion, or rejection on the part of the sheep. Preaching to the same audience weekly, to those who are filling the collection basket, presents additional restraints on the messenger and his message. If attendance ranks high on the list of favorable results, then the message will have to match the expectations of the audience. The message will assume the character and mindset of the attendees. For this reason the message will shrink and move in the direction of what the audience can bear. The messenger delivers their message not his, and certainly not Jesus' message.

One advantage Jesus had was his mobility, plus his non-dependence on a fixed income from a fixed audience. Jesus moved from village to village proclaiming his message of salvation without any suppression of the message. There were naysayers everywhere, but his messages were delivered intact. If they were not received well, he left that town shaking the dust from his feet. There was a two-sided rejection—one from those who rejected Jesus' message and the other from Jesus himself. In the end Jesus had the last word. Moreover, his message suffered no abbreviation or diminution. Conformity came from the audience and not from Jesus, else Jesus left town.

The message from the pulpits today is not one built of steel. Over the centuries it has walked away from the strong hand of Jesus. The pulpit is filled with sound, and sometimes and in some places with fury, but it is not the sound and fury of Christ. Jesus' today was about tomorrow. He never came to stay; he never established a homestead and everything he said and did was about his Father and his Father's place. His today was always tomorrow—Tomorrow with his Father. Today is quickly and suddenly over, and tomorrow is "just a day away." Today, today, today, today's a great day, but tomorrow is the greatest. Jesus preached this message endlessly. His forecast for life was, "I am the resurrection and the life, he who believes in me, even though he dies, will live." He prohibited any surrender of his message and its absoluteness. The sacraments, in particular, are harbingers for tomorrow. If "grace" through the sacraments has any significance at all, it is about tomorrow's lifeline. Christianity guarantees a tomorrow experience. Today is just preparatory. Jesus is today for the tomorrow that is forever.

If Jesus had a voice today, he probably would not last long in an average church setting. He would not be uncomfortable, but those in the pews might express disgust and dismay and treat him as his Nazareth townsfolk did when he opened up Isaiah and declared himself "of God." When Jesus, the mere carpenter's son, declared himself of God, by God, from God, and was God, but would not perform miracles on their behalf, he lost favor with the townsfolk and barely escaped their vengeance. But he was not one to run from trouble. How can God not confess his lineage? How can Jesus not override human resistance? How can Jesus whittle down his divine person and mission and still claim divinity as his blood line? Jesus stood up to human threats and challenges. He never took the fifth amendment. He steadfastly stood absolute. Jesus, indeed, was an ABSOLUTIST. Nothing he said conformed to a thin line. He maintained an absolutist position throughout his many declarations: "I am the way and the truth and the life. No one can come to the Father except through me."(J.14:6) "Very truly I tell you, unless you eat the flesh of the Son of Man and drink his blood, you have no life in you."(J.6:53) "Whoever disowns me before others, I will disown before my Father in heaven."(Mt.10:33) Jesus was an absolutist with ultimatums. The message was clear and the delivery was adamantine.

The clerics who preach the gospels today have adopted a gospel of moderation filtered through the eyes and ears of numerous public agenda driven powers. Jesus' Christianity is not the norm nor the message. Accosted, they will claim that Christianity is about love and friendship. They will insist that nothing supersedes the demand for peace. They insist on good works without condemning bad works. They will demand diversity without division. Their claim at moderation is that Jesus is for everyone and no one is excluded, even though Jesus never said he was for no enforcement and that his morality allowed innumerable loopholes. The pulpits speak softly and carry no stick. It is all a rehearsal for "Christianity-as-you-like-it." It is all an overture to moral mayhem. Because "their God" is not a dictator: he directs; he leads; he recommends; he loves; he let's us be. His pulpit people all follow this other God. In order not to offend the offenders of the gospel, in order not to ostracize the heathen from inclusiveness, in order to keep pro-choice "amoral," in order not to separate the sheep from the goats, the preachers in their pulpits deliver a soft mono-lithic message of peace and harmony. "Let's just all get along." The Jesus of Matthew, Mark, Luke, and John is buried in the catacombs where only candle light dimly reveals the essential truths of the past.

But Jesus of the gospels is not a religion. He is not an insti-tution, or doctrine, or theology, or philosophy, or language, or morality. He exceeds all measurements and all maximums. He is recognizable in the sacraments but he is goes far beyond these events. He is the way, the truth, and the life. "Come follow me" is not an invitation to a membership in a club, but an absolute incorporation into his and his Father's divine reality. He wants us to join his divine family.

There is no future for the human race "unless" it joins the divine family. Jesus came to invite and create that oppor-tunity. His invitation is both opportunity and necessity. It is not an opportunity as an option, but an opportunity as an indispensability. You cannot live now without oxygen, and you cannot live later without the divine life. You came by way of two parents this time, but next time it will only happen by way of Christ. Again, this is opportunity as indispensability, not opportunity as option. Jesus made this claim very emphatically and the word he chose always was "unless." "No one can see the Kingdom of God UNLESS they are born again." (J.3:3) "UNLESS you change and become like little children, you will never enter the kingdom of heaven." (Mt.18:3) "UNLESS you eat the flesh of the Son of Man and drink his blood, you have no life in you... Whoever eats my flesh and drinks my blood has eternal life, and I will raise them up on the last day." (J.6:53-54) "I am the vine you are the branches... No branch can bear fruit in itself, it must remain in the vine. Neither can you bear fruit UNLESS you remain in me." (J.15:4) "No one knows the Father EXCEPT the Son." (Mt.11:27). Jesus' "unlesses" are ultimatums. They are clear and emphatic demands allowing no exceptions or exemptions.

But these "Unlesses" do not make God an autocrat, or dictator. If creation was dictated by God, it appears logical and consistent that he can dictate the requisites for eternal life. The first came freely, the second comes freely if chosen. God, therefore, rightfully holds a position of autocracy. Nothing happens without his hand. And as a consequence Jesus, his Son, comes with his Father's authority to expect compliance from mankind. The ultimatums that Jesus delivered were in effect unconditional conditions for this future and final creation.

If those who preach the gospels fully believe that Jesus did in fact deliver these ultimatums, then it seems appropriate that they in turn advance those same ultimatums in their respective churches and in their writings.

Generally, we are wired for our specific and unique functions. Childbirth could not be accomplished by a woman unless she was "wired" for that challenging task. Men are wired for manual labor and for a competitive life in the workplace. Any individual who evolves into an undercover profession must be mentally wired in order to survive the dangers. God wired Adam to tireless labor and Eve to anything but a pain free childbirth. The wiring was essential to the task. You cannot light up a building unless it is wired and no building will receive heat unless proper ductwork is installed throughout the rooms. Today more than ever the software in a computer governs its entire function. If we claim to be Christians, then becoming wired to Christ is essential for our functioning as Christians. Moreover, how can we preach Christ unless we are wired to Christ, and truly hardwired indeed.

The great misfortune of the day is that more and more the preacher is wired to the culture more than he is to Christ. Various and many churches and church leaders have seceded their authority to the culture. Culture rules. However, without being hardwired to Christ, their message of Jesus is anything but his. The message has been eroded over time by prevailing ideologies, a generous and loose understanding of Jesus' ultimatums, a distorted assessment of the meaning of love, a grandiose application of the word "peace," and overall a willingness to concede Jesus to the masses. Jesus had boundaries. These boundaries did not include everything and everyone. His boundary started with his Father, then to those who would "come follow him" without reservation. He was hardwired to his Father and, in turn, he demanded everyone who believed him would be hardwired to him. If Jesus is the only gateway to the Father, there are no exceptions. Becoming hardwired to him is the only way to eternal life. Those who in the past died for the name of Jesus were the many who were hardwired to Christ. Those who live by his model and truth also are hardwired to Christ.

The world is full of self-interested people who commit evil and do violence and have no awareness of their injury to others and have complete disregard for those who have less possessions and opportunity. Jesus stepped into a world that was led by a self-righteous band of religious leaders who lived selfish lives and protected their fiefdoms by putting burdens on others. Their oligarchy decided the truth and their enforcements determined the survivors. Jesus turned them upside down. He decried oligarchies of all kinds—political, social, cultural, intellectual, and religious.

Groups are dangerous entities because they create a governing status quo and subject members of the group to an assembly of dictates that become static principles of behavior and likewise truths. In "religious" groups they can prevent the individual his/her freedom and growth toward the Creator who is the only arbiter of truth. The group adopts a philosophy and doctrine that all members must adhere to with threat of expulsion. Adherence to group membership beliefs and rules are key to the organization. Sometimes the doctrine is harsh and sometimes it is soft, however, in every circumstance adherence is obligatory. The group dictates the belief, or lack of. It dictates the direction of the belief and the intensity of the belief. It allows few exceptions and exemptions to the belief. It is group belief and group thought. Christian Churches are groups of people dedicated to the Christ they hold in common by reason of their leadership teachings and leadership demands. The scriptures are a common thread held by all but not commonly developed by all; scripture is commonplace but not with common understanding. In effect each group develops Jesus and his message differently, some more seriously and others more leniently. In the end, the group decides who Jesus is and what he wants.

In Jesus' world the only membership there is is membership in the divine family. It is not an organization, or religion, but a lifestyle. It is oxygen on a divine level. It is more than a belief, Jesus becomes part and parcel of consciousness. Jesus comes and never leaves. His residency never ceases and his influence advances. Once he is invested in consciousness, he takes center stage in one's life, creating a dynamic position in the way one lives, thinks, and acts. When Jesus left everything in the hands of the apostles after his resurrection, they became somewhat self-absorbed in their lives, confining themselves to Jerusalem and not venturing out into the vast available land of the Gentiles. Jesus felt compelled to meet Paul head on and bring him into his evangelization work. Here was a man who, after having nothing but contempt for Jesus, becomes absorbed with Jesus. Here was a man whose consciousness became immersed in Jesus. There was no group thought in Paul. He was not a member of any crowd. He was charismatic and unique in his work on behalf of Jesus. Here was a man who could say with complete conscious conviction, "Christ is in everything and is everything." (Col.3:11)

The primary reason why there is a vacuum of thought and energy and action on behalf of Jesus in the world is because those who claim the leadership titles in Christianity are housed in a group that is tied to conformity. No one is allowed to leave the plantation. The group has wrapped itself in a safe dialogue and that dialogue must be adhered to by all. And that dialogue is part culture, part political correctness, part monetary appeal, and part Jesus. Nothing is pure Jesus and pure selfless truth. Preaching to a crowd what it wants to hear is not the same as preaching to the crowd what it should hear. If Jesus had preached to the crowd what it wanted to hear after he had miraculously fed them with a few loaves and fishes, he would not have preached about his flesh as real food and his blood as real drink. If the truth has value and urgency, then it ought to be heard and spoken confidently and fearlessly. Paul was just the man for that. He possessed the charisma of Jesus and used it without crowd approval.

When Jesus met Paul, everything changed. Paul became enamored with the Son of God and the rest is history. Paul became a consummate follower of Jesus: "I have been crucified with Christ and it is not I who live, but Christ lives in me; and the life which I now live in the flesh I live by faith in the Son of God, who loved me and gave himself up for me." (Gal. 2:20). Paul's ability to breathe Christ with such devotion and passion is because the entirety of his conscious life was overtaken by Christ: "I live, not I, but Christ lives in me." Paul became the most ardent leader for Christ in the first century, and without a doubt his relentless example of leadership for Christ still survives today, but not necessarily at the top.

After looking at the current landscape of Christian leaders across America, it would be hard to find just one, let alone a handful, of those who would with vigor and determination denounce those in public political office who support the Killing of the Unborn. Certainly among Catholic Bishops one cannot find any kickback against Catholic politicians who vote for Abortion, who support those who profess agreement with Abortion, who argue for the freedom to choose Abortion, who willingly support funding Abortion, who support Abortion in the extreme even at birth, who vote against candidates for judgeships who profess a Pro-Life position, and, lastly, who campaign openly as Pro-Abortion proponents. These same politicians are nurtured with the Eucharist on Sundays and buried with ceremony and praiseworthy eulogies in the presence of clergy and bishops when they die. Such is the standard of Christian morality set by the leaders of the Catholic Church in America. And such is the moral standard set by the Catholic leaders of this country. No one is willing to stand against a barbaric crime against the innocent Unborn and against humanity. Jesus once said, "Suffer the little ones to come unto me." He never said, "Suffocate the little ones in their mothers' wombs."

Chapter 19

CONSCIENCE ABORTED

ONE FUNCTION HIGHLY RESPECTED FOR ITS sacrosanct place in human life is conscience. It has authority to make final decisions and judgments when the individual is confronted with difficult and contested situations in life. On a daily basis, however, conscience need not be employed. It lays fallow most of the time because it appears most life activities do not require serious evaluation. Eating and sleeping do not require a ruling from conscience. Nor do many other daily functions. Instinct suffices to lead the individual forward in life. And when instinct does not rule or direct, then normal circumstances of time and place draw out the decision for action.

What is clearly in evidence is that conscience does not play an active role in daily life. For the most part it lies dormant behind the forces of instinct, concupiscence, and self-interest. An appetite has more authority than a reflective thought. Visual contact with something can induce more propulsion than a thinking concept. We are led by something rather than we decide something. Conscience generally is relegated to forming a judgment about something after having reviewed the evidence of all of the circumstances. This can be time consuming and in many cases irrelevant when there is no time for review.

For all practical purposes conscience is of very little consequence in most of life's undertakings.

Outside of innate impulses in our lives, the established
forces in a person's life lie outside. Feeding and cleaning begins
by others. Language and learning follow the same pattern. A
reservoir of do's and don'ts come from external measures. By
the time a person reaches the "age of reason," the world outside has left its long imprint. Enormous formation has taken
place by the time the age of seven is completed. Seven years of
external influences have filled the person's mind for an entire
lifetime, many of them never to be reversed. What has the individual contributed to its formation when all these early years
have been stuffed with everyone else's influences and/or baggage? Spoken or unspoken the world has brought the human
sapling into a conscious responsible existence. The individual is
what its environment has created. In all of this individual conscience does not make a pronounced appearance.

At the age of seven the individual is a walking and talking
replica of its surroundings. It doesn't think on its own and it
doesn't judge on its own. It mimics the voices and actions of
its influences. We learn our responses and repeat them. We are
trained to be good and told not to be bad, or not to get caught.
At this point individual conscience does not have a say. We are
not thinking on our own, we are imitating others. There is no
conscience formed as yet. We become what is expected of us,
or we learn what others do with impunity.

Conscience, however, in essence, is not a rote response
mechanism. It is highly sophisticated and highly informed and
develops interiorly within the individual. It does not mimic
society, or crowds, or parties, or gangs, or even families. It
develops away from the crowd and away from any power
seeking dictatorial adherence to itself. Conscience stands alone

and rejects intrusion or coercion from a source or force that will not accept its idolatry.

This ideal image of conscience does not come inevitably in the lives of every human being on earth. This ideal image is perhaps only for a few and seldom developed in the masses of people who follow someone's party line. The reason for this underdevelopment is simple. We are conformists. Human life tends in the direction of "fitting in." Establishment rules and ideas receive top billing and deviancy from these rules gains no favor. The military is an example of "No Deviancy Allowed." Party Politics is another major force for "No Deviancy Allowed." Group after group that insists on performing with one standard and one voice for the sake of its dominance and power will demand absolute conformity. The group rules. Power resides in the entity, not the individual. Any Communist Dictatorship gives superabundant evidence of not only conformity rules, but tyrannical conformity absolutely rules. Deviancy in a Communist Dictatorship ends with imprisonment and death. There is no soft conformity, there is no partial conformity, there is only absolute conformity. The Party "Conscience" defines everything for everyone.

Wherever power is the primary purpose for existence, then the ritual of conformity dominates the lives of those who seek that power. If power is sought absolutely, then conformity is demanded absolutely. The quest for power overrides everything else and everyone else and subjects individual conscience to hard labor. The gulags are full of private consciences that advertently or inadvertently stood erect against the tyranny of brutal conformity. Because power rises rapidly in the human environment, the exercise of conscience stays hidden out of sight and under wraps. Power becomes power because it essentially overwhelms everything around it. Power is not power unless it can destroy effectively and absolutely. If power cannot annihilate its opposition, its power remains un-established. Herod went after the new born baby in Bethlehem because he could not tolerate any challenges to his power. The only way to guarantee impervious power is the annihilation of anything that stands as a threat. Jesus was a threat when he was born because he was referred to as the newborn king and he was a threat later because he was referred to as the Messiah. Both times Jesus with his titles of king and messiah showed himself as a threat to those in power and eventually was destroyed.

Tyranny abounds in all avenues of life. On every level and in many degrees tyranny forces itself on humankind. As a consequence we labor in vain to enter our conscience amidst a mix of threats and danger. We submit and surrender rather than "take up arms against a sea of troubles." Bodily harm and death are not desired outcomes when conscience demands action, nor are harassment and slander desired conditions when conscience begs for contest. Hamlet said it well when thinking over his options and methods to take on his uncle who had killed his father and usurped his father's throne: "Thus conscience does make cowards of us all, and thus the native hue of resolution is sicklied o're with the pale cast of thought, and enterprises of great pitch and moment with this regard their currents turn awry and lose the name of action."

Conscience in each human being is a slow starter, and at best is seldom activated. If we assume that conscience essentially has the truth as its objective, then we have to admit that the average human being stands off to the side of conscience because both the truth and conscience will expose you to danger. Conscience can produce a lot of truth and along with it a lot of dangerous consequences, hence the truth is not always welcome. Witnesses brought to court are reluctant to tell the truth for fear of reprisals by those convicted. Conscience pleads for exemptions when the truth impacts life and limb, and money. "Not me, not now, maybe later, let someone else do truth's bidding."

Power is the antithesis of conscience. Wherever power presides, there is no conscience. Power surfaces to destroy conscience. Dictatorships of all kinds, in any form and every avenue of life, exist to destroy conscience. If truth and conscience are companions, then power becomes unnecessary because the truth replaces power and conformity with the impact of the evidence. Truth is evidence not power; it does not need a hammer to create adherence. Jesus was, and is, the antithesis of power. Jesus and power are mutually exclusive. If he had needed power to convey his message and preserve his life, he could have called on his Father for absolute overwhelming power: "Do you think I cannot call on my Father, and he will at once put at my disposal more than twelve legions of Angels?" (Mt.26:53) If God, the Father, had wanted power to rule, the coming of Jesus was unnecessary; he could have sent famine and pestilence and sword bearing surrogates to change mankind. But he did not. He sent Jesus with the truth and a Supreme example of powerlessness.

Jesus came to awaken conscience with the truth, to raise the individual to the good without enforcement. There were enticements, but never enforcements. His promise of paradise to the "Good Thief" was an enticement; his promise of a hundredfold to the Apostles was an enticement; the promise of resurrection and immortality to Martha and Mary, and new birth through baptism to Nicodemus, then himself as the Bread of Life, and his wish for salvation to mankind rather than judgment, were all enticements without enforcement. Jesus pursued justice without compulsion, repentance without retribution, and truth without enforcement. With the beatitudes he inspired the human conscience to excel above and beyond itself.

Conscience is a fragile commodity in a world of power brokers. They are everywhere. Jesus even included his family as one of them. "Who are my mother and brother and sister?" he queried. "The one who does the will of my Father in heaven." Conscience must derive its truth from the Father and from above, and from the one whom the Father sent. Every time Jesus performed celebrated healings and miracles and his audience wanted to make him a king, he vanished out of sight. He kept a great distance from power. Neither did he seek his own glory and station in life, nor did he conform to anyone else's eminence and station in life. Power is a destroyer, and conformity is a loser. Conscience must travel between these two in order to safeguard the search for truth.

Today one of the most forbidding places for conscience is in the political power climate. The very place where government exists to make laws for society is the place that keeps no laws. Today's government for the people, by the people, and of the people, is a place exclusively for the party, by the party, and of the party. Power, driven by the party's self-aggrandizing ideology, is the one and only objective. There are no rules and no shame. Anything and anyone can be destroyed in the quest for power. One party can absorb all the time and money it wants to defeat opponents and their supporters. It is a place where there is no conscience. Truth is rubbed out. It suffocates under the lies, distortions, and slander that party mobsters create. Under the guise of politics and people's business, they operate a deceive-and-destroy machine that has for years gathered an army of entrenched bureaucrats who bow and fulfill their demands through the millions of agencies and regulations they create. If government means honesty and truth and justice, we are in the wrong country.

Jesus was wary of all earthy power. He admitted that all power on earth came originally from his Father, but he also warned that not all power was "of his Father." The power seekers pretend they are our benefactors and watchdogs, but in reality are the foxes who hunt down the innocent for slaughter. Jesus slammed the power brokers: "'Woe to you, teachers of the law,... you have neglected the more important matters of the law—justice, mercy, and faithfulness." (Mt.23:23) Yes, Woe to you MAKERS of the Law who violate every code of justice for your personal power gains. In the very beginning of Genesis the devil offers Adam and Eve a chance to match God's power by inviting them to eat of the one tree in the middle of the garden, "For God knows that when you eat from it your eyes will be opened, and you will be like God, knowing good and evil." (Gen.3:5) Power and evil have from the beginning of time formed a bond of solidarity that never leaves the planet. And today it is more visible than ever.

The one difference today is that there are no armies, no gestapos, no gulags, no guns and swords to take power from the unsuspecting. No, it is done without weapons of force, or a shot being fired. It is done with the mouth of the Media. Power is done without a club, but with cacophonous and perverse propaganda. People fall not from bullets but from the reverberating lies of disinformation and defamation. Eve listened to the devil's propaganda and became enamored with his promises. God had told her that eating of the one tree in the middle of the garden would cause death, but the devil reinterpreted that to mean that you will not die, rather "your eyes will be opened, and you will be like God, knowing good and evil." (Gen.3:5) With clever wording he adjusted the truth by claiming that God lied and hid the truth. God was holding back on some critical information, namely, that they would become self-sufficient and powerful knowing all truth about good and evil and therefore match God in his wisdom. They chose the devil for truth rather than God. Adam and Eve allowed the devil entry into their lives. That was their most costly mistake.

The present day primary Media, under the guise of Journalism, formerly a business that reported facts and evidence, runs a ponzi scheme that daily slices and dices the news to fit into its preordained outcomes for moral issues, individuals, political power, religion, elections, social and scientific and medical developments, and everything else it touches. Nothing is outside its ability to elevate or corrupt. Because of its historical status and preeminence on the airwaves, it controls what is heard and how it is heard. It reports only what its predicate is. If the predicate is Abortion, then a pro-Life March of Half a million people in the Capital receives not five seconds of coverage. If the predicate is immigration, then the reporting is not about the unmanageable crime and drugs entering through the porous borders but that borders are illegal, not the illegals entering illegally. If the predicate is a Me-Too Accuser, then the reporting is 100% per hour if its about a conservative and 0% if it's a Democrat. A conscience in this environment will never be correctly informed with a constant barrage of defective reporting and, worse still, with a premeditated predicate of lies and slander and false prosecution by the editors and bosses of the major media. If information is gathered from the people of the major outlets, then conscience will be confronted with the same lies that Adam and Eve found themselves in the Garden. It's the same journalism, by the same malefactor, he just goes by different names.

One of the most important tasks we have in life is deciding who to believe: the devil or God; parents or teachers; family or friends; church or state; individuals or party; this friend or another; one media over another; and the list goes on. There is no one absolute believable person outside of God who can deliver the truth in its perfect state, and since God has left it in our hands we are dependent on other sources. That's why we become conformists, believing that others have the truth we are looking for. They are older, better informed, started before we did, have bigger and better degrees, have more money and influence, command more power, look more credible overall, and lastly belong to a group or party that speaks with loud sounds. We submit rather than object, and we conform rather than question.

The decision to submit or conform is not derived from reason, but from emotion. Attachments are first and foremost emotional. Nothing is devoid of emotion, and nothing escapes the clutches of emotion. A truth can be explained with logical precision, and it can be demonstrated with pages and pages of evidence, and it can have the endorsement of God, but if a person has been locked in by a preceding emotion, there is no exit from that emotion. The truth will not matter and it will be summarily denounced. "All the king's horses and all the king's men" will not put the truth ahead of the emotion. Emotion controls the truth beyond any injection of reason and evidence. This precisely is why conscience is at risk in a world of deflated reason and inflated emotion. You adopt what you feel and you believe what your emotion dictates.

For the most part emotion rules conformity. But it is not any emotion. In the litany of emotions the most suited for conformity is hatred. If there is nothing else in common among a group of people and someone wants quick and immediate unification of purpose, all he has to do is find an object of hate and the group will be galvanized into action. Since hatred is fundamentally irrational, it requires no prosecution of thought and argument. It need not give evidence and fact. All that is needed is an accusation of an alleged threat and hatred will emerge. Pin a crime on someone without evidence and fact and you can hang him tomorrow. Hatred does not require evidence. It is an emotion without restraints or boundaries. All that is required is someone with a microphone and a shrill mouth who denounces someone else as a threat and danger, an "enemy of the state," or an "enemy of my freedom." Under Hitler the Jews suffered and died under the force of hatred; under slavery and segregation blacks were hated and chained for centuries; under imperialism the Japanese hated and destroyed millions on the Asian continent; today this country celebrates its hatred for the Unborn through millions of Abortions every year. Hatred works without justification and logic. With hatred you don't have to prove a negative. The devil surmised this when he told Eve that God wanted to deprive her and Adam of a special knowledge about good and evil that would put them on equal footing with God; here was a reason to despise and depose God.

Hatred substitutes for reason. It makes the irrational rational. A collective conformity gathered together under the impulse of hatred satisfies for conscience. When hatred leads the pack, the conscience of millions, perhaps billions, of people stands idle and acquiesces to the evil that occurs. There is no conscience, there is conformity. The devil, or Hitler, or Stalin, or Planned Parenthood, creates a threat and unleashes it with vitriol. American "news" outlets have waged a war of hatred for four years against Trump with nothing but false accusations and distortions to create an atmosphere of distrust worthy of removal. Lies inform just as truth does, but to someone predisposed emotionally to the lie then believing the lie is simple and easy. Slander is easily created and quickly believed because it satisfies our taste for the negative. Slander has more zest than truth.

Conscience reacts more quickly to emotion than it does to reason. We are emotional before we are rational, and we are constantly walking on emotion not reason. Conscience is not the faculty we claim it is. Conscience is not the pristine power we may have believed it is. As long as it resides in the body of a human being, it is subject to error and corruptibility, and enormous malevolence. If we have preserved some high minded conception that conscience looks for objective truth by which to act, we are living in a fantasy. Conscience in a human being is no better or more trustworthy than the scales of justice with the devil's hand on the scale. Conscience does not conform automatically to truth, nor does it seek justice blindfolded, nor is virtue its intended goal. Conscience conforms to the emotional, self-seeking, uninformed, easily duped, ambitious and/or slothful embodiment inside each person. It is not a faculty with angelic wings. It craves and cowers just as the person it pretends to lead into righteous behavior. A conscience in concept form can be defined as a faculty seeking and conforming to objective truth and goodness, but once housed in the human being it becomes subservient to the occupant who is encumbered with concupiscence, self-aggrandizement, self-righteousness, and a plethora of objectionable self-serving propensities.

What is generally referred to as conscience is in reality self-interest and self-promotion. However, conscience in its divinely designed state is not a self-serving faculty. It serves the individual with a compass that directs it outside and beyond itself. Good is not just for me. Goodness is not just my livelihood. If God is for everyone and for everything and in everything, then goodness becomes a shared commodity: it's communal. The first and greatest commandment is to love God and it's immediate follow up is to do to others as you would to yourself. It is a solidarity commandment. Goodness is a verb acting for the betterment of God and neighbor. If conscience derives its character and characteristics from the first commandment, then it is always and essentially about acknowledging the blessings and benefits of God, neighbor, and self. The good of others has equal validity with my good. The divinely designed conscience encompasses God, neighbor, and self in all of its undertakings. If conscience is "about right action," it is first about "who is in the action." I am not the only one in the action, and God is not the only one in the action, and the neighbor is never left out. Life is a chorus. We are one of the chorus and conscience takes pleasure in bringing all three together for the good of all.

If there is any conformity connected with conscience, it comes from a God who is always connecting us to himself, and to life and nature and humanity. The divinely designed conscience drags an individual out of solitary confinement into an awareness that sees goodness in who God is and what he has created. It shuns selfishness and egotism and self-indulgence, and above all avoids harming and destroying other people for the sake of its own power. Awareness of God is an awareness of others, and vice versa. The more conscience recognizes and values God and others, the closer it comes to its original specifications and design. Recognizing God in this complex world draws the individual out of a small, selfish shell that has kept him in lockdown to a minutia of wants and ambitions and expectations instead of the world God wants him to see. God has more to offer than we can offer ourselves. Jesus had that very charisma—the ability to open hearts, minds, and conscience to the valuable things of this world and the most valuable things beyond this world. When he went along the shore of Galilee and encountered Andrew and Peter who were catching fish in the mere dozens and Jesus told them that if they came with him they could catch men in the hundreds and thousands, they were intrigued and followed him. Jesus advanced a bigger narrative than the one Andrew and Peter saw for themselves. If conscience is not informed from above and beyond itself, it shrinks and surrounds its own wagon believing that "life, liberty, and the pursuit of happiness" is a springboard to self-made goals: "What is good for me is good for me." It's just an introvert speaking to the introvert inside. Without conscience the introvert remains attached to the good for himself, with little for others if any. But with a properly transformed conscience he adopts God's values and behavior.

For any revitalization of conscience to occur it must be formed from intelligences beyond the mere patterns and tendencies of human nature. The emotional weights of human nature will drag it down and justify every aspect of personal conduct. Human nature leans toward the emotional and irrational, not the rational heading in the direction of the spiritual. Conscience resides in a nature that is flawed and prone to self-justification. It is a nature that can shift 180% in seconds from a consciously mature individual to a person emotionally beyond control. As long as the conscience stays trapped in the confines of the individual's temporal weaknesses and wants, it quickly harbors resentment for people and things outside. It easily surrenders to prejudice, discrimination, negativity, hostility, vengeance, and retaliation. Human nature makes us "needy"; conscience, however, when and if informed from depths beyond itself, attempts to transform that overbearing nature into something God-and-Other oriented: "Whoever finds their life will lose it, and whoever loses their life for my sake will find it." (Mt.10: 39).

When Jesus spoke of "being born again from above," his reference was not to a mere washing with a symbolic baptismal water, but to a birth through a divine action of the spirit. It is occasioned from above but is in league with consciousness. If conscience is to take root in God's world with God's values, then consciousness has to provide the pathway to that world. We are spirit in a world of flesh and matter, but we are also evolving in the spirit every day that we are in the flesh. That evolution occurs through the assistance of consciousness. We are conscious and we are spirit. We come to know the spirit through consciousness. God may be invisible but he is not unknown. Consciousness is a revealing faculty that transfers the spirit into our minds and hearts and emotions, with the ultimate effect of developing conscience. Consciousness broadens the individual far beyond himself. Consciousness is the door to spirit and to the many other/world awakenings that occur throughout life. Baptism is not a dead experience, meaning that we are more than washed and reborn; consciousness draws us into invisible regions that acquaint us with God's life in the spirit: "They will all be taught by God.," (J.6:45) has the ring of God's intervention in our life.

If we are evolving, then we are surely evolving in spirit and the evidence for that is the ever frequent messaging that comes through consciousness. We are God-driven and that results in a value system that creates and orders our conscience. Consciousness is a limitless and transformative faculty. To be conscious is to be aware and in that awareness comes waves of inspiration that tell of God, of his supremacy and power, his love and mercy, his goodness for all mankind, his munificence and engagement in our lives. Consciousness is our roadmap to God. As consciousness develops, conscience arises to take responsibility for the thoughts and actions we commit along the way.

There is only one caution. Not everyone has the same access to this roadmap, nor the same degree of capacity and interest. Not everyone has the same drive and passion to allow God an open door to and through consciousness. For some consciousness is simply an enigma, a mystery hole that never brings anything to light. For some consciousness is too tedious to bother with so they remain attached to the impulse of the day. Others use consciousness to empower themselves and deviantly destroy others. People consciously create good and others devise evil. But no matter what with consciousness we can trace ourselves back to God and his values.

Intermediaries are not required intercessors. If that were so, God would be locked into human filters who could and assuredly would derail his presence and influence. This has been in evidence from the beginning of time. Consciousness defies anyone to presume authority over God. If access to God is guaranteed through consciousness, then he can manifest himself at his will not through some surrogate. Abraham had multiple direct encounters with God. Moses exceeded those of Abraham. The prophets all had their encounters. Jesus directly reached out to Paul years after he had left this earth. The saints throughout the ages followed God's directives without human intervention, many times in defiance of ecclesiastical authorities. The apparitions at Lourdes, Fatima, and Medjugorje have all occurred by a direct intervention of God. St. Thomas Aquinas' endless volumes of theology manifest a consciousness filled with the things of God.

Anyone who says God is not present in our lives spreads an enormous falsehood. To deny God in our consciousness is tantamount to denying the very other end of consciousness—God Himself. We are at one end of the line (stream of consciousness) and God is at the other. To be human is to be conscious on a spiritual level. That means we are in God's neighborhood. Out of sight does not mean out of mind. That means we are conscious on a metaphysical level. Consciousness is sight, on a metaphysical level. Eyes are for material objects, consciousness is for the metaphysical ones. We see God with a different vision, one that carries us beyond space and limited horizons. Every child knows who his parent is, and vice versa; similarly, he knows instinctively and intuitively that God is the one original power in his life. Consciousness confirms that conviction. The conviction is the evidence. "I know because I know." Proof is an absurdity and a redundancy. If I am conscious, then I know that life is of God, by God, and for God. When we suddenly know that Jesus "speaks with authority," it is because consciousness has already manifested that fact. You hear something you already know. My consciousness has already revealed it.

Conscience follows consciousness. The more God becomes a dramatic factor in one's life, the more conscience becomes a guide for the good, the more it establishes the values of justice, mercy and love in that life. Without God in that consciousness, the less goodness and justice will pervade that life. If we are led by others, we will be subjects of their value systems, their visions, their emotions, and their distortions, even their crimes. ("Who is my mother and who are my brothers?" No One.) God has to be the centerpiece of our consciousness in order for conscience to enact his justice and righteousness in our lives. If in the end conscience has the final word for our actions, it will only provide a moral outcome if God is first and primarily in consciousness. Without God as the centerpiece of consciousness, there is no conscience with a morality founded on divine principles. The Ten Commandments came publicly and directly from God through Moses and established the foundation for a divine morality. God has not been truant in his presence and involvement in mankind's morality. He is not truant in the personal life of each individual who possesses a consciousness that has God at its focus of attention. Jesus' focus and attention on his Father is to be a paradigm for our focus and attention on him and his Father. A certain perfidy arises when consciousness leaves out the most quintessential occupant of that unfathomable function. With faith we confirm and agree that God is the center and beginning and finality of our consciousness. With a conscience that is attached to a consciousness that celebrates his residency, morality finds direction and authenticity. "So who is my mother and my brother and my sister?" The one who finds Jesus' Father and does his will.

So when we say that conscience in order to act correctly must be informed from outside, we are not saying that that information is necessarily from outsiders who constitute a secondary authority, or who are delegated authorities by reason of appointment or a degree, we are saying that we must be informed from the essential authority, who is God himself. Consciousness is not a tabula rasa that contains nothing but an empty hole. Truth is of God. It is his absolute domain. And consciousness comes with a predisposition to God and his truths. We are not foreigners to the truth of the One who established creation. The 56 signers of the Declaration of Independence were of disparate faiths but they all agreed that, "We hold these truths to be self-evident, that all men are created equal, that they are endowed by their Creator..." They all agreed not only that the right to liberty and self-determination came directly from God but that this revelation also came directly from God. They got it from the source itself—God himself—in spite of their enormous differences of faith practices, ethnicity, professional backgrounds, and age.

Consequently, if conscience is in search of truth, it cannot occur without God's truth. God is the primary source of truth, no one else. Searching for truth without God makes the endeavor a fallacious search. Surrogates mismanage and often falsify the truth. They are tertiary authorities at best and must always be filtered and verified before given credence. People are not the direct source of truth. A conscience, freed from the overreaching pressures of family, friends, teachers, parties, media, church leaders, and the forces of culture and society, will overall arrive at the truth God has already established there if listening to the essential voice in consciousness surfaces first and foremost We are God made and God informed, and if we submit ourselves to the truths of body and spirit deeply installed in our consciousness we will perform as God intended us to. We are not derelicts; we are simply derelict from the truth already in place in our hearts and consciousness.

Finding the truth from God is the challenge of a lifetime. He doesn't talk to us in words and speech. But he does inform. There is a code of truth built into our consciousness that resides patiently there waiting for our exploration and usage. Without our direct access to it we are left in the hands of those who would exploit us.

Chapter 20

JESUS, THE UNIFIER? REALLY!

CORRECTLY SPEAKING THE MOST AUTHENTIC information we have about Jesus is in the gospels of the New Testament. Indeed at times it seems Jesus appears in person through the quoted words and parables of the text. The language is loud and clear, forceful and unequivocal, firm and unashamedly one-sided, even absolute. Jesus comes alive in his many discourses. Moreover, his words mold a message that continues consistently and persistently without deviation from the textual essence he brought from his Father. He is always on cue. And above all the message statements are designed for all people and all generations with no exceptions. He is never intimidated and always intense.

In spite of the overwhelming consistency and unyielding direction of Jesus' words, the reception of Jesus' words and the unwaveringness of those words has not been passed on through the centuries. Though Europe first received and exercised an attachment to Jesus, the depth of his words were seldom incorporated into the lives of those recipients. Jesus was heard through the voices of men and women who saw Jesus in many suits, and it was not a Pauline suit. Jesus evolved according "to men," not according to his Father. There is a world that carries Jesus' banner on church walls, and there is a Jesus who does not live in graphics but lives fearlessly in a mind and action that defies arrogance and self-indulgence. Actually, it is probably safe to say that if we obliged Jesus by living Jesus according to Jesus it would not be safe living on this earth.

Throughout the evolution of "Jesus on Earth" the propelling activity has been, not the distortion of Jesus, but the disarming of Jesus. If you propose Jesus as Jesus really is, you end up with too much Jesus. That is simply unacceptable. Jesus says too much and asks too much. Therefore, he has to be managed. There is something good about Jesus and there are many things too much good about Jesus. If Jesus is brought forward in his originality, he will suffer the loss of an audience. People will not only stop listening, they will leave. The rule is: "You fit Jesus to the people, not people to Jesus."

Centuries of Jesus in the churches has molded a Jesus of comfort and agreement. He has been absorbed and refined to fit our capacities. But there is more than that. He has been molded, shaped, designed, and recast, and even restructured to fit our needs and expectations. He is not Jesus from the Father, he is Jesus of the people, for the people, and by the people. Hence Jesus has been groomed into a model of peace and tranquillity, into an icon of love and self-surrender. Jesus is Goodness personified and wants everyone to experience that goodness, no matter anything else.

For so many people, especially Christians, Jesus stands as the epitome of universal unity. When you think Jesus, or you say Jesus, or you pray in Jesus' name, a sense of cosmic unity is invoked. Jesus brings people together. You do not think division. You think only "sheep," without goats. You see olive branches and Christmas trees. This notion of Christianity is inbred in those who come into the Christian world. Churches are considered "safe places," or "sanctuaries," a place where theoretically no pursuer may enter. Those who attempt to separate and divide become the outcasts, people you must at all costs keep at a distance. Hence, any aggressive talk about the Killing of the Unborn that leads to serious confrontation toward those Christians who are willing to walk softly around the issue is quickly criticized and dispatched. Since for many Christians Abortion is a "private matter," a "matter of choice," something that is allowed by the decision of he court, it is a non-starter topic and only opens up division and ill feelings if the evil of Abortion is approached. If unity at all costs is invoked, goodness has to move to the sidelines in order to allow evil a preeminent place at the table.

All these years the voices in pulpits have taken Jesus' whip and turned it into a plough share. His "Woe to you Liars" has been quieted. His "casting people into Gehenna" has been placed on hold. Everyone talks about peace, but he said he brought a "sword." There is so much talk about Jesus being a unifier, but how can that be when he is always pushing people around and getting in their face and declaring that if anyone disowns him, he "will disown him before my Father in heaven." And lest we forget, if someone wants to get to God, that someone must go through him; access to the Father is exclusively through him—"no one knows the Father except the Son and anyone to whom the Son wishes to reveal him." (Mt.11:27) Once you take away Jesus' autocratic tone, you have a different Jesus.

When reading the New Testament carefully and closely one comes away with many impressions that do not necessarily correspond to the common denominators of Christian churches in America. More and more the Jesus of today's pulpit is disarmed. He has been made into the image of man's image of the "pursuit of happiness" rather than the pursuit of God. The word of God in the pages of the gospel is often subjected to dismemberment in the minds and mouths of so many professional clerics. It is not so much what they say as it is what they do not say and what they leave out. A word instead of a whole phrase, a sentence outside of a paragraph, a single thought separated from its context disengages the entire message. If you say love and leave out law, you have disarmed the message. If you say "Jesus loves," and leave out "Jesus condemns," you disarm Jesus. Likewise saying "Jesus unites" is not the whole story, not even close to the true story.

If Jesus was a unifier, what is the Parable of the Weeds doing in Matthew's gospel? Dumbfounded the apostles asked Jesus the same question. This was his answer: "The one who sowed the good seed is the Son of man. The field is the world, and the good seed stands for the people of the kingdom. The weeds are the people of the evil one, and the enemy who sows them is the devil. The harvest is the end of the age, and the harvesters are the angels. As the weeds are pulled up and burned in the fire, so will it be at the end of the age. The Son of man will send out his angels, and they will weed out of his kingdom all that causes sin and all who do evil. They will throw them into the blazing furnace, where there will be weeping and gnashing of teeth. Then the righteous will shine like the sun in the kingdom of their Father. Whoever has ears, let them hear." (Mt.13:37-43) Again, if Jesus was a unifier, why single out the goats from the sheep? His answer was: "Truly I tell you, whatever you did not do for one of the least of these, you did not do for me. Then they will go away to eternal punishment, but the righteous to eternal life." (Mt. 25:.45-46)

Jesus was not a unifier. He demanded adherence, not unity. Next he demanded compliance. You were either with him or against him. Unity for Jesus meant that there was only one way to the Father, and that was through him. Furthermore, there were demands placed on his followers, and that was doing the will of his Father. Theft and injury and harm to others, perjury and slander and lies, adultery and drunkenness and murder were not the "will of the Father." The good and the bad do not mix, nor do righteousness and evil mix. There is an irreconcilable separation between good and evil, between murder and selflessness, between slander and truth. Jesus was on one side only and never attempting to mingle the two or suffer an accommodation. Those who attempt to consolidate good and evil, to bring good and evil under the same tent, do irreparable harm to Jesus and his Father's message. One very noticeable trait in Jesus was his quest to expose evil and separate it from good. His time on earth shined the light on evil incessantly. In the Book of Genesis the tree in the middle of the Garden of Eden was tagged by God as the "tree of good and evil." Apparently God wanted Adam and Eve to recognize the distinction between good and evil. The Fall starts with their willingness to disregard God's admonition about evil. And what the devil accomplished was getting Adam and Eve to accept an evil as good, to fail at distinguishing one from the other, a problem the world cleverly employs when advancing evil as good, or finding good in evil.

In order to advance unity as a primary goal among human beings, the task going forward requires that evil be covered up as good and its lethal and toxic characteristics be washed over with the appearances of good. Unity without goodness is the cry of today's politics and the toxic calls of the elite media and social media giants. Unity without a moral structure in place is the devil's utopia.

When Jesus stated, "May they all be one," he was just hours away from his arrest by the Jews and his subsequent death. He was speaking to the apostles and making a final statement about their resilient fidelity and their persistent commitment to him. Indeed, he went out of his way to thank his Father for the disciples he gave him. His gratitude was profuse. One has the impression that in this final discourse that occurs in Chapter 17 of John's gospel Jesus is addressing his Father as though he were present in the room with them, and that he wants very much to praise the apostles and praise his Father for the bond they have together. The message of unity he dramatizes is not a unity of global proportions, but restricted to himself, his Father, and his followers. Only those "who believe" fit into the scope of his words. Jesus with absolute clarity defined that direction: "I have revealed you to those whom you gave me out of the world. They were yours; you gave them to me and they have obeyed your word. Now they know that everything you have given me comes from you. For I gave them the words you gave me and they accepted them. They knew with certainty that I came from you, and they believed that you sent me." (J.17:6-8)

"May they all be one" is certainly the theme exhibited in this final moment of Jesus' gathering with the apostles. He awards his Father with resounding praise for the "exclusive bond" his Father has established with those he has given him. It is NOT an "inclusive bond" that becomes an open ended automatic relationship with anyone. The bond has fixed boundaries that is reserved for those the Father has brought to Jesus. It is not for just anyone or everyone. "May they all be one" does not apply universally to mankind. It is directed to one specific group, and that group Jesus identifies is "to all those you (Father) have given me." Jesus throughout this final moments of his time with the apostles demonstrably connects "May they all be one" with "to all those you have given me." If the context of "May they all be one" is separated from "to all those you have given me," the result is a distortion: his message in essence fails and he is disarmed of the truth. Jesus was not here on earth for a kumbaya event; he left that to the crazies of Woodstock. The only group cited by Jesus for inclusion in this unity pack were the apostles and "all those who will come to believe in Jesus through the work of the apostles." Believing in Jesus is the way to the Father, but, according to Jesus, it all starts with the Father, who is first and foremost the only way to the believer.

In so many ways this final dinner, perhaps banquet, is an awards dinner for the apostles who for three years were treated to the same obstacles Jesus was, and, in spite of everything, arrived at this climactic moment to receive this ceremonial accommodation from him before his Father, all because they believed that he truly was the Son of God and that he was sent by his Father. The final analysis is that this Passover banquet becomes a unity dinner for Jesus and the apostles who are officially inducted into the same relationship Jesus has with his Father. This is the Oneness Jesus celebrates that night, "so that they may be one as we are one."

To many in the Christian world these final words of Jesus conjure up a state of universal unity. "Let's all be one" is translated as a slogan for peace. The most vocal among us push for a world without division. Coexistence is the operative word among those who demand unity no matter what. Little do they know that they do so at the peril of righteousness. Goodness and truth and honesty are prerequisites for unity. Unity without value is loss of purpose and principle. "Let's all be one" is ostensibly a slogan of peace, but in too many realities it is the preamble to slaughter. People who yell unity in the midst of lawlessness and falsehood attempt to cover up their radical evil. If Jesus had wanted unity at all costs he never would have called the Pharisees a bunch of Vipers; he would have refrained from using a whip in the temple; he certainly would have had more restraint in calling out the goats among us; and sending people to Gehenna would probably have been stricken from his vocabulary. Today if unity among people of any inclination and persuasion means compromise and surrender in order to satisfy crowd appeal, then we have lost the Jesus of the gospels.

So many forces of the world are at work to shame us for not uniting together for the sake of peace. What they are really asking us is that we go back to the Garden of Eden and believe the snake is not there.

Chapter 21

PIETY VS. MORALITY

IF THERE IS ONE UNIVERSAL EXPRESSION
common to most, if not all, human beings it would be prayer.
Christians pray, Hindus pray, Native Indians pray, Tibetans pray,
and Jews have been praying since Abraham. The Romans and
Greeks prayed too, even the ones on Mt. Olympus. Praying
is a staple among human beings because we do not have the
answers and we are looking for the answers and no one around
us seems to have the answers. Praying is not a religious phenomenon; in its very essence it is an attempt to control and
forecast the unknown.

We pray for a lot of things. We pray for good weather. We
pray for work. We pray for a healthy new baby. We pray for a
good spouse. We pray for good grades and a winning team in
sports. We pray to escape harm and disease. We pray to avoid
bloodshed and catastrophe. We sometimes pray for war and at
other times to end war. Prayer is all over the place. Some even
pray for evil, or that evil people would stop being evil. We certainly prayed for the end of Hitler and Stalin and Moa Zedong
and Pol Pot and Idi Amin and the Hutus. Nothing falls short
of prayer.

Churches overall specialize in prayer. Song and prayer is
their focus. Church service is fundamentally a prayer service. It

suffices that we gather in church to hear the Bible speak familiar words—brotherly love, peace above all, kindness and forgiveness without exception, be thoughtful and civil—then pray for all of the above. Everything is wrapped in pleasant words and soft tones. We come for an easy message and upbeat song. We pray to escape the dangers and evil of the world, and all of the uncertainties of tomorrow. We use church for comfort and prayer and above all to hear what we want to hear. Churches make God's Voice softer and more agreeable. But it wasn't always that way.

Over the years and perhaps for decades the laws of God have been turned away from their initial meaning. Commandments once detailed strong directives for righteous behavior. There were majorities of the population that accepted the original meanings of those commandments. Churches spoke openly and firmly about obedience to the commandiments that God had delivered to earth. A consensus for good behavior generally persisted in the public eye. We could agree almost unanimously on a variety of topics of moral consequence. The church in the past spoke with determination against evils of weight and injury to others. Of course, this was all before Roe v Wade and the takeover of the information sources by the media and the profound dive by the culture into the pit of hell.

There are no moral authorities of prominence anymore. The churches, in particular, the Catholic Church, have been driven into a whisper mode. When a church can declare something "intrinsically evil" but not pursue and condemn in uncertain language those who commit "intrinsically evil acts," then we know that any real force of morality has been silenced. There are lone voices speaking about the evil of Abortion, but there are no voices of magnitude that speak and condemn those who promote, vote into law, and fund the "intrinsic evil" of Abortion. The Catholic Church with its mighty platform will not take on the in-your-face platform of the Democrat Party and specifically condemn the Catholic Democrats who support and campaign for Abortion. The morality of the Catholic Church has been reduced to a whisper, hidden away in the pages of its theological documents and only opened and read by a few frocked clerics.

In Church on Sunday we "pray for an end to Abortion" and there it ends. The Unborn Babies are remembered every week before they are executed in the Womb every week. The sellers of Abortion and those who vote for the sellers of Abortion are all gathered together in the same churches every week along with those who protest Abortion lobbying God for an end to Abortion. The praying is a sham, an outrage. To stand in a holy place and ask God to pray for an end to the Killing of the Babies in the Womb with the very people who the next day go out and support and elect the very people who perpetuate that Killing is an intrinsically evil act in itself. An accomplice falls into the same crime as the commissioner of a crime, and suffers the same guilt.

In the last several generations the Churches of Jesus Christ have literally cast off their moral armament. They have retreated to their sanctuaries and devoted themselves to prayer. Piety has become their strong suit and only suit. Whatever morality they continue to endorse is kept in books and quiet prayers. No cleric can be found with gloves on to fight for moral rectitude. If there is one, he is kept indoors.

It is Piety that prevails overall. The political loudmouths have managed cleverly with the ever powerful forces of the Media Big Mouths to shove the Churches into the limited spaces of the church sanctuary. According to them this is where the First Amendment puts them—out of sight and confined to a prayer place. And dutifully the church hierarchies have complied and accepted their quiet, private roles in the sanctuary.

It would be hard to imagine today a man like Bishop Fulton J Sheen hiding in some sanctuary away from the limelight of television not denouncing the butchery of Abortion, unless, of course, his Vatican superior kept him shackled and silenced.

Churches have truly become the dwelling places of mystics, who desire consolation not confrontation, where nothing is inimical and nothing deserves the pointed finger of shame. If these same churches are the offspring of Jesus Christ, they have lost their founder's message. Jesus was not a mystic devoted to epiphanies, but the Son of God who came to exercise an exorcism over the spectrum of human evil. Jesus was always dealing with an enemy. Not just the Pharisees, or Herod and Pilate, or Judas and sometimes Peter, but the whole culture of greed and the selfishness of his own townspeople. A morality of righteousness always has an abundance of enemies and very few friends. In the gospels as Jesus' story develops, Jesus gathers more and more enemies. If you want to be loved by the crowd, you have to join the crowd. Jesus belonged to NO crowds. He was the loner from heaven pointing fingers at every evil he encountered and never moving aside in silence. Once Jesus left Nazareth and started his mission the gloves came off and he spoke with rapid fury; "Woe to you..., hypocrites."

Nothing of a reserved voice could be ascribed to Jesus. His findings of fault among men deserved and received judgment and condemnation. If good behavior, right behavior, and just behavior have priority in human life, then that priority demands enforcement. Morality without enforcement has no meaning or viability. It pales out of existence. It dies before it is announced. Jesus never said, "IF you do this." Jesus said, "UNLESS you do this!" "IF" never entered his mind. "UNLESS" was the only operative word. The only IF is "If you want to go to heaven," then it becomes, "UNLESS you do these things."

Jesus exercised a Commander-in-Chief style attitude toward everything and everyone around him. He had a recognizable authority that escaped no one. He had a commanding persona that drew people, especially his enemies. When you adjudicate something in public before witnesses that no one can otherwise contest, you have stolen all attention. Jesus only conformed to his Father and his Father made no excuses for anything. His task was to enforce his Father's will. God's law without enforcement is no law; it dies without enforcement. It becomes meaningless. When God banished Adam and Eve out of the Garden of Eden he started a pattern of enforcement. When God told Noah to build the arc, the end purpose was to punish a sinful mankind for rejecting his laws. The Israelites wandered for Forty years in the desert for their reluctance to remain faithful to God's name. David was punished for his adultery and murder of Uriah. Jesus, the very Son of God, was sent to admonish and punish the waywardness of mankind. God deplores evil. His remedy is punishment. There are consequences for those who disobey.

What has taken place these last years of the twentieth century and then beyond is the weakening of the principles of morality and the authority of church leadership. The church once held a commanding position in the moral lives of its followers and even carried significant weight outside the range of its spires. Church edifices were a reminder of Jesus' presence in the world and a recognition of his statutes. The buildings once stood tall and symbolized an authority above and beyond this earth. The churches are still here and the spires still stand high, but the reverence for the rule of law and obedience to Jesus' declarations of morality have been suffocated by the ruthless and reckless distortions of the truth. Moral authority has no longer any enforcement mechanism coming from the churches. The culture along with and foremost the Mephistophelian Media and all of its surrogates and sycophants have unleashed the devil's mind and mouth on society. Anything sacred and moral has been smashed to the ground. The devil has accomplished with this mankind what he could not with Jesus: "The devil took him to a very high mountain and showed all the kingdoms of the world and their splendor. 'All this I will give you,' he said, 'if you bow down and worship me.'" (Mt.4:8-9) The devil fooled Adam and Eve, and, "Guess What," he's done a better job today.

Moral authority without enforcement has no existence. A hammer without its handle is lifeless. Laws without enforcement have no force. Laws without cops and judges will not survive. "Down with the cops," is civil anarchy, and, "Down with the commandments," is moral anarchy. This is what this Media/Culture has achieved. They have planted their toxic seeds in the minds of the Democrat Party. Right is wrong, and wrong is right. They have accomplished a complete moral makeover with the mouths and the powers of the Democrat Party declaring absolute authority.

In this civil/moral mayhem the churches, however, have found a niche. They still have their sanctuaries. With prayer and bowed heads they can go about raising their thoughts and words to God. Since they have completely lost moral distinction and moral authority, they have no place else to go. One such acknowledgement of this is detailed in the clever casuistic surrender of the Catholic Church's required resistance to the Killing of the Unborn in the Womb. In recent months the Catholic Bishops of America enmasse in their annual directives to Catholics have outlined a blueprint for "Informing Consciences" in preparation for the Presidential Election. In a lengthy document of 53 pages they enumerated many important issues of concern in the upcoming election. It ran the gamut of social and moral concerns, insisting in its Paragraph #42 that the church is not a "ONE" issue church: "As Catholics we are not single-issue voters. A candidate's position on a single issue is not sufficient to guarantee a voter's support. Yet a candidate's position on a single issue that involves an intrinsic evil, such as support for legal abortion or the promotion of racism, may legitimately lead a voter to disqualify a candidate from receiving support." Notice the word "may" in the concluding portion of the directive. Not "must." Not "absolutely must" disqualify a candidate. The entire matter is left to the individual without a clear resolution to the matter of an intrinsic evil, which should unconditionally block out a candidate who votes and promotes the Killing of the Unborn.

It would appear that if an authority of some weight pro-posed a document specifically to "inform the conscience" of its members, it would behoove that authority to offer clarity and honesty in matters regarding "intrinsic evil." To declare an issue of such magnitude as Abortion an "intrinsic evil act," then place that same act in a political limbo where a voter "may" or "may not" select a candidate who advocates for Abortion seems to negate the entire purpose of "informing the con-science." On one hand "to declare" an act "intrinsically evil," then walk away from condemning any form of support for that evil ranks as moral ineptitude. God did not declare in the Fifth Commandment "Thou May Not Kill," he wrote in stone, "Thou Shall Not Kill." The act was condemned, not optioned. And yet we have the leaders of the Catholic Church and many and most of the other Christian Churches that say little or nothing about the intrinsic evil of Abortion that deserves extrinsic and unqualified direct condemnation.

When God delivered the Ten Commandments to Moses, they were etched on two tablets of stone and eight of the com-mandments began with, "Thou Shall NOT...". God had removed all ambiguity about the seriousness of the acts involved. One commandment was not juxtaposed against another, allowing choices and preferences between them. Each one carried its own weight and moral obligation. People who commit murder and those that commit adultery are held accountable and no one escapes the wrath of either crime.

What the churches have dispensed with in these latter years is the wrath of God in all matters evil, and especially in matters "intrinsically evil." In advising its sheepfold this past August in its document entitled, "Forming Consciences for Faithful Citizenship," the college of Catholic Bishops of America also carefully crafted a "substitution clause" for Catholics preparing to vote in the great election of 2020. Regarding the matter of Abortion as an "intrinsic evil," a voter may decide to vote for a candidate who advocates for the Killing of the Unborn if he/she deems that there are other "morally grave reasons" to vote for that same candidate: Paragraph #35 of the document states, "There may be times when a Catholic who rejects a candidate's unacceptable position even on policies promoting an intrinsically evil act may reasonably decide to vote for that candidate for other morally grave reasons." What we have here is an endorsement of every Catholic who votes for Abortion supporting Democrats as long as he or she can claim a grave moral issue that that candidate favors. Any one of the following could suffice: climate change, open immigration, saving sanctuary cities, shutting down fossil fuels, free health care for all, free college education, even capital punishment. As long as one of these is elevated to a "morally grave" status, the Abortion candidate can receive your vote. This has been the prevailing attitude of the Catholic Bishops of America for the past 47 years, giving men like Joe Biden and John Dingell and Andrew Cuomo the ability to escape the wrath of supporting a crime against the Unborn. An "intrinsically evil act" is checkmated by a "Climate Change" substitution. "Thou Shall Not Kill" the Unborn Is balanced by one's advocacy against capital punishment.

When God spoke on Mt. Sinai, he spoke clearly and emphatically. There were no excuses allowed, no alternatives, no uncertainty, no leniency, no justifications, and no "morally grave reasons" for committing an "intrinsically evil act." There was no quiver in God's voice. There was moral certainty and clarity in God's delivery. The moral dilemma we face today stems from the near takeover by the culture of Christianity. The public lying, the falsehoods, the slander, the promiscuity, the greed, and above all the Killing of the Unborn in magnitudes unbelievable is due to the wasting away of the Christian church. Greed and gluttony and slander are staples in society and we hear so little about it. The Hollywood actors and Media Mouths and Moguls have created a culture of indecency in our social and domestic behavior and in politics they have created an empire of lies and falsehoods. Even the devil could take lessons from them. When a leading politician like Harry Reid can boast with glee that he lied about accusing Mitt Romney of paying no taxes, he glibly said, "Well, it worked, didn't it? We won!" Nightly the world is subjected to the incestuous mouths of Media Pharisees whose tongues of poison destroy everyone inside the Womb and everyone outside the Womb.

All of this forced submission on Christianity leaves the Christian Church of America relegated to Easter and Christmas, mostly indoors and out of the mainstream of life. The Viper that once got Adam and Eve evicted from Eden has now succeeded in banishing the voice of biblical honesty and morality. Instead crawling through our audio/visual senses are the faces and voices of the Cuomos, the Lemons, the Maddows, the Schumers, the Pelosis, the Schiffs, and the other multitudes who prey on and annihilate the very essence of truth and morality. Without leadership Christianity is history past. Without a strong shepherd the evils of wickedness poison the consciences of feeble humanity. In order for the blessings of

Jesus' words to be delivered forcefully in the world a leader must stand and inject the truth into the very veins of susceptible minds. For Christianity to be vital and effective, its leader must literally assault the minds of men and women with God's authority. For three years Jesus brought his Father's authority and assaulted the evil he encountered. The path to his Father was one of belief and obedience with no substitutions for evil, and that same path with the same force must be rekindled today.

Until a leadership of some strength and mighty passion is found, Christianity will linger in the background of societal life. It will remain locked in its prayer services and constantly undermined by the incestuous dominance of the Media and its Democrat allies. The snake that left Eden has overtaken the Democrat Party and has grown to gargantuan proportions and will not leave until a destroyer of greater proportions is found. May that destroyer soon appear and claim dominance over such flagrant and craven evil.

Until Jesus' voice and passion for honesty and truth and righteousness reenters Christianity, we will be subjected to the unremitting evil of the snake from Eden.

Chapter 22

ONE FINAL WORD

IF THERE IS ONE THING CHRISTIANITY IS uniquely associated with it is submission. Martyrs have been known to universally submit to their oppressors, dying rather than surrendering their beliefs and principles. "Turn the other cheek," is a familiar quote associated with Christianity. Under Nero Christians were food for the lions because they would not worship the emperor. If there is one common trait to be found among Christians, it would be classified as a willingness to back off and submit rather than fight. Christ himself is the best example of non-aggression, and the cross verifies that. His coming as a baby in Bethlehem and his ignominious death in Jerusalem exemplifies a person of submission, and with enormous repetition he said, "I have come to do the will of my Father in Heaven," implying perhaps that he was not here for war but for peace. When Peter cut off the ear of the guard in the Garden of Gethsemane, Jesus corrected him and told him to put up his sword. In addition he told everyone present that if he had wanted to retaliate he could have called up 12 legions of angels to defend him. None of which happened.

At the Sermon on the Mount one of the final Beatitudes Jesus intoned offers an alternative to retaliation: "Blessed are they who are persecuted for the sake of righteousness, for theirs is the kingdom of heaven." Jesus clearly supports non-aggression. There is submission written all over the history books of Christianity, plus in the multitude of books on piety and prayer and theological tracks, love as opposed to anger is the approved avenue to Christ's way of thinking. Any imitation of Christ follows the path of submission. According to the general takeaway of the Beatitudes it appears that submission becomes a constitutional requirement in Christianity. Indeed, for those who join a religious order it becomes a lifelong vocation.

When you have an organization such as the Catholic Church with its hegemony of authority—Pope, Cardinal, Archbishop, Bishop, priest, and volumes of Vatican congregations, plus the innumerable books on dogma and then the Catechism—the only working adhesive device keeping order is submission. Adhering to authority is the sine qua non of Catholic Christianity. "Follow the leader" is the best advice. The assumption is that if we want to follow Christ, we best follow his appointed authorities, and since they come with the added power of the sacrament of sacerdotal ordination, our submission to their authority comes with even deeper obligation. Since they represent Christ, their authority is incontestable.

But this appearance of submission in Christianity is erroneous. Christianity was not created for submission, it was created for the truth. The Beatitudes do not lead to submission; they lead to perfection. Love is not a pushover, and it certainly was never designed as an infirmity. Love in its essential nature is resilient, not submissive. Likewise peace, if it must be reached at all costs it must never consign itself to inaction. In the face of evil, the greatest evil is to allow plough shares to remain plough shares.

Without doubt the most fallacious and perverse identity anyone can give Jesus is that he was a submissive man. Quite to the contrary, Jesus submitted to no one. He submitted to no man, to no group, to no religion. No one gained any advantage on him, his message, or his mission. His alignment fell exclusively to his Father and the Spirit, all others were scrutinized and suspect, and for good reason. The reprimand Jesus gave Peter, "Get behind me Satan," applies aptly to every member of the Fallen Race, and then some. Jesus reserved his trust only for his Father. He may have died for mankind, but never did he submit to any member of the Fallen Race.

On the contrary, Jesus came to engage the human race from top to bottom. Everyone was on his radar. He was constantly in the open. From the time he left Nazareth he never ceased healing and preaching. He was a marketplace man. At one moment he was seen and heard healing an individual and the next moment he was in the midst of thousands feeding them with a mere two fish and five loaves. At no time was Jesus out of sight, and never in hiding, and absolutely never conceding.

His portfolio of rejections covered every level of life. If you cheated, you were called a Cheater. If you lied, you were called a Liar. The hoarder with warehouses of goods received a sentence of death. Judas was better off "never being born." Simon, the Pharisee, received a tongue lashing for accusing Jesus of not washing his hands while he himself cared nothing for cleansing his own soul. The men who accused the woman taken in adultery were summarily dispatched with a scarlet letter on their own heads. Jesus never hesitated in passing out a range of caustic accusations on those who stretched the bounds of morality. Numerous times Jesus dispatched the devil from those possessed—Lucifer was one of his favorite targets. But Jesus' most favorite targets of all were the Hypocrites, the Pharisees, who were ravenous wolves walking around in sheeps' clothing: "Woe to you teachers of the law.... You Snakes. You Vipers." The money changers got a whipping also. And Herod, the "Fox," got not a word from Jesus, only a deadly silence.

Jesus spoke his mind without intimidation. Jesus' moral outrage was delivered indiscriminately across every avenue of evil. He operated publicly daily and no one escaped his critical eye or his deliberate words.

Jesus often said that his "Kingdom was not of this world," but he never implied that this kingdom on earth did not belong to his Father and was subject to his Father's rule, and, furthermore, that Jesus himself came to shine a light on evil and reveal it and destroy it:

> "What came to be through him was life,
> and this life was the light of the human race;
> the light shines in the darkness,
> and the darkness has not overcome it." (J.1:3-5)

The "truth," above all things rose highest on Jesus' list of tasks to proclaim on earth. This truth mission started with his announcement that "he was the one to come," that his Father in heaven had sent him, and that he was the Son of God. None of this ever left him from declaring it in the open before vast throngs of listeners, nor before the suspicious minds of the Sanhedrin. If anything would have induced him to back off from this claim and silence his insistence on his divinity, this would have been the one. But he did not. Divinity had come in person to earth and it would not deny itself or submit to a rescindment. When the Sanhedrin questioned and condemned him for his claims of divinity, he boldly affirmed his lineage with his Father. In spite of the threat of death, he maintained his position as the Son of God. Submission and truth were opposing strangers in Jesus' lexicon.

For anyone to believe that denunciation does not befit Christianity, that someone has never read the New Testament and knows little about the Jesus who inhabits the gospels. Once

Jesus left Nazareth he was loaded for bear. Personal perfection was certainly on his mind, but never at the expense of eradicating evil behavior. Two things Jesus did unceasingly were the proclamation of his divine Sonship and his denunciation of evil. He came with impeccable authority from his Father and he used it to accost every form of evil. After all if he had come all the way from heaven with his Father's commission to deal comprehensively with Fallen Man, he had to confront man's depravity. Jesus showed no restraint where chastisement and punishment were required. A quick reading of Matthew 23 and Luke 11 demonstrate this claim conclusively. The laws of God are front and center for Jesus. Deviants are defied and held in contempt.

The Christianity that has arisen over the past several generations has become a shadow of the culture and has backed itself into a corner out of the limelight and away from the condemning mouths of the Liberal Media and all of its allies. Its long-standing and persistent hold on the commandments and the stringent principles set down in the texts of the gospels has been neutered by the many forces in the public sector. The "morality" of the culture has overridden the commandments of God. Christianity has labored in vain to restrain the takeovers by Hollywood and CNN and the Social Media maggots, along with the Democrat Party Trumpeteers, who daily devour justice and honesty and truth. With no shame and all bravado they (Everyone of them) subject Babies in the Womb to death; Marriage has become a multi-gendered event; Patriotism is a dirty word; Sex is a cinema-after-dinner-entertainment; Lying has become the language of Politics; the quest for Power outranks any pursuit of honesty; then there is Socialism and its elevation to sanctity (accompanied by Papal Approval); above all, Climate change has replaced the apocalypse; and, lastly, the Constitution with its separation of church and state protection clause has become a renunciation clause of the church by the state. If there is any force left in Christianity, it is kept under wraps deep inside the portals of the church, hidden not only from the public but from the members as well.

We call ourselves a Judeo-Christian Country, but evidence of such has vanished rapidly before our eyes. The Voice that Christianity once had in commanding moral rectitude has been snuffed out by a Political/Media structure that allows no discussion or debate about issues it has abusively sequestered. Once you have literally stolen the very life of the Unborn in the Womb with sheer impunity, you have STOLEN THE AUTHORITY OF GOD. You have RAPED HIS ONE-OF-A-KIND POWER. The giving or taking of life belongs to no man. It BELONGS TO GOD. For a Black Robed Society of Seven to have usurped the Plenipotentiary Jurisdiction of God demonstrates the sheer arrogance of human justice because it believes that the Separation of Church and State means the Separation of State from God, from God's Laws, from God's Creative Power. To GOVERN WITHOUT GOD is to govern as the Devil. To Govern without his Truth is to govern without any truth. If this country was endowed and therefore founded by the Creator, it is therefore ruled and governed by his laws and his reality. You may be able to separate a particular church from the State, but you can separate nothing from God. If God is out of the picture, then the entire picture is mastermind by the devil.

To embrace openly the death of the Unborn is not a matter of choice, it is a matter of murder. When Christianity stands by and allows its members to harbor an allegiance to this practice of the Killing of the Unborn, then that Christianity has suffered a paralysis of morality. It simply means that Christianity has resigned its moral authority to the culture of convenience and criminality. In the end the Church no longer condemns immorality, immorality condemns the Church. This is not the gospel of Jesus, nor the letters of Paul, nor the Voice of the man in the Wilderness calling all men to repentance and self-discipline. The Christianity that Paul and Barnabas spread among the Gentiles in the first century brought forward ONE Jesus who consigned everyone to ONE and the same morality. Paul did not tolerate variations of morality. He was well aware that Fallen Nature existed, but he was not one to let it remain Fallen, or excuse its Fallenness, or promote its Fallenness.

Today Christianity is about staying put and accommodating the loudmouths in the Democrat Party and the bigger loudmouths in the Media. Today Christianity is devoted to staying out of the way and accepting its "non-essential" role in society—seen but not heard, heard but not listened to, and if listened to without effect. The whole purpose of separating (extinguishing) church and state is to create singular access for the state to ONE Rule, ONE Power. This has nothing to do with advancing democracy, but everything to do with dictatorship. The Democrats and the Media have convened an alliance to forge a dictatorship that rules out democracy, morality, church, and God. By inducing impotence in every challenger outside of themselves, they can and have arrived at an absolute dictatorship over all things and all men and women. This is why and how this conglomerate of Democrats and Media have erased the fundamentals of morality in Christianity.

Christianity and democracy are very fragile endeavors, perhaps better designed for heaven than for earth. They both encompass a world of ideals—love, goodness, fairness, equality, and so many more. Both operate in the name of truth and justice. Christianity leads into democracy and democracy performs well when it follows Christianity. But neither is safe from the dictatorship of evil. Each has a handicap. For Christianity it is truth, for democracy it is justice. The evil forces of Fallen Men defy truth and justice, and continue relentlessly to defeat both. Without restraints and without regard for human frailty, evil advances its lies and deceits and enterprises over a trusting human condition that quickly succumbs to its rule. Christianity walks a path of resigned endurance and democracy follows a path of lengthy legal jurisprudence while evil systems storm through every barrier with slim resistance and little contest. Christianity pushes love and non-resistance and democracy is restrained by its requirement of "innocent until proven guilty." All the while evil marches into the culture, into society, into minds and hearts, into the deep fabric of emotion and spirit, and claims a footing over life. Both Christianity and democracy have demonstrated that they are inadequate to the task. They fail because neither resisted…, and not soon enough. The one thing evil counts on is our good faith and impotence.

However, this was not the Jesus who preceded Christianity. Jesus did not come all the way from his Father's house to tell us to be pious and pray. He did not come to suggest impotence. He was not Mr. Congeniality, he was Mr. Cogent. When Jesus came out of Nazareth he did not merely name evil, he pointed a finger at the evil doer and befittingly denounced him. Jesus' crosshairs were loaded with perpetrators. When Jesus championed those referred to in the Beatitudes, "Blessed are they who are persecuted for righteousness," he did not say retreat from righteousness; persecution does not come by retreating from doing what is right, but by resisting those who commit evil against righteousness. If Christianity has a role to play in the lives of ordinary people, it must both forgive and oppose evil, and by opposing condemn it, and that includes condemning the perpetrators, with their names in CAPS. Evil is not some mere concept that appears in books of morality, it is an act of destruction committed against others. The act requires exposure and the actor must be detailed and condemned.

If the gospels are read carefully, anyone can see that Jesus contested with evil throughout his ministry. It started at the very beginning when he left the desert: the devil approached him with his offers of submission and Jesus handily rebuked him. Page upon page of the gospel reveals Jesus in the market-place healing those with physical diseases and thwarting those with diseased minds. He meets humanity in the open, outdoors, in public, face to face, ready to cure and to confront. He is never indoors hiding his message and his authority. His Father sent him to unburden the deprived and burden the depraved. And he did it with steadfast courage and undeterred determination and leadership.

The book of Genesis opens with the beautiful story of creation and then in short fashion as it unfolds we rapidly learn that the essential story revolves around good vs evil, and for all subsequent pages from the Old into the New Testaments the theme remains the same: it is a struggle between good and evil. Prophets come and Kings go and evil continues to prosper. Evil is in the forefront. Fallen Nature maintains a foothold on the story and nothing happens that does not demonstrate its malevolence. Somehow God witnessing all this folly caused him to interject his Son. Thus Jesus arrives at the time of the monstrous Herods and delivers a new covenant to mankind. The covenant is not a doctrine of disarmament as so many followers of Christianity believe, but a mandate for action. The Sermon on the Mount delivers a litany of action points that cover the entire spectrum of life. Doing good, becoming good, delivering good, does not create a physical or mental disability. On the contrary, it moves us to action. We enjoin evil, not step aside for it. Jesus exemplifies that very action. He is in the world, for the world, not of the world, but very often whenever necessary against the world. Jesus is anything of a pushover.

Today and so often Christianity is found aiding and abetting the trends of the culture. We have witnessed how Christianity over these many years has been removed to the background of authority in matters regarding morals and the fundamentals of truth. People do not much bother consulting Christianity for anything anymore. Its voice is soft and subdued and conditioned for Sunday services. It is not the voice of the man in the desert, "Make straight the path of the Lord." In more recent months, for example, the Catholic Bishops of America have written into their Conscience "Informing" Document a "justification clause" for Catholics who are inclined to vote for a candidate who actively professes an Abortion position. They stipulate that Abortion is an "intrinsically evil act," but then provide an escape hatch for their members by allowing them to find another gravely serious matter that their preferred candidate supports, and thus opening the door for them to vote for the Abortion candidate. Climate change would suffice for a substitution, or capital punishment or even racism (however these are defined today). This allows Catholics to vote for Joe Biden in spite of his declared and actively executed position on Abortion. Babies be damned, you can still vote in "good" conscience for Joe Biden if you are a Catholic.

Jesus came to "make straight the way of his Father," not to satisfy the way of any group, nor the way of any church, certainly not the way of any political party. He was exclusively a member of the trinity and no other group. He listened to no one else and trusted NO ONE ELSE. Fallen Nature was his target of concern at every level. Evil found anywhere was evil condemned anywhere. His task was to harness the powers of truth and apply them directly without reservation or political correctness. Jesus did not stay away from evil doers "just because they were too big to handle." The Pelosis, the Durbins, the Leahys, the Dingells, and the Bidens, just to name a few, were all his special targets if they chose the evil barbarity of Abortion. Something "intrinsically evil" cannot be washed into a corner and allowed to hide in some sort of "private pro-life" cloud. A public figure gets public treatment, not a public waiver. That is the difference between Jesus and those of the leading Ecclesiastics of the Christian Churches. Jesus swept nothing under a carpet.

The underlying menace in every act of evil is the LIE that creates it and permits it. Nothing evil starts without a lie, an excuse, a "private" justification. Theft, adultery, slander, and even murder, start with a lie. It is a protective device to shield against the moral calamity of the act. The moral thermometer of the country has been overtaken by the domineering forces of the Media and the Democrats who have installed their flag of lies over every institution on the land. Slander and lying is the single method of conquering and destroying democracy and morality. Own the airwaves and you own the world. The lie works wonders when delivering evil. This was best demonstrated by the words of a former leading Democrat senator who after being questioned about his false statements about Mit Romney's taxes said, "Well, it worked, didn't it? We won!"

What is missing in all of this moral destruction is the outrage from a Christian centered institution that carries the name of Jesus on its church doors and the cross on its steeple tops. It is not enough to pray for five minutes for the Unborn on Sunday, then have those same praying members spend the rest of the week advocating, endorsing, and voting for the very people who commit and fund the Killing of the Innocent in the Womb.

When John in the desert arrived, he came with a VOICE "proclaiming the straight way of the Lord." His Voice then became Jesus' Voice—fearless, confident, powerful, and mighty in its delivery of the Truth. Jesus delivered a message of hope and repentance for those who believed, and a message of outrage for those who refused his Father's will and his Father's laws.

For Forty-seven years Christianity has stood by inertly allowing its members to participate in the "intrinsically evil act" of Abortion without a declaration of judgment and condemnation. This forbearance has now morphed into a dictatorship of evil that not only includes the barbarity of Abortion but a plethora of slanderous evils that issue daily out of the incidiary mouths of Democrats and the Media. At this moment in history there are no forces powerful enough to sanction and overcome this dictatorship of evil that openly and brazenly wages war against the very truths "we hold self-evident." This dictatorship has no boundaries and submits to no laws, has declared itself unleashed from the constitution, and has pilloried the very laws of God. It steals and cheats and lies without any restraints. Winning power is no longer necessary, taking it is all that matters.

If we are to believe Jesus came from his Father's house with an olive branch preaching piety and prayer, we have identified the wrong Jesus. Jesus came to unnerve the bully, frighten the wicked, warn the rich, stop the adulterer, cast out the devil, separate the sheep from the goats, awaken us to the final days of judgment, with utmost diligent care for the least of the least, and with unrestrained emotion condemn the Hypocrites who flaunt God's laws and impose their own. Jesus did not bring placebos from his Father's house, nor platitudes, he brought one stern message: "Make straight the paths of the Lord."

Christianity has now been here among us for a long time and has attempted to lead us in the paths of righteousness also for a very long time. The thousands and thousands of churches it has erected attest to its influence and vast monetary support. But something dreadfully evil has snuffed out its voice of late. It walks a path of silence and submission. It prays and remains quiet in its "separated" state. Billy Graham has passed. Bishop Fulton J Sheen has long been gone. One has to believe that instead of leading with a Voice of Righteousness, it has become itself a Whisper in the Wilderness. We have no Shepherd. We have no Shepherd proclaiming above the cacophonous voices of evil "the way the truth and the life." Jesus, where are your shepherds!

Lastly, and most unfortunately, the Christianity of yesteryear has been stolen by the Democrat Party. The Church, by submission, has allowed the Party of moral destruction to apply its tyranny over the sheepfold of its flock without a word of outrage. The Jesus who is the title holder of Christianity has been banished from public spaces and refused a place at the table of truth. When evil becomes good you have crossed over into the land of Lucifer. Evil has been crowned king, and virtue and goodness are kept at bay. There are no longer any safe places for good and truth. Evil has stolen the title to power. Evil has been retitled as good. In the first Garden the devil enticed Adam and Eve into believing that evil substituted for good and if they ate it they would know more than God. Evil of grotesque proportions has now taken center stage. With the shrill voice of the Devil you can destroy the life of the Unborn, and with the same shrill voice you can hurl the truth into the abyss. All you need is a lie.

When John saw a group of Pharisees spying on him in the crowd at the Jordan while he baptized, he had these parting words for them:

> "You brood of vipers! Who warned you to flee from the coming wrath? Produce good fruit as evidence of your repentance. And do not presume to say to yourselves, 'We have Abraham as our father,' For I tell you, God can raise up

children to Abraham from these stones. Even now the axe lies at the root of the trees. Therefore every tree that does not bear good fruit will be cut down and thrown into the fire" (Mt.3:7-10)

John's Voice will never be snuffed out. In spite of his beheading, the One Crying in the Wilderness will never cease proclaiming, "Prepare Ye the Way of the Lord." Jesus is no myth. He and his Father are plenipotentiary and no fake power will ever overtake their preeminence and majesty and mystery.

If Christianity is of Jesus, it will never submit. Falter, yes, but never submit. If Jesus is its cornerstone, it will rise above its ashes and proclaim the only "way and the truth and the life."

About the Author

THE AUTHOR HAS PASSED MANY GENERATIONS on earth and can list several degrees and postgraduate degrees that need no enumeration. He has been very blessed in life with a highly dedicated mission-minded wife and two successful grown children with outstanding spouses and eight most remarkable grandchildren. He was baptized at one month of age and has stayed connected to Jesus his entire life. He was an educator earlier in life followed by a lengthy business career. He has learned and observed that the most important accouterments in life are truth and self-discipline. John the Baptist exemplified both; he entered life before Jesus and he died just before Jesus with the title of "the greatest man ever born to woman." He had the honor of introducing Jesus to the world and the rest is history. They both died defending the truth with an enormous proclivity to self-discipline.

CPSIA information can be obtained
at www.ICGtesting.com
Printed in the USA
BVHW071117230421
605721BV00003B/260